ODESSA

ODESSA

Genius and Death in a City of Dreams

CHARLES KING

W. W. NORTON & COMPANY

New York   London

For information about permission to reproduce selections from this book,
write to Permissions, W. W. Norton & Company, Inc.,
500 Fifth Avenue, New York, NY 10110

For information about special discounts for bulk purchases, please contact
W. W. Norton Special Sales at specialsales@wwnorton.com or 800-233-4830

Manufacturing by Courier Westford
Book design by Helene Berinsky
Production manager: Julia Druskin

Library of Congress Cataloging-in-Publication Data

King, Charles, 1967–
Odessa : genius and death in a city of dreams / Charles King. — 1st ed.
p. cm.
Includes bibliographical references and index.
ISBN 978-0-393-07084-2
1. Odesa (Ukraine)—History. 2. Odesa (Ukraine)—Social conditions.
3. Odesa (Ukraine)—Biography. 4. Jews—Ukraine—Odesa—History.
5. Social change—Ukraine—Odesa—History. 6. Cultural pluralism—Ukraine—
Odesa—History. 7. Cosmopolitanism—Ukraine—Odesa—History. 8. Genius—
Social aspects—Ukraine—Odesa—History. 9. Cruelty—Social aspects—Ukraine—
Odesa—History. 10. Death—Social aspects—Ukraine—Odesa—History. I. Title.
DK508.95.O33K5 2011
947.7'2—dc22
2010038000

W. W. Norton & Company, Inc.
500 Fifth Avenue, New York, N.Y. 10110
www.wwnorton.com

W. W. Norton & Company Ltd.
Castle House, 75/76 Wells Street, London W1T 3QT

1 2 3 4 5 6 7 8 9 0

For the Martens family:
Karl, Karleen, Jay, and Jerry,
and to the memory of Eldon, Marie, and Leland,
whose ancestors, with bravery and hope,
left the Russian plains for the American prairie

[A] great city is a kind of labyrinth within which at every moment of the day the most hidden wishes of every human being are performed by people who devote their whole existences to doing this and nothing else.

STEPHEN SPENDER, *World within World*

Odessa knew what it meant to bloom. It now knows what it means to wither—a poetic fading, a little lighthearted and totally powerless.

ISAAC BABEL, "Odessa"

Have respect unto the covenant: for the dark places of the earth are full of the habitations of cruelty.

Psalms 74:20

CONTENTS

Contents

PART III

Nostalgia and Remembrance

AUTHOR'S NOTE

Odes, Odesa, or Odessa? The city has been known by many names in Yiddish, Ukrainian, Russian, and other languages. Today mapmakers often prefer the Ukrainian version—Odesa—given that the city has been situated inside the independent country of Ukraine since 1991 (and the Ukrainian Soviet Socialist Republic before that). I use the spelling most familiar to English readers—Odessa—a convention that masks no particular cultural agenda.

In general I have opted to use spellings that are easy on the eye when rendering foreign names or phrases in the text. The more academic versions are used in the notes and bibliography. The Russian word for a person from Odessa is *odessit* or *odessitka*, which has sometimes been rendered into English as "Odessite." I use the more sonorous "Odessan."

Most works of literature are quoted in their readily available English translations. Other translations from Russian, Romanian, and French, unless otherwise indicated, are my own.

Until 1918 Russia used the Julian calendar rather than the Gregorian one. That distinction left the Russians thirteen days behind the West in the twentieth century, twelve days behind in the nineteenth, and eleven days behind in the eighteenth. Dates for events in the Russian Empire are given according to the old system.

IF BY SOME MIRACLE this book finds its way to the families of Vera Nikolaevna Sepel or Nicolae Tănase, whose story is related in chapter 9, I would be very grateful to hear from them.

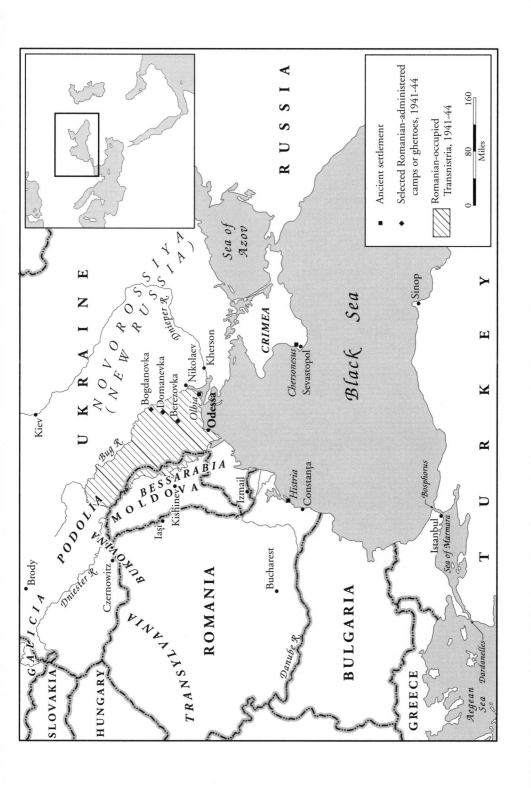

Legend:

■ Ancient settlement

◆ Selected Romanian-administered camps or ghettoes, 1941–44

▨ Romanian-occupied Transnistria, 1941–44

Miles: 0 — 80 — 160

Labels on map:

RUSSIA

UKRAINE

NOVOROSSIYA (NEW RUSSIA)

Sea of Azov

CRIMEA

Black Sea

Kiev

Dnieper R.

Bogdanovka
Domanevka
Berezovka
Nikolaev
Olbia
Kherson
Odessa

Chersonesus
Sevastopol

Sinop

Bug R.

PODOLIA

BESSARABIA

MOLDOVA

Izmail

Histria
Constanţa

Brody

GALICIA

Dniester R.

BUKOVINA

Czernowitz

Iaşi
Kishinev

TRANSYLVANIA

ROMANIA

Bucharest

Danube R.

BULGARIA

GREECE

Istanbul
Bosphorus
Sea of Marmara

TURKEY

Aegean Sea
Dardanelles

SLOVAKIA

HUNGARY

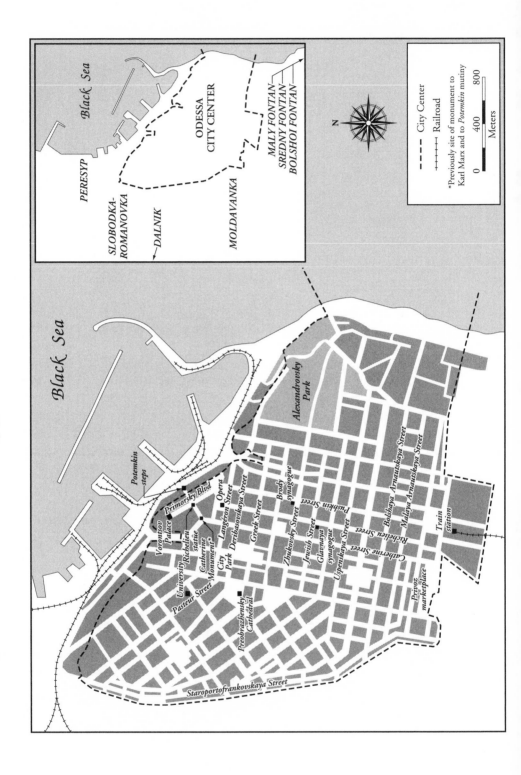

ODESSA

INTRODUCTION

Mark Twain felt supremely at home when he visited Odessa in the late summer of 1867. He had come to the Russian port city on the world's first long-distance pleasure cruise, a jaunt across the Near East related in *The Innocents Abroad*. After a twenty-hour run across the Black Sea on the American steamer *Quaker City*, Twain stepped ashore to see Odessa's cascade of stone steps—one of the most famous staircases in the world—beckoning him from the docklands to the upper city. At the top, looking like a casual visitor peering out over the harbor, the diminutive statue of the duc de Richelieu, one of the city's early builders, held out a welcoming hand. Twain puffed his way to the heights and gazed out over the grain silos and quays below. Behind him rose the city center, buzzing with the business of trade, shipping, and exchange.

Broad, well-kept streets intersected at right angles. Low houses of two or three stories flanked the boulevards. Plain facades plastered in blues and yellows reflected the sunlight that bounced ashore from the calm waters of the Black Sea. Acacia trees lifted their branches over sidewalks that teemed with people taking in the summer air, while dust clouds roiled with each passing carriage. "Look up the street or down the street, this way or that way," Twain wrote, "we saw only America!"[1]

That was an odd way of seeing things. Twain was standing in a city that had been scouted by a Neapolitan mercenary, named by a Russian empress, governed by her one-eyed secret husband, built by two exiled French noblemen, modernized by a Cambridge-educated count, and celebrated by his wife's Russian lover. It was one of the largest cities in Russia and the empire's preeminent commercial port, even though it was situated closer to Vienna and Athens than to Moscow and St. Petersburg. The population was almost a quarter Jewish.

Not long after Twain's trip, the city witnessed some of the most horrific antisemitic violence in Russian history. Jews were literally murdered in the streets in repeated outpourings of hatred and fear. Much later, in a forgotten chapter of the Holocaust, Odessa's Jewish community—by then a third of the city's population—was nearly destroyed by the largest wartime program of planned killing committed by a country other than Nazi Germany, in this case, Nazi-allied Romania. What Twain saw in the streets and courtyards of Odessa was a place that had cultivated, like his homeland, a remarkable ability to unite nationalities and reshape itself on its own terms, generation after generation. What he missed was the city's tendency to tip with deadly regularity over the precipice of self-destruction.

At the time of his visit, Odessa was still developing the identity that its boosters would embrace and its detractors decry: a taste for the witty and the absurd; a veneer of Russian culture laid over a Yiddish, Greek, and Italian core; a boom-and-bust economy; a love of the dandy in men and the daring in women; a style of music and writing that involved both libertine abandon and controlled experimentation; and an approach to politics that swung wildly between the radical and the reactionary. It would eventually transfer many of those habits and values to new locales, from the jazz clubs of Leningrad to the borscht-belt banquet halls of the Catskills and Brighton Beach. In the four countries that have governed it—the Russian Empire, the Soviet Union, Romania (as an occupying power), and now Ukraine—Odessa has stood out as a mixed and rambunctious city, an island of difference perched between sea and steppe, yet a place continually threatened by its own mottled personality. "Odessa did not have any tradition, but it was therefore not afraid of new forms of living and activity," recalled the Zionist activist and Odessa native Vladimir Jabotinsky. "It developed in us more temperament and less passion, more cynicism, but less bitterness."[2]

From its founding in 1794 all the way to the present, Odessa has struggled to survive somewhere between success and suicide. Like many vibrant seaports and multicultural urban spaces, the city has continually sought to unleash its better demons, the mischievous tricksters that are the vital muses of urban society and the restless creators of literature and art. But it has often loosed its darker ones instead, those that lurk in alleyways and whisper of religious loathing, class envy, and ethnic revenge. When things worked, Odessa nurtured intellectuals and artists whose talents lit up the world. When they didn't, the city's name became a byword for fanaticism, antisemitism, and deadly nationalism.

This book follows the arc of Odessa's story from its imperial beginnings, through the punctuated tragedies of the twentieth century, to its passage into the realm of myth and longing. It traces how generations of native and adopted Odessans built a city with a uniquely incorrigible disposition, a place that became Russia's most ambitious port and the inspiration for writers from Alexander Pushkin to Isaac Babel. It weaves together the city's history with some of the individual lives, both well known and obscure, that made it a beloved and legendary hometown for Jews, Russians, Ukrainians, and many others.

How does a city thrive? And how does it do so in ways that give it a distinct reputation—a spirit or identity that makes denizens into local patriots? How does a piece of real estate get transformed into a way of being rather than just a place to be from? Many cities, especially ports and boomtowns—New Orleans and Naples, Las Vegas and

Liverpool—have reputations that lend themselves to easy and familiar labels, but only a few become modes of living and doing. Today, it is easy to be nostalgic about the cosmopolitan idyll that Odessa has tried heroically to represent. Odessans themselves have made a profession of it. But the harder truth is that this city, like all others with some claim to greatness, disappoints as much as it inspires. The monstrous aspects of its identity have won out as often as the more noble ones, and far more than the gauzy version of its past normally allows. In the end, Odessa's experience reveals the creative power as well as the everyday difficulty of being diverse. In the exacting art of urban flourishing, teetering between genius and devastation may be the normal state of affairs.

PART I

City of Dreams

CHAPTER 1

The Sinister Shore

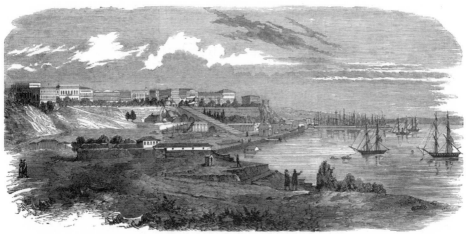

ODESSA.—THE HARBOUR AND BOULEVARD.—(SEE NEXT PAGE.)

City on a hill: A nineteenth-century engraving of the
Odessa city center and port. *Author's collection.*

Visitors don't arrive in Odessa so much as stumble upon it. From the landward side, the city appears unexpectedly on the Pontic steppe, an ancient grassland now covered in Ukrainian farms and the detritus of Soviet industrial agriculture. The slight roll in the landscape, dipping into dry draws and ravines that cut down to the sea, hides the city until you are well inside it. "Here is the steppe, and a yard further the city," noted a German traveler more than a century ago, "and one might almost fancy it exercised no influence whatever on the surrounding country."[1]

From the sea, Odessa rises atop a range of low cliffs, with the city center coming into view only once a ship is around the prominent headlands that hide the bay. Tall apartment blocks dot the outer suburbs, but the older parts of the city seem oddly absent until a ship turns its bow toward the small lighthouse at the end of the mole. "Europe was once more before our eyes," recalled a French visitor in the 1840s upon seeing the public buildings silhouetted against the sky.[2] The same sentiment would echo again and again among both locals and strangers. The low roofs and wind-blown trees announced a dreamlike city rising out of nothing, a surprising blip on the blank horizon formed by steppe, sea, and sky.

Odessa is still best approached from the water, the way that the earliest recorded visitors to the Black Sea world—the ancient Greeks—would have experienced it. Here, the coast sneaks into view, appearing as a low ridge of dun-colored limestone bluffs that can turn dull orange or even pink in full daylight. It must have been a tremendous sight for seafarers from the Aegean, who had hugged the coast for days staring out at the monotony of wavy grassland and rippled sea, the one barely distinguishable from the other. It is still an astonishing view. The broad bay opens azure from the blue-black sea, flanked by craggy promontories rising a hundred feet or more above the beach.

On some parts of the Black Sea coastline, the land ends in imposing mountains, wooded and alpine, that tumble straight into the water. In others, it falls away suddenly as immense limestone cliffs, the dark waves crashing noisily against the gray-green walls. Yet around Odessa, in the sea's northwest corner, the water doesn't so much meet the land as complete it. The flat earth slips gently into the brackish shallows. The sea floor, choked in places with seaweed and algae, forms a continuation of the steppe, once a vast prairie of undulating feather grass and fescue, now divided into strips of plowed and planted farmland, the soil burled in blacks and browns.

Yet if anyone in antiquity found the cliff-top location of modern-day Odessa remarkable, they failed to mention it. The wide-open bay would surely have been known to the ancients, but none of the extant written records gives an unambiguous account of long-term settlement there. Other modern cities on or near the Black Sea—the grimy port of Constanţa in Romania, the storied Russian naval station at Sevastopol, and the jewel of the Black Sea world, Istanbul—all have ancient pedigrees. Beneath modern concrete and asphalt lie Greek, Roman, and Byzantine ruins. But Odessa has none of this. The site had little to offer beyond a bay open to harsh northeasterly winds. When you see the city from a cruise ship or ferry, you are looking at a recent creation, a place that for two hundred years has both reveled in and regretted the fact that it has no history.[3]

Explorers found more attractive destinations in other parts of the Black Sea. Arriving in shallow-draft rowed vessels, perhaps in the early first millennium BCE, sailors from the Mediterranean gradually colonized much of the Black Sea coastline, beginning with the south and eventually extending their reach to the north. The draw was substantial. The southern and eastern coasts yielded precious metals. The legend of Jason and the Argonauts' search for a mysterious golden fleece may have recalled a time when Greek traders scoured what are today the coasts of Turkey and Georgia in search of gold that natives sluiced from the fast-running rivers of the Pontic Alps and Caucasus. The north provided contact with the flat interior, which in turn offered access to the grains that were cultivated by the non-Greek peoples already living there when Mediterranean sailors first ventured north from their warmer, saltier sea.

Herodotus, the Greek historian of the fifth century BCE, either visited the Black Sea himself or, more likely, heard some of the tall tales about the region that flowed southward all the way to his hometown, Halicarnassus, along the western coast of modern-day Turkey. Already by his day, the Black Sea was a place of mixed cultures and allegiances. The area north of the sea was the realm of

the Scythians, a word that Greek writers used as a catchall for different non-Greek tribes of herders, farmers, and nomads, united
to a degree by commonalities of custom and belief. In his *Histories*, Herodotus describes the peoples living at the mouths of the
Dnieper, Bug, and Danube rivers, near the future Odessa. The Cal-
lipidae and the Alizones, he says, were a "Greco-Scythian tribe,"
the offshoots of marriages between Greek colonists and inlanders,
who resembled the Scythians in their dress and manners but grew
onions, leeks, lentils, and millet, some for their own consumption
and some for export.

For Herodotus, the Dnieper River—which he knew as the
Borysthenes—represented a kind of boundary. To the east lived
rogue bands of Scythians who had little regard for outsiders. There
were the Androphagi—literally, "man-eaters"—who were said to
live on the edge of a vast desert. Other peoples marched across
treeless prairies or engaged in almost constant warfare and slave-
taking. To the west, Scythians and Greeks intermingled freely,
enriching themselves through commerce with the Mediterranean.
The flatlands watered by the Borysthenes and its tributaries were
a veritable paradise, a river system that was "the most valuable and
productive not only ... in this part of the world, but anywhere
else, with the sole exception of the Nile."[4] Lush pastures unrolled
themselves along the riverbanks. Great schools of fish churned in
the shoals. Tidal flats nearer the coast yielded salt that was used to
pickle fish for transport to the south, a delicacy lauded by Greek
and Roman gourmands—"even though it causes severe flatulence,"
warned Pliny the Elder in the first century CE.[5]

The physical remnants of this civilization—part native, part
Greek and Roman—can still be found along the northwest coast of
the Black Sea, at archaeological sites such as Olbia, Chersonesus on
the Crimean Peninsula, or Histria in Romania. Stone houses lined
narrow streets, some even paved and fitted with complex drainage
systems. Rocky breakwaters reached out into the sea, welcoming

ships from the Mediterranean and small sailboats coming from other cities, commercial emporia, and distant outposts. These cities were destroyed, resurrected, and refashioned over the centuries following the first Greek forays, yet the archaeological digs still give modern visitors a sense of what it was like to live there in antiquity—a place that Mediterranean Greeks considered to be the true edge of the world.

Cities such as Olbia, Chersonesus, and Histria lasted for perhaps half a millennium. They grew and expanded in some periods and fell prey to raiders in others. Relations between colonists and locals not only gave rise to cordial trading relations but also produced bloody warfare. While many Greeks tended to see the peoples of the region as uncouth, unlearned, and prone to violence, some observers found the foreign colonists themselves to be the source of social problems. "Our mode of life has spread its change for the worse to almost all peoples," commented the Roman writer Strabo, "introducing amongst them luxury and sensual pleasures, and, to satisfy these vices, base artifices that lead to innumerable acts of greed."[6]

Strabo was himself a product of the Black Sea world, born just inland from the southern coast in the old Greek colony of Amaseia, today the city of Amasya, Turkey. Reared in a Greek-speaking environment, in the green valleys that lead down toward shimmering stone beaches, he was perhaps predisposed to see his own part of the world with more sympathy and nuance than were many outsiders. The poet Ovid, for example, was exiled to the sea's western coast in 8 CE as punishment for offending the emperor Augustus. Accustomed to the comforts of his native Abruzzi or his villa on the Capitoline hill in Rome, he found the site of his enforced *relegatio* singularly unappealing. The Black Sea's name in Greek and Latin— Pontus Euxinus—meant literally "the sea that welcomes strangers." But Ovid's view was clearly different. "They call it hospitable," he wrote curtly in a letter from the Pontic coast. "They lie."[7]

Barbarians walked freely about the cities, their long beards covered in icicles during the harsh winters. Raiders from the interior descended with fury on the communities of Greek-speaking seamen, frontiersmen, and political exiles who inhabited the settlements. In the continual tug-of-war between hinterland and seacoast, the former came to dominate by the late Roman period. A region that Greek authors had once compared to Egypt—which they believed to be the most civilized society outside the Greek world—was again beyond the ken of most foreigners.

A millennium later, in the thirteenth and fourteenth centuries, Italian city-states revived the ancient connections between the Mediterranean and the Black Sea. The great military and commercial powerhouses of the late Middle Ages and Renaissance, cities such as Genoa, Pisa, and Venice, extended their reach beyond their own waters and established global empires of profit that leached into the Black Sea world and beyond. The sea provided an essential water link to the heartland of Central Asia and, farther still, the overland passage to China.

Italian towns and cities, most built on top of older Greek foundations, flourished as nodal points in a vast commercial network. Just as Greek sailing ships had returned laden with grain and preserved fish, Italian trading companies crisscrossed the sea in their fat-hulled vessels carrying silk, furs, and slaves from among the Tatars, Circassians, Georgians, and other peoples—a substantial source of profit to European powers seeking servants as well as oarsmen on naval and commercial galleys. They overshadowed the dominant political power at the time—the Byzantine Empire, centered in Constantinople—and effectively bankrolled the Greek-speaking Byzantines as traders and creditors, a fact not lost on contemporary writers who decried their "arrogance" as "masters of the Black Sea."[8]

At this stage, the wider Black Sea region was a part of the world so intimately familiar to Genoese sailors, Venetian tax collectors, and Florentine financiers that adventurers such as Marco Polo could write about it with studied nonchalance. "We have not spoken to you of the Black Sea or the provinces that lie around it," he wrote in the late thirteenth century, "for there are so many who explore these waters and sail upon them every day . . . that everybody knows what is to be found there. Therefore I say nothing on this topic."[9]

Polo was writing primarily about the southern and eastern coasts, which gave access to the riches of Central Asia, the Indian subcontinent, and China. If the northwestern corner of the sea had been one of the breadbaskets of antiquity, providing barley and millet to Athens and other Greek city-states at the height of their power, it was the eastern parts of the sea that benefited from the growth of global commerce during the Renaissance. Generations of businessmen made and lost fortunes in the Italian outposts at Caffa in Crimea and Tana on the Don River. A detailed Florentine business guide from the early fourteenth century, Pegolotti's *La pratica della mercatura*—a combination of *Rough Guide* practicality and chamber-of-commerce boosterism—listed wax, iron, tin, copper, pepper, spices, cotton, cheese, oil, apples, silk, saffron, gold, pearls, caviar, and cattle hides as some of the many commodities shipped through the Black Sea ports.[10]

Yet that commerce in turn rested on the same kinds of relationships between coast and hinterland—mutually beneficial yet also often fraught—that had allowed Greek colonies to flourish in antiquity. For Italian sailors and merchants, the inland partner was no longer the Scythians, who had disappeared centuries earlier into a fog of migrations, intermarriages, and invasions. It was now one of the many nomadic and settled peoples that had exerted control of the steppe in the millennium separating Herodotus from Marco Polo: the Tatars.

The Tatars were the successors to the Golden Horde, the last remnant of the great movement of peoples out of Central Asia that had accompanied Genghis Khan in the early thirteenth century. After the breakup of Genghis's empire, the Golden Horde laid claim to much of the western Eurasian steppe and governed a massive imperial landscape traversed by Turkic herdsmen, Italian merchants, emissaries from European heads of state, and intrepid Christian missionaries. European visitors invariably condemned the barbarity of the Mongol-Tatar nomads, whose customs and traditions seemed to represent the antithesis of learning and civilization. But Europeans' own recorded experiences often flew in the face of their prejudices.

In the 1240s, the rotund friar John of Plano Carpini was dispatched by Pope Innocent IV to establish relations with the Mongol-Tatar khan. Friar John was convinced of the nomads' barbarous ways. "The slaughter of other people is accounted a matter of nothing with them," he wrote. But his own eyewitness report reveals a cosmopolitan culture of erudition and exchange, albeit one that was often on the move, as the Mongol-Tatars followed their herds of sheep, cattle, and horses across the steppe and down to the shores of the Black and Caspian seas. As Friar John prepared for his long-awaited audience with the Mongol emperor, he was embarrassed to learn that the emperor's secretaries were able to write in Arabic, Russian, and Tatar—whereas John himself knew no other written language but Latin. With considerable back-and-forth, the group managed to render the emperor's multilingual thoughts into a Latin text that John could at last ferry back to the pope.[11]

In time, the Golden Horde, like its larger Mongol predecessor, fell prey to internal dissension and dynastic rivalries. It eventually broke apart, forming a new patchwork of small khanates scattered across Eurasia. These, in turn, struggled for control over trade routes and resources with some of the emerging Christian powers of the region: Muscovy, which was prospering north of the steppe zone and managed to throw off Mongol-Tatar dominance in the late fourteenth century, and Lithuania, which had also begun to expand at the expense of the Golden Horde, claiming even the lower reaches of the Dnieper River in the 1360s. The eastern nomads who had once threatened Europe—sparking desperate long-distance diplomatic missions like that of Friar John—were no longer the conduit of commerce they had been in the late Middle Ages. Business with China slowed, and Italian trading centers around the Black Sea withered.

Beneath these grand geopolitical changes, as tracts of territory shifted from one great power to another through decisive battles or royal successions, the lives of fishermen, merchants, farmers, and nomads continued from season to season. An army on the march ruined crops. Locusts ate what remained untouched. Cattle failed to calve, or spring lambs came earlier than expected. The arrival of ships flying unknown flags signaled some imponderable change beyond the sea. The sensible localness of Odessa was prefigured in the fate of its earliest and truest ancestor, a small windswept settlement lying at the meeting place of rival empires.

BEFORE IT BECAME Odessa, Khadjibey was an out-of-the-way village situated on the heights overlooking the Black Sea. Its origins are obscure, but local lore maintained that it was founded by an eponymous Tatar chieftain, Hadji I Giray. Seeking support against internal rivals and nomadic incursions, Hadji allegedly ceded a portion of his western territories to the Grand Duchy of Lithuania, a military and political powerhouse whose lands stretched across much of modern-day Lithuania, Belarus, and western Ukraine. The village of Khadjibey entered nominally into the Lithuanian domain, but in practice life probably went on as usual. Tatar villagers herded cattle, feuded with rivals over grazing lands, and traded livestock and grain with peoples farther inland, from the distant Poles and Lithuanians to the nearer Moldovans.[12]

If the Lithuanians were the dominant force in the early fifteenth century, when a place called Khadjibey first appears in written sources, a century later a new set of influences came rushing in from the south. The Muslim Ottomans had created a voracious empire after the conquest of the Byzantine throne at Constantinople in 1453. Originally a set of allied Turkic-speaking tribes that long before had migrated out of Central Asia, the Ottomans gradually conquered or assimilated the panoply of Christian communities, Greek-speaking villagers, and migrant shepherds who lived on the margins of Byzantium. At their head was the sultan, a dynastic title carried by rulers who traced their lineage to Osman I in the 1290s—a chieftain from whose name the English term "Ottoman" is derived. Although Islamic at its core, the Ottoman state evolved as an empire in the truest sense of the term: a collection of peoples and territories loosely bound together by an overarching political leader and governed by an enormous machinery of taxation, tribute, and war-making.

By the time the Ottomans marched into Constantinople, the Byzantine Empire had nearly melted away on its own. Over the

The port of Odessa, from an early-twentieth-century postcard. *Author's collection.*

centuries, it had become a ghostly shell of the glorious eastern Rome of centuries past. Ottoman armies had already spent many summers on the march across southeastern Europe, bypassing the imperial capital and placing pressure on the Christian kings and princes of the Balkans, from Serbia to Moldova. But by the 1520s, with Constantinople subdued, the Ottoman sultan was able to secure the full acquiescence of the major powers in the region, who promised fealty in exchange for his recognizing their authority in their own lands. The coasts of the Black Sea were now under Ottoman suzerainty, even if the sultan often had to rule indirectly through local notables. The sea itself, with Ottoman warships commanding access to the Mediterranean via the Bosphorus and Dardanelles straits, was the watery domain of the world's greatest Islamic empire.

Villagers in places like Khadjibey, whether they knew it or not, were now Ottoman subjects. That news did not always convince the locals, however. Pirates from north of the Black Sea frequently targeted Ottoman ships, even hitting the Ottoman heartland in Anatolia and occasionally menacing Constantinople. These raiders grew up out of the frontier society that defined the coastal borderlands of the empire—a mixture of former Polish-Lithuanian or Muscovite peasants, local Muslims, and nomadic herders, some of whom coalesced into distinct communities given the catchall label "Cossacks." Cossack groups emerged in the mid-sixteenth century as a key power at the intersection of Polish-Lithuanian and Ottoman authority, offering their services as freebooters—the word "Cossack" probably derives from *kazak*, a Turkic word for "free man"—to whichever sovereign could pay the highest fee. Although a substantial livelihood came from raiding and piracy, Cossacks were a true multipurpose frontier people, farming, herding, and fishing in the grassy lowlands and estuaries of the Dnieper and other rivers.

The French artillery engineer Guillaume de Beauplan, who

witnessed Cossack raids in the seventeenth century, left a graphic
description of the Cossacks and their waterborne lives, painting them not as the legendary cavalrymen they would eventually
become, but rather as able and daring seamen, commanding small
river craft that could be reoutfitted for voyages across the sea. As
he wrote in his *Description of Ukraine*:

> Their number now approaches some 120,000 men, all trained for
> war, and ready to answer in less than a week the slightest command
> to serve the [Polish] king. It is these people who often, [indeed]
> almost every year, go raiding on the Black Sea, to the great detri-
> ment of the Turks. Many times they have plundered Crimea, which
> belongs to Tatary, ravaged Anatolia, sacked Trebizond, and even
> ventured as far as the mouth of the Black Sea [Bosphorus], three
> leagues from Constantinople, where they have laid waste to every-
> thing with fire and sword, returning home with much booty and
> a number of slaves, usually young children, whom they keep for
> their own service or give as gifts to the lords of their homeland.[13]

As the Cossack raids illustrated, in the seventeenth century at
least, the Ottomans exercised little direct control north of the Black
Sea, except during seasons of war when troops might descend on
local villages to burn crops or requisition livestock. Even then, the
Ottomans depended on a web of relationships of treaty, tribute, and
vassalage with Christian sovereigns as well as the Muslim Tatars of
Crimea. Agreements were as often breached as honored. Constantinople's inconstant hold on the northern coast lasted until yet another
imperial power, Russia, moved southward to challenge the sultan's
notional hegemony. The riches of the sea and its hinterlands—
including grain, sheep, cattle, and timber—had been an inducement
to imperial rivals for centuries. But the sea also offered two things
that the Russians in particular desired: ports that were ice-free for
most of the winter and potential access to the Mediterranean.

Under Peter the Great, Russia launched a series of military forays against the Ottomans and their clients. Most of Peter's southern expeditions, in the 1690s and 1710s, came to little. But one of his successors, Catherine the Great, was able to combine strategic daring, technological innovation, and careful diplomacy to present a sustained challenge to the Ottomans and the Crimean Tatars, a remnant of the old Golden Horde based on the Crimean Peninsula and exercising some sway along the northern coast of the Black Sea.

In a series of military campaigns from 1768 to 1774, Catherine pushed back Ottoman armies and secured territorial gains that made the Russian Empire an emerging Black Sea power. The empress took control of old Ottoman fortresses at Kinburn, Yenikale, and Kerch, vital choke points that commanded access to the Dnieper and Bug rivers, as well as to the shallow, fish-rich Sea of Azov. Under the terms of the Russian peace treaty with Constantinople, the Crimean Tatars were proclaimed independent of Ottoman authority, although they were permitted to recognize the sultan as caliph, or earthly spiritual leader of all Muslims. Russian-flagged ships were allowed to enter the Black Sea from the Mediterranean, an essential boon to commerce in the Russian lands north of the sea.

The empress ordered a massive shipbuilding campaign to outfit a new commercial and naval fleet. New towns grew up in the areas now under Russia's control, small but promising hamlets that were soon attracting merchants and immigrants from across the empire's uncertain borders and even from across the sea. As one observer noted at the time, "These towns . . . as well as numerous villages which have suddenly reared their heads in a country formerly inhabited only by lawless banditti, or traversed by roving hordes, are filled with Russians, with Tartars reclaimed from their wandering life, and with numerous colonists, particularly Greeks and Armenians, who migrated from the adjacent provinces of the Turkish empire."[14]

Settlements were rising farther inland, along the southern reaches of the Dnieper and Bug rivers, but in backward places such as Khadjibey—coastal villages, Cossack settlements, and Tatar camps—the martial designs of kings and sultans were probably less important than the advent of rain, the seasonal migration of fish, or the availability of freshwater and salt licks during the winter trek from steppe to coastal meadow. An early frost or the lavish wedding of an elder's daughter might leave more of a mark than the faraway coronation of a new ruler or the fall of an imperial capital to invaders. All this began to change in the late 1780s, when a new war between Russians and Ottomans focused attention on the part of the sea that travelers and traders had often bypassed—the shallow inlets and grasslands of the northwest, including the dusty cliff-top village of Khadjibey.

CHAPTER 2

Potemkin and the Mercenaries

Founding father: *Portrait of Admiral Osip de Ribas*
[José de Ribas] (1796) by Johann-Baptist I. Lampi,
© *The State Hermitage Museum, St. Petersburg.*

"Rather than sign the secession of thirteen provinces as ...
George has done," Catherine is reported to have said of her
contemporary, Britain's George III, "I should have shot myself."[1]
Russia had expanded toward the Black Sea, but Catherine saw her

empire's natural frontier as lying even farther to the south, well into Ottoman lands, perhaps even to the Mediterranean. George III, along with other eighteenth-century monarchs such as Joseph II of Austria and Louis XVI of France, ruled domains that stretched across Europe and around the world. Catherine was not to be out-done by their imperial acquisitiveness. From the coast of the Black Sea, she reckoned, Russia could realize its longer-term aims of removing the sultan from his throne in Constantinople and replac-ing him with a Christian (and Russian) prince. The rise of a new Byzantium under Russian protection would then mark the end of Islam's reign on the borderlands of Europe.

In 1783 Catherine had taken a further step southward by for-mally annexing Crimea, backtracking on the independence that the region had been guaranteed less than a decade earlier. The imme-diate results were disastrous. Tens of thousands of Crimean Tatars fled to the Ottoman Empire. Their fellow Muslims soon called for the sultan to intervene on behalf of the embattled refugees now overwhelming the Turkish ports. But the plight of starving, typhus-ridden Tatars, however galling to the sultan, paled before an osten-tatious display of Russian power stage-managed by Catherine's personal and political partner—Prince Grigory Aleksandrovich Potemkin.

Towering and auburn-haired, Potemkin had been present at the advent of Catherine's reign, first attracting the empress's atten-tions in the early 1760s. He was then a dashing figure in an impe-rial guards regiment, she the ambitious consort of a boorish and ineffective tsar, Peter III. When Catherine engineered a coup to depose her husband, Potemkin joined the ranks of those loyal to the new sovereign. As the troops prepared to march on the Peter-hof Palace outside St. Petersburg, Potemkin boldly edged his horse over to Catherine's position. The two exchanged friendly words, and the empress laughed at the skittishness of his horse.

He soon parlayed this familiarity into a position as gentleman of the bedchamber—at this point, merely a courtly rank rather than a profession. He could now engineer further encounters with Catherine in the mazelike corridors of the Winter Palace. At every meeting, Potemkin would fall to his knees, declare his undying love, and rashly kiss the hand of one of the most powerful monarchs in Europe.[2]

Some of the tales of Catherine's sexual proclivities are apocryphal, but she was clearly a ruler who enjoyed the company of men—intimately, energetically, and not always serially. Under Catherine's protection, Potemkin received a post in the empire's fighting forces during the first Russo-Turkish war of her reign. He returned from the frontlines a hero, bearing the title of lieutenant general and basking in the glory of citadels captured, Ottoman armies routed, and new lands acquired for the empress, with whom he had corresponded, off and on, throughout the conflict.

Around the time the empire was formulating its peace treaty with the Ottomans in 1774, Potemkin became Catherine's lover and court favorite, a position that gave him unimpeded access to the empress's bedchamber and, by extension, to the affairs of state. There were other favorites both before and after him, and Potemkin's signature injury—the disfiguring loss of an eye—may well have come about from an encounter with one of the men he shunted aside, the obstinate and philosophical Grigory Orlov, father to Catherine's illegitimate son. But Potemkin accomplished something that none of his rivals quite managed: to build a relationship of eroticism and genuine affection—sealed in what may have been a secret marriage—while also making himself indispensable to the running of an expanding empire.

Throughout the 1770s and 1780s, Potemkin became the chief architect of Russia's breakneck development of the southern borderlands. He remained in this position long after he had ceased to be Catherine's preferred lover. He created new naval arsenals along the coast, including the port at Sevastopol, which even today remains the seat of Russia's Black Sea fleet. Germans, Albanians, Greeks, and others were given special privileges to establish farming or trading communities on the steppe and in seaside towns and river ports such as Kherson and Nikolaev.

The regions that fell to Catherine's armies were gathered into a new administrative unit known as *Novorossiya*, or "New Russia." Like New Spain, New France, and New England, New Russia was an experiment in imperial implantation. Colonists were sent to explore and settle the virgin territory. Mapmakers and geographers were dispatched from the learned Academy in St. Petersburg to catalog the natural wealth and exotic natives. Vast tracts of land—of uncertain boundaries and indefinite content—were bestowed upon stockinged and befrilled aristocrats who could now add an exotic marquisate or baronetcy to their list of honors. "[T]hey have been vaguely informed of their having been distributed among several lords," a new landowner remarked of the indigenous Tatar shepherds, "but . . . they do not exactly understand what it means."[3]

To illustrate—and market—the transformation of the prairie and coastlands, Potemkin organized a massive display of imperial pomp in the late winter and spring of 1787. In the style of Cleopatra, Catherine the Great promenaded south from St. Petersburg, across the Eurasian flatlands, and down to the Dnieper River, where her retinue embarked on the waterway that meanders across Ukraine toward the Black Sea. A convoy of fourteen carriages and 184 sledges carried dignitaries over the snowbound steppe. Once they reached Kiev, a flotilla of seven large galleys, more than eighty other boats, and three thousand crewmen and guards ferried them down the Dnieper toward their final destination, the old palace of the Tatar khan at Bakhchisaray in Crimea.

The guests comprised a veritable who's who of European nobility, from assorted princes and counts to the king of Poland and the emperor of Austria. The staterooms on board the galleys were outfitted with Chinese silk and Oriental-style sofas. Every time one of the guests exited or returned, a small orchestra of twelve musicians signaled the departure or arrival. Once in Bakhchisaray, the guests were assigned to the living quarters once occupied by the last of the Crimean Tatar khans and his harem, a treat that thrilled even the most worldly travelers.

For the delectation of the entourage and the thousands of spectators, Potemkin organized delights and surprises along the route. He installed English gardens on the virgin steppe, complete with mature, transplanted trees. Huge tents, garlanded and pearl-studded, served as dining halls. Regiments of Cossacks and loyal Tatars paraded before Catherine to pay homage. Silver-clad horsemen from the Caucasus Mountains thundered past in feats of martial skill. Lanterns shone from trees while bonfires lit up the night sky. Near the city of Kremenchug on the Dnieper River, a magnificent re-creation of Vesuvius rained down fire and brimstone on the peaceful prairie.[4]

Although masterful, Potemkin's stagecraft could not cover up the fact that the new lands were, in reality, something other than the wondrous paradise that now seemed to stretch out before the European heads of state, ambassadors, and aristocrats in Catherine's retinue. This part of New Russia had only recently passed from Ottoman to Russian control. The peasants and herders who inhabited the flatlands, hill country, and coastline were awed more by the flamboyance of the procession than by the freedom and rational governance that the Russians now promised. As one of the European nobles on the journey, Charles-Joseph, prince de Ligne, wrote at the time, "The empress, who cannot run on foot as we do, is made to believe that towns . . . are finished, whilst they often are towns without streets, streets without houses, and houses without roofs, doors, or windows."[5] Potemkin did not construct fully operational, idealized peasant villages, in the style of his contemporary, Marie Antoinette. But his enthusiasm for painting the southern prairie in the best-possible light did produce the derisory label "Potemkin villages" to describe the diverting entertainments, barely functional towns, and orchestrated displays of loyalty he created for his *Matushka*, the imperial "beloved mother," as he called Catherine in his most intimate letters, using a common term of endearment for the sovereign.

After tooling down the Dnieper, visiting Crimea, and lodging in the palace at Bakhchisaray, the Russian delegation returned to St. Petersburg, leaving the steppe much as it had been before. During the voyage downriver, a squadron of Ottoman ships had been drawn up at the mouth of the Dnieper. Their mission was not to prevent the Russians' descent to the sea but rather to provide a bellicose counterdemonstration to Potemkin's lavish parade. "This I consider as a pretty prognostic of a pretty war with which I hope we shall soon be gratified," enthused the prince de Ligne.[6] He was not to be disappointed.

<hr />

IN EARLY AUGUST of 1787 the Ottoman government presented an ultimatum to Russia demanding the immediate return of Crimea, recognition of Georgia—an Orthodox Christian kingdom in the Caucasus—as a protectorate of the sultan, and the right to routinely search Russian vessels passing through the Bosphorus. The terms were ludicrous from Catherine's point of view. After all, the entire point of Potemkin's grand journey had been to inspect Crimea and other lands that she now considered her own. Moreover, the right to travel freely into the Black Sea under a Russian flag had been secured in the last peace treaty, signed nearly a decade and a half earlier.

When Russia rejected the ultimatum, the Ottomans declared war. Both empires raced to ready their army and navy for assaults on strategic choke points on the estuaries of the Bug and Dnieper rivers, as well as along the Dniester River and on the delta of the Danube. Fortresses were resupplied. Potemkin took personal command of an army of more than a hundred thousand men—a motley collection of noble officers, Cossacks, peasants impressed into a lifetime of military service, and even a hastily assembled cavalry of Jewish lancers.[7] Catherine's triumph in the earlier war drew numerous soldiers of fortune to her cause in the second. Some were noble and well bred, like the prince de Ligne. Others were lowborn adventure-seekers. The war provided a chance not only to serve a successful Christian sovereign in the Orient, but also to profit from the wealth that the newly opened Black Sea seemed to offer. Both these inducements appealed to one famous mercenary: John Paul Jones, the naval hero of the American Revolution.

His work for the newly independent United States now finished, Jones traveled eastward to serve as commander of a Russian squadron in engagements with the Ottoman navy. Jones had made his reputation in America through a series of successful attacks on British warships; he is today revered as the founding father of the U.S. Navy, his remains encased in a lavish shrine in Annapolis, Maryland. But Potemkin was unimpressed. "This man is unfit to lead: he's slow, lacks zeal and is perhaps even afraid of the Turks," he wrote to Catherine. "He's new at this business, has neglected his entire crew and is good for nothing: not knowing the language, he can neither give nor comprehend orders."[8]

Jones had been a brilliantly successful captain in the Atlantic, but his skills were essentially those of a pirate: the ability to lead a small contingent of men aboard a single ship in order to confront a single adversary. His abilities as a commander in a more complex struggle—especially among the haughty, intrigue-ridden, and multilingual European officer corps into which he had placed himself— were questionable. "Jones was very famous as a corsair, but I fear that at the head of a squadron he is rather out of place," wrote Charles of Nassau-Siegen, another foreign officer in Catherine's employ.[9] Jones reacted petulantly to any perceived slight from his aristocratic brother-officers and spent much of his time in Russia arguing over rank and chain of command. "Never, probably, did any commanding officer commence service under circumstances more painful," Jones complained. "My firmness and integrity have supported me against those detestable snares laid by my enemies for my ruin."[10]

Whatever reputation Jones managed to salvage from his Russia years was in large part owed to the good judgment, operational savvy, and decorum of one of his lieutenants, another mercenary named José de Ribas. During the war with the Ottomans, de Ribas proved far more adept than the storied American captain at securing his fortune on the Russo-Turkish frontier, as well as his place in history as Odessa's true founding father. His mixed background and improvised life were emblematic of the city he helped to establish.

José Pascual Domingo de Ribas y Boyons—known to Russians as Osip Mikhailovich Deribas—was born in Naples in June of 1749, the son of the Spanish consul and his aristocratic Irish wife. A port city of breathtaking views, nestled in a natural amphitheater before the brooding cone of Mount Vesuvius, Naples had for centuries been a pawn in political struggles among Spain, France, and Austria. In the 1730s the city at last became the seat of an independent kingdom, ruled by a Bourbon dynasty and momentarily safe from the machinations of other foreign empires.

Naples soon embarked on an era that would see its greatest flowering. The Bourbons patronized the arts and restored medieval and Renaissance-era buildings to their former splendor. But beneath it all swirled an underworld of urban destitution, cultish saint-worship, corruption, and creative debauchery, all surrounded by a benighted countryside that Jesuit priests dismissed as "the Indies over there."[11] Naples was "the most beautiful country in the universe inhabited by the most idiotic species," quipped the Marquis de Sade on a visit to the city when de Ribas was in his early twenties.[12]

Whether it was to escape the gilded squalor of Naples or to seek adventure abroad, de Ribas found himself in the position of many upwardly mobile men in the late eighteenth century: looking longingly to the east, toward Russia, as the next great opportunity. Like John Paul Jones, he must have found the chance to gain a military commission, serve a legendary empress, and fight the infidel Turk a singular inducement to decamp to Catherine's domains.

De Ribas had served a short stint in the Neapolitan army in the late 1760s, and in 1772 he secured a post as a junior officer at the close of Catherine's first war with the sultan. Afterward, he remained on the margins of the empress's court. He was one of the many young men hoping to gain the favor of a monarch who relished her role as defender of Christendom against the supposed barbarities of Ottoman rule. It was a role Catherine embraced. "If you had similar neighbors in Piedmont or in Spain, who brought you annually plague and famine . . . ," she is reported to have said of the Ottomans, blaming them for a host of natural ills on the Black Sea steppe, "would you find it agreeable that I should take them under my protection? I believe then you would indeed treat me as a barbarian."[13] The men she welcomed into her court shared that vision, seeing themselves as crusaders against the cultural and religious darkness—Islamic, despotic, and seminomadic—looming to the south. In St. Petersburg they also found themselves in one of the great centers of Enlightenment-era culture, with heated conversations on liberal philosophy, rapier-sharp witticisms delivered in conversational French, and games of whist that extended late into the night.

The difficulties of liberating and remaking the southern borderlands would have been familiar to a Neapolitan mercenary. After all, de Ribas had seen both the triumphs and the failures of perpetual reformism in his Italian hometown, itself both provincial and southern. From his brief wartime experience, he was also familiar with fighting on the stormy Black Sea, the sweltering plains of southern Russia, and the swampy estuaries—or limans—of rivers such as the Bug and Dnieper. When a new war came in 1787, he was assigned a task that must have been particularly unwelcome: liaising between Potemkin's headquarters in the field and the unit commanded by the hapless Jones. Still, it was a chance to join in the opening salvos of a war rather than trail in at its conclusion, as he had done before.

De Ribas was present at one of the most important and most gruesome episodes of the Russo-Turkish conflict, an engagement in which he served alongside the disoriented and indecisive John Paul Jones. In midsummer 1788, de Ribas was Potemkin's liaison officer with Jones at the Battle of the Liman, an encounter on the Dnieper estuary before the ramparts of two fortresses, Ochakov and Kinburn. The former was held by the Ottomans, the latter by the Russians; the twin outposts faced each other across a narrow water inlet connecting the Dnieper with the Black Sea. Jones was given command of a detachment of oar-powered boats outfitted with small cannons. Their task was not to engage Ottoman warships head-on but to lure them into the shallows, where they would be stuck fast in the mud and offer easy targets to Russia's heavy guns and incendiary bombs. "Humanity recoils with indignation and horror from seeing so many wretched creatures perish in the flames," Jones wrote to de Ribas during the fighting.[14]

The senior officers bickered and prevaricated, but the combination of overwhelming firepower and difficult sailing conditions led to a Russian victory. More important, the battle paved the way for the Russian taking of Ochakov in December, an even more horrific slaughter that produced so many Turkish dead that the Russians simply piled the bodies on the frozen estuary in massive blood-soaked pyramids. The victory, hard won and merciless, was repeated over the next two years against other garrisons farther to the west. Ottoman positions along the Black Sea coast fell in succession after grinding sieges. Brilliant seaborne maneuvers underscored the might of Russia's newly built fleet of sailing ships, bristling with cannons.

Despite his role in these events, Jones ended his Russian career in ignominy. After numerous run-ins with Nassau-Siegen and other aristocratic officers, he was transferred from the southern fleet by Potemkin and returned to St. Petersburg. With the war still raging, he was drummed out of Russia altogether, accused of forcibly deflowering a twelve-year-old girl. His defense was not to disown the affair—a matter usually glossed over by American historians—but rather to deny that it was rape. He admitted in a statement to prosecutors that he had "often frolicked" with the girl for a small cash payment, but that "I can assure you with absolute certainty that I did not despoil her of her virginity."[5] He died in penury in Paris a few years later, a broken man in a faded uniform, still pestering foreign diplomats with plans for new naval campaigns in faraway lands.

De Ribas, by contrast, proved to be a supremely capable, loyal, and decorous adjutant. He worked assiduously to soothe relations between Jones and the European officers, especially Nassau-Siegen, as well as with Potemkin. He dealt with cases of insubordination and drunkenness by talking firmly with the offenders rather than exacting immediate punishment. His performance was noted and rewarded. Potemkin personally transferred him from the navy and placed him in charge of an army detachment under the operational command of Count Ivan Gudovich, one of the most decorated and accomplished generals in the southern theater.

In Gudovich's outfit, de Ribas was made commanding officer of a battalion of Nikolaevsky grenadiers, an elite unit founded by Potemkin himself in honor of St. Nicholas, one of Russia's patron saints. The battalion was composed of just over eight hundred men, including soldiers from three different Cossack regiments. In the summer of 1789, Russian forces were massing for a new series of attacks on Ottoman positions along the sea's northwest coast.

Nearly forty Ottoman vessels lay at anchor offshore from the village of Khadjibey, including two large multimasted warships, or *chebeks*, propelled by both sail and oar. They were the backup force for the small garrison now quartered in the village. Over the years, the Ottomans had improved the fortifications there, adding a stone-walled citadel and a few outbuildings. The village grew to supply the needs of the troops, while Tatar nomads still wintered their flocks on the grasslands beyond. However, the diminutive buildings hardly earned the portentous name the Ottomans gave their outpost: Yeni Dünya, or "new world."

That August, Russian troops under Gudovich and de Ribas approached with caution. The garrison seemed quiet. But the wide bay that opened before the Yeni Dünya facility provided a safe anchor for what remained of the Ottoman fleet, and with the considerable Ottoman firepower located within cannon shot of the coast, the Russian commanders were understandably cautious about how to proceed. "I'll decide how to bring [the Russian fleet] out and how to approach Khadjibey by land so as to seize it and to provide support for our vessels there," Potemkin wrote to the empress from the field. "This matter requires ... great skill and bravery. Placing my hope in God, I have called upon His help and shall try to entirely surround the enemy." The challenges were taking their toll on his health. "My piles, however, are giving me a bad headache," he concluded in his field report.[16]

Finally, after ordering a well-planned reconnaissance, in September of 1789 Potemkin learned almost by surprise that de Ribas's grenadiers had marched up to the walls of Yeni Dünya and claimed it for Catherine. It was, in fact, one of the great non-battles of the war. The entire affair lasted no more than half an hour. The Ottoman garrison, a few-dozen startled soldiers and their senior officer, surrendered on the spot. The ships at sea remained silent. A few days later, a force of some twenty-six Ottoman ships-of-the-line—large-scale fighting vessels—appeared off the coast and fired some cannonballs ashore.

But after a few engagements of this sort, the ships retired. Their captains seemed satisfied to have secured a few tall tales of their heroically lame defense of a small fortress against underwhelming odds.[17]

Meanwhile, the Russians set about surveying what they had conquered almost by happenstance. There was little to report. Khadjibey consisted of a few barracks and five or six small houses. One of them, slightly better kept than the rest, served as the residence of Ahmed Pasha, the garrison commander. The Yeni Dünya citadel was protected by a few crenellated walls and towers, but it had no ditch or other obstacle to prevent the walls from being stormed.[18]

It was not much on which to rest a career, and de Ribas himself never claimed that the Battle of Khadjibey was anything more than good fortune married to the lack of resolve of the Ottoman troops and naval squadron. He would go on to serve in a much more illustrious capacity. The following year he was instrumental in the taking of several Ottoman strongholds on the Dnieper and Danube rivers, battles whose credit even the vainglorious Potemkin was willing to distribute. "I cannot praise Major-General Ribas enough," Potemkin wrote to his empress. "Along with his excellent bravery, he is filled with unspeakable fervor"—a word that appears frequently in Potemkin's descriptions of the Neapolitan officer.[19]

De Ribas was soon returned to naval service and given command of his own oared flotilla. In perhaps the most important single engagement of the war, he helped plan the attack on the key Ottoman fortress at Izmail, a victory that secured the Danube delta for Russia. He eventually rose to the rank of admiral (bypassing his erstwhile superior, the disgraced Rear Admiral Jones) and took command of the entire Black Sea fleet. Even Lord Byron, who featured the Russo-Turkish conflict in his epic *Don Juan*, recorded de Ribas's role in the war:

> *But the stone bastion still kept up its fire,*
> *Where the chief pacha calmly held his post:*

Some twenty times he made the Russ retire,
And baffled the assaults of all their host;
At length he condescended to inquire
If yet the city's rest were won or lost;
And being told the latter, sent a bey
To answer Ribas' summons to give way.[20]

———————————

EVEN AFTER THE GORY and glorious conquest of fortresses from
Ochakov to Izmail, the diminutive Khadjibey remained on de
Ribas's mind. At the end of the war, the village became formally a
part of the Russian Empire, relinquished by the Ottomans in the
peace treaty of 1792. The site had gone overlooked for centuries,
but it mattered now, at the close of the eighteenth century, in ways
that generations of Greeks, Italians, Tatars, and Ottomans could
not have foreseen.

Khadjibey and the fortified Yeni Dünya were situated near the
mouths of several major rivers: the Danube, Dniester, Dnieper, and
Bug. A detachment of infantry or dragoons stationed there could
conceivably control the mouths of the widest, most navigable rivers
in eastern Europe. In the interior, nomads were losing out to settled farmers. The village was a natural gateway to the herds of cattle
and sheep grazing along the southern rivers, to the orchards and
farms situated in the inland regions of Podolia and Volhynia, and
even to the distant trade fairs of Poland and the Baltic Sea. With
appropriate planning and construction, the wide bay could house
a serviceable harbor. Given the comparatively mild climate, ships
that anchored there would have a nearly ice-free winter, something
that virtually no other Russian port at the time could boast. Docks
had already been created farther to the east, in the cities of Kherson and Sevastopol, but neither of those ports provided the immediate access to the open sea and the link with established overland
trade routes that Khadjibey seemed to offer.

Shortly after the war, de Ribas approached the empress Catherine with a plan. The old garrison town could be transformed into the jewel of her new southern possessions. With enough money and de Ribas's notorious fervor, a purposeful city could rise like a beacon at the edge of the sea. The greatness of her reign, evident in the new edifices of St. Petersburg and in the European customs of her court, would have a southern exposure.

Catherine was evidently taken with the idea. On May 27, 1794, she issued an edict to de Ribas recognizing the "profitable situation of Khadjibey on the Black Sea and the advantages connected therewith." She ordered its development as a commercial and shipping center and personally named de Ribas the chief administrator—the *glavny nachal'nik*—of the project. "As Our trade in these lands flourishes, so the city will quickly fill with inhabitants," pronounced the empress.[21]

The Neapolitan soldier of fortune was now tasked with building his own city from scratch, one that would be all that his native Naples was not—fresh, modern, rationally organized—as well as the favored property of one of the world's great empires. It was to be a new city built around a broken-down fortress that the Ottomans had themselves named, coincidentally, the "new world." De Ribas may have been the person who suggested that the city be called Odessos, picking up the name of an ancient Greek colony that had once existed farther down the coast. He may have had his own fondness for antiquities. The lost city of Pompeii, buried by the eruption of Vesuvius in 79 CE, had been unearthed near his hometown only a year before de Ribas was born, spurring widespread interest in the ancient world and making Naples one of the foremost centers of neo-Hellenism in the arts, literature, and philosophy.

In any case, "Odessos" would have fit with the emerging Russian practice of resurrecting ancient traditions along the coastline. The other cities founded or expanded by Potemkin were given russified versions of Greek names, some of them more fanciful than others. Old Tatar villages had been rechristened "Sevastopol" ("the august city") and "Kherson" ("the city of gold"). Crimea became "Tavrida," the Russian spelling of Tauris, a name that would have been familiar to Euripides and Herodotus. Within a year of his appointment as chief of the city-building project, de Ribas was already urging Russian diplomats to talk up the advantages of the facilities in old Khadjibey. Fortifications had been erected to protect the building works from Ottoman reprisals. More than a hundred stone houses and other administrative buildings took the place of Tatar hovels.[22]

According to a story that is as fitting as it is unverifiable, the empress made one lasting change to de Ribas's original plans. All the new foundations on the steppe and coasts of the Black Sea had masculine names. Odessos, commanded the most powerful and self-consciously modern woman in Russian history, should be changed to "Odessa"—the feminized version of a name forever associated with the ancient Odysseus, the wily warrior and navigator. By January of 1795, when St. Petersburg finally got around to issuing a gazetteer of the official labels for the lands taken from the Ottomans three years earlier, the document affirmed that the town "the Tatars call Khadjibey" would be firmly fixed as "Odessa."[23]

CHAPTER 3

Beacon

Одесса. Дерибасовская улица.

Green spaces and fashionable shops: Deribasovskaya Street, from a
nineteenth-century postcard. *Author's collection.*

The most famous thoroughfare in Odessa is Deribasovskaya
Street. It is a green, pedestrianized walkway, tree-lined and
pleasant, with a park and commemorative statues, a bandstand, and
a fountain that spurts in time to music. It is one of the main destinations for a city that comes out for cool-of-the-evening strolls
and gentle public wooings, the same ritual promenade that takes
place on summer nights from Madrid to Istanbul. Deribasovskaya

lies at the heart of historic Odessa, flanked by nineteenth-century storefronts and ornate facades. Cafés choke the sidewalks in the warmer months, and amid the children with melting ice creams and sunburned Ukrainians and Russians returning from the beach, you might find a billiard table plonked in the middle of the street, with an enterprising Odessan trading trick shots for small donations.

The street is a tribute to de Ribas himself—his name is wrapped inside the Russian adjective—and he is still considered the city's truest founder. As he envisioned things, Odessa was to be a light-house of civilization and commerce on the edge of Russia's expand-ing empire. De Ribas managed to secure Catherine's personal support for enlarging the Ottoman fort and beginning work on a jetty to provide protection for ships coming into the harbor. The empress died suddenly in 1796, however, leaving the Odessa project without a clear patron and advocate.

De Ribas soon found himself caught up in the political intrigues that followed Catherine's death. The new tsar, her son Paul, was passionately devoted to undoing much of what his mother had achieved. She had studiously kept him at arm's length throughout her reign, fearing the pent-up ambitions of an heir who was already in his early forties by the time the old empress fell ill. He looked with disdain on his mother's camarilla of courtiers, advisors, and lovers. Pet projects were allowed to languish. Old associates were pushed aside or placed in administrative positions that limited their power. One contemporary observer claimed that the purge included some eighteen thousand men dismissed by the tsar from state service, along with another twelve thousand who resigned voluntarily—a mark not only of the depth of change under Paul but also of the bloated state service created by his mother and Potem-kin (who had died five years earlier).[1]

The Odessa project was falling by the wayside. State funds promised for ambitious building plans and port facilities never materialized. De Ribas's dream of creating an eastern Naples—a port that would be grander and more prosperous than his native city—was fading. De Ribas was frustrated at the tsar's inattention, but he had little power to alter what seemed certain to be Odessa's fate: to become no more than a Russian version of the minor Ottoman fortress-town that he had easily conquered the previous decade. Even de Ribas seemed to lose interest as the obstacles to building Odessa grew during Paul's reign.

Fortunately for Odessa, de Ribas's personal frustrations with the new tsar were widely shared. Paul I made considerable enemies among the Russian nobility, and he ended his short reign as the victim of a palace coup and regicide. There is some suggestion that de Ribas might have had a minor role in planning the end of Paul's time on the throne—and his life—in 1801. But even if he had been a bit player in the drama of imperial succession, he was not around to see the climax. He died several months before Paul was deposed.

The new tsar, Alexander I, came to power intent on returning to his grandmother's policy of encouraging ties with Europe, tugging the empire toward modernity, and developing the southern borderlands of New Russia. Alexander had good reason to begin rethinking New Russia's place in imperial development. The international turmoil brought about by the French Revolution highlighted the importance of the natural resources that Catherine's conquests had bequeathed to his empire, particularly the grain fields and cattle herds of Europe's eastern borderlands. Overland transport across Europe was long, expensive, and—with armies now crisscrossing the continent—frequently dangerous.

The rise of Napoleon, who promised a pan-European and French-dominated order in the wake of revolutionary change, only exacerbated the problem. To starve his enemies in other parts of the continent, Napoleon slapped a ban on the export of grain from Hungary, a move that increased the demand for wheat and barley from other sources. At the same time, there were new ways to profit from Russia's surplus foodstuffs. Ottomans were caving to Euro-

pean pressure and allowing foreign ships to travel unimpeded into
the Black Sea via the Dardanelles and Bosphorus straits. Russian-
flagged vessels had already been granted that privilege in the early
1770s. In 1784 access was extended to Austria, in 1802 to France,
and soon thereafter to Britain, Naples, Ragusa, the Netherlands,
and other trading powers.

These circumstances combined to make de Ribas's original
vision for Odessa more timely than the Neapolitan mercenary
could have imagined. The Black Sea now "became the common
domain of the Nations of Europe," wrote Robert Stevens, a contemporary American visitor, "and Odessa the centre of vast speculations. . . . The very circumstances, that paralysed commerce
elsewhere . . . acted upon Odessa in an inverse ratio."[2] New funds
were appropriated for enhancing port facilities and realizing de
Ribas's earlier building plans.

With this renewed attention to the south—and Russia's key
role as a trading partner and ally against the looming threat of
Napoleon—European interest in the new port skyrocketed. When
Russia was at peace with France, shipping flowed freely from the
major European ports. When it was at war, Russia found ways of
supplying precisely the goods that were most in demand. Europe's
misfortunes were Odessa's gain, and money from across the continent swirled around the city: Dutch ducats, Venetian sequins,
Spanish dubloons, Turkish piasters, Viennese thalers.[3]

Fortified wines from Spain and France, silk from Florence and
Genoa, olive oil and dried fruits from the Levant, and nuts and
fine woods from Anatolia were offloaded from cargo ships. Sacks
of grain and stacks of cowhides from the prairie took their place
in the ships' holds for the return journey.[4] New breakwaters shel-
tered cargo ships from destructive winds, while newly built docks
groaned beneath casks and bundles. Both seaborne and overland
commerce made Odessa the centerpiece of an expanding international network that tied the city more to its European counterparts

than to the imperial metropolises of St. Petersburg and Moscow. The deplorable state of Russian roads meant that the overland journey from Moscow to Odessa could take up to forty days in bad weather, while a traveler could get from London to Odessa in as few as twenty-one days, via Hamburg, Berlin, and Cracow.[5]

Like the New Russian region of which it was now the effective capital, Odessa was following a path from distant colonial outpost to commercial center. De Ribas's vision had spurred the city's founding, while Alexander I presided over the initial boom in New Russia that revived Odessa's role in the southern empire. But much of the real credit for its takeoff goes to a French aristocrat on the lam.

IN THE TUMULTUOUS final decades of the eighteenth century, Russia became a haven for down-and-out European nobles, bored adventurers, and impecunious philosophers, musicians, and artists seeking patrons in an empire that had only recently discovered its European vocation. Armand Emmanuel Sophie Septimanie du Plessis, duc de Richelieu, was one of them. Born in September of 1766, Richelieu was a member of the great family of French nobles and heir to a long tradition of state service. His great-uncle, Armand Jean du Plessis, Cardinal Richelieu, had been the famous and powerful chief minister to Louis XIII.

Well educated and urbane, lean and slightly stoop-shouldered, with arrestingly dark eyes and hair, the young duc reportedly bore a striking resemblance to the cardinal. The Richelieu name alone guaranteed access to the French court. In time he developed a reputation for constancy and honest dealings, both of which were rarities in the gilded and intrigue-ridden world of late-eighteenth-century France. After an early arranged marriage, Richelieu remained uxorious throughout his many subsequent years of travel and state service.

Before the age of twenty, he had inherited from his grandfather the role of First Gentleman of the Bedchamber to the French king, a senior position at court. He soon became a trusted advisor to Marie Antoinette, even begging the royal family not to return to Paris when news of the revolution reached Versailles. That association nearly cost him his life. After the mobs of Paris descended on the Bastille and French aristocrats were marched to the guillotine, Richelieu escaped eastward, to Russia. There he joined the cloud of European nobles swirling around Catherine and Potemkin. He served in minor roles during Catherine's second war with the Ottomans, alongside Potemkin, de Ribas, and John Paul Jones. He was lightly wounded during the storming of the fortress at Izmail and in return received the expected military decoration and gratitude of the empress herself.

As a veteran of courtly machinations in Versailles, Richelieu skillfully weathered the uncertain years following the death of his new patron and the brief reign of the petulant Paul. When Alexander became tsar in 1801, Richelieu was thus in a good position to seek a major role in the reformed administration. Given the growing importance of France—both as a trading partner with New Russia and as an occasional enemy of the Russian Empire—appointing someone with French connections to a position in the south made good sense. In 1803 Alexander named the thirty-seven-year-old Richelieu to the post of *gradonachal'nik*—city administrator—of Odessa, with responsibility for all military, commercial, and municipal affairs. He soon found himself journeying southward to take up the new assignment on a piece of territory that, as he recalled in his memoirs, probably overstating the case, was still "a desert inhabited only by hordes of Tatars and by Cossacks who, rejecting all civilization, sow terror through their brigandage and cruelties."[6]

When he arrived, Richelieu discovered not so much a city, despite the robust commerce, as an architectural drawing—all plan and relatively little substance, with streets and foundations laid out in the chalky dust of the plain. One of de Ribas's lasting contributions had been his insistence on self-conscious urban organization. Odessa is young by European, even by American, standards. A city that we now think of as typically old world was founded three years after Washington, D.C. Both cities' central districts are eighteenth-century fantasies of what a city should be: rationally laid out on a grid of symmetrical streets intersected by long, wide avenues and dotted with pocket-sized parks. The avenues provide edifying sight lines over great distances. The parks are places of relaxation and civic-mindedness, with statues and monuments that extol the virtues of duty, honor, and patriotism. It was a thrill for later visitors to Odessa—such as Mark Twain in the 1860s—to stand in the middle of a broad thoroughfare and see the empty steppe at one end and the empty sea at the other, just as visitors to Washington can connect the dots of the Capitol, the Lincoln Memorial, and other prominent landmarks via the major avenues and open spaces.

Preobrazhensky Cathedral, from an early-twentieth-century postcard.
Author's collection.

Richelieu found this basic town structure already in place. De Ribas had worked with a Dutch engineer, Franz de Voland, to design a city based on a grid pattern, or at least as much of one as could be squeezed into the ravine-cut landscape on which Khadjibey was situated. Nearly two-dozen administrative buildings fashioned from the ubiquitous limestone rose beside hundreds of wooden shops, grain magazines, and earthen huts.[7] But the mass of people that soon flooded into the town contrasted sharply with the designers' emphasis on order and rationality. Peasants lined the wide streets hawking their produce and seeking occasional work on the docks. Sailors cavorted while their ships were in port. The growing population—seven to eight thousand people when Richelieu took office—was putting pressure on public order.[8] In response, Richelieu organized a campaign to reshape city administration, improve sanitation, and erect a series of public buildings that would polish a place that was still little more than a colonial outpost, albeit one with a logical street plan. "To perfect, to encourage, and to finish: that is the spirit of the current regime," noted a contemporary French observer.[9]

Within only a few years after assuming his post, Richelieu had built a theater and public schools, including a *gymnasium* for merchants' sons, a relative novelty in an empire where education was still a privilege of the upper classes. He established a library and a printing press, which published works in several languages (all overseen by the official state censor, housed in one of the first government buildings to be erected). Throughout the city, he ordered the planting of trees along streets and in parks, creating a green oasis in the flat expanse of blue-black sea and dun-colored steppe— and personally berated citizens when they failed to water the new plantings.[10]

The American merchant Robert Stevens waxed lyrical about the changes he had seen in the first few years of Richelieu's tenure, and how spectacular the differences would have appeared to the old inhabitants of Khadjibey. As he wrote in a manifesto on the advantages of commerce with Odessa, "At this epoch could one of the primitive inhabitants of this country, one of those wandering Tartars, could he have been suddenly transported, into the midst of this city, witnessing the public and private prosperity, the elegance and grandeur of surrounding objects, he could not be made to believe he was not viewing, works of enchantment."[11] In relatively short order, Odessans became as status conscious as people in other major cities. "Today a one-horse carriage is the final form of humility, the last reserve of the strictest economizing," wrote a French marquis, Gabriel de Castelnau. "That is to say, no one goes on foot."[12]

But for all Richelieu's civic-mindedness, Odessa could not escape its location. As a burgeoning entrepôt, the city was open to outsiders like no other port in the empire. The ships that dropped anchor in the inner harbor often carried an unseen cargo lurking deep inside the bundles of textiles or crates of dried fruit. The perils of epidemic diseases, and Russia's nearly century-long fight against them, became another of the hallmarks of Odessa's frontier identity.

———————

IN THE BOILING August of 1812, people were falling sick in Odessa at a rate no one had witnessed before. On August 12 a female dancer in the local theater died after an illness of only thirty-six hours. Three days later, a second performer died. A third soon took ill. A few days more, and two servants and an actor were dead as well. All had the same symptoms: a mild vertigo and headache, followed by nausea and vomiting, then fatigue and dizziness, a burning thirst, and swollen, painful carbuncles in the armpits and groin. Death followed in less than six days.[13]

Large-scale infectious diseases such as cholera and the plague were a fact of life around the Black Sea, much as they were in any region where landscape, climate, robust trade, and variable immunity created propitious breeding grounds and transmission routes for microbes. The Black Death—a highly contagious microbial infection that wiped out a quarter or more of Europe's population in the 1340s—may have made its leap to the west aboard cargo ships leaving the old Italian ports of Crimea. After Catherine the Great incorporated the region into her empire, returning Russian soldiers and seamen often unwittingly transported disease from the pestilential south to the towns and villages of central Russia. For the cities of New Russia, especially those that regularly welcomed ships from the plague-afflicted ports in the Ottoman Empire, diseases threatened to jump easily from quayside to town center.

For that reason, one of Richelieu's specific assignments, laid out by Tsar Alexander in his initial orders to the new *gradonachal'nik*, was to "choose a suitable place for the construction of a quarantine facility and accelerate its construction."[14] In fact, a quarantine system had been in place in Odessa nearly from the city's founding. Ships' cargoes were checked and fumigated with sulfur dioxide or other chemicals. Passengers were required to spend at least fourteen days in isolated observation in the old Ottoman fortress, a period of time thought to be sufficient for symptoms to become manifest.

Quarantine officials at the time had little inkling of the specific causes of the bubonic plague—the *Yersinia pestis* bacillus and its chief vector, the flea—but they knew that some routes of transmission were more likely than others. Bacilli traveled on fleas, fleas on rats, and rats on ships, which, when docked in the harbor, would be drawn to the granaries and rubbish-strewn streets of the city center. People, too, could become vectors. In a city already becoming famous for its corrupt customs officers, a few infected but asymptomatic passengers could always avoid the quarantine regulations—perhaps for a small, informal fee—and pass unnoticed up the hill and into the heart of the city.

Early on in the August outbreak, stories circulated about an actress in the local theater who had received a ring, wrapped in a small fluff of cotton, from an anonymous admirer. Cotton—a prime hiding place for fleas—would certainly have been subjected to inspection and fumigation, but the actress's admirer, recently arrived by ship, had somehow managed to smuggle the ring and its wrapper past port authorities. That was why the major symptoms—the painful carbuncles, or buboes, from which the bubonic plague takes its name—were first reported by actors and actresses working together on the city's only stage.

Richelieu, who had just returned from a tour of Crimea, was due to take a field command in the war against Napoleon, but he wisely decided to remain in the city. He ordered an investigation into the illness. City officials soon reported that there had been a spate of suspicious deaths in the last several months, but since the dead were mainly peasants and servants, their fate had gone unremarked. It was only once men and women in the public eye began to succumb—those performing in the theater Richelieu himself had built—that the scale of the problem became evident. By that time the plague had already insinuated itself deep into Odessa's population.

The Grande Armée of Napoleon was already menacing Moscow far to the north, but Richelieu delayed his departure for the front, reckoning that fighting the local and unseen enemy was more pressing than fighting his fellow Frenchmen on the outskirts of Moscow. He called together several doctors and sought their advice. They were divided on the cause and seriousness of the illness. Some argued that it could not possibly be the plague. No sailors had been reported ill, and there was no news of the disease raging in Constantinople, which had usually been taken as a signal to be particularly careful with ships hailing from the Ottoman capital.

But the mere suggestion that the plague might have made an appearance in the city determined Richelieu to act. On August

26 he ordered all buildings where people might gather in large numbers—churches, the commercial exchange, courts, the custom house, and the theater—to be closed. Markets were allowed to remain open, but new regulations were put in place to prevent loitering. The smell of vinegar wafted through the sparsely populated bazaars, as merchants soaked their money in the liquid to kill whatever pestilence was thought to carry the disease.

As with any epidemic, information was the chief weapon. Richelieu ordered the city divided into several districts and assigned deputies to make daily reports, based on household surveys, of the progress of infection in their territory. The quarantine zone was extended far inland, to the Bug and Dniester rivers, as well as on roads and drover paths leading to the north, and the length of quarantine monitored by officials: twenty-four days for individuals without baggage and twelve weeks for those with merchandise or suspect goods.

Notwithstanding these precautions, the number of deaths soared. District inspectors reported as many as twenty people dying each day. Outbreaks were now seen in surrounding villages as mothers embraced infected children and husbands tended to dying wives, flouting restrictions on contact with the infected. Physicians, racing from household to household to provide terminal care to the dying, were themselves falling victim.

At this point, Richelieu took a daring decision that probably secured Odessa's future. He ordered the city's borders to be sealed and established a general quarantine in all neighborhoods. It was a bold, even foolhardy, move. He had virtually no military forces at his disposal to enforce the quarantine. Most soldiers were at the front. Richelieu eventually managed to secure a detachment of five hundred Cossacks, but they were given the nearly impossible task of invigilating a city whose population had swollen, in the previous seven years of Richelieu's tenure, to around thirty-two thousand people.

The new regulations came into effect on November 12. All doors and windows were to remain closed. Only people in public service were permitted to leave their homes, and even they were required to have a special identification ticket. To provision the shut-down city, police and commissary officials conveyed food through each district twice a day. Meat was dipped in cold water and bread was fumigated before distribution. Each house was inspected twice daily, and anyone exhibiting signs of illness was taken to a separate surveillance area until he either died or, much more rarely, recovered.

Wooden carts crawled through the streets conducting those who were to be removed for observation. Red flags announced that the cart was hauling the living, black flags that the victim had already expired. Prisoners were dragooned into serving as ferrymen for the dead and dying. Wearing oil-drenched overcoats as prophylactics against the disease, they trudged through the deserted streets, their corpse-bearing carts trailing behind them.

"I was present at these scenes of sadness," wrote the French traveler Auguste, comte de Lagarde, "and I have viewed with bitterness the despair of those prepared to give up all they had in order to escape death."[15] Another observer described the eerie stillness that enveloped the port and the changes in everyday social relations that the disease seemed to spawn:

> People were almost afraid to breathe, lest the contagion should be floating in the air, — fires were lighted, and odoriferous substances burned before their doors: . . . [T]wo horsemen, posted in every street, paced it slowly in opposite directions; the functionaries addressed each other only at a distance; letters, when received, were fumigated and delivered by means of a stick slit at one end, being refumigated before they were opened and read; all the exterior marks of friendship were forbidden, and no one dared to make enquiries after his relations or friends, for fear of hearing that they had died of the plague.[16]

The city, once bustling and full of life, now ground to a halt. Fumigation fires filled the streets with acrid smoke. On the out- skirts of town, freshly dug mass graves created false hillocks on the flat steppe. When those pits were full, piles of human bodies were put to the torch. Even Richelieu himself, who wandered freely about the city throughout the epidemic, was occasionally seen to pick up a shovel and dig graves when the workmen tired or feared for their own safety.

With the rate of death increasing, Richelieu finally ordered the docklands — the jumping-off point for the infection and the locus of its greatest toll — to be razed. Smoke billowed from the piers that de Ribas had worked to build and from the array of warehouses that peppered the quay. Despite the regulations on public gather- ings, some citizens ventured outside, past the Cossack pickets, to watch the spectacle of their city's ruin. Ships at sea witnessed the fat column of smoke rising in the distance, dark evidence of the city's self-immolation and a beacon warning them to keep away.

After nearly two months of general quarantine, on January 7, 1813, citizens were finally allowed to venture out of doors, although customs and quarantine barriers around the city remained in place and were never completely removed. Suspect houses were emptied or torched. Richelieu's harsh methods, rather than stoking fear and disorder, had almost miraculously caused the plague to burn itself out. From August 1812 to January 1813, the number of people infected was 3,331, of whom only 675 recovered, a death toll of just over 10 percent of the city's population.[17]

A city that had imagined itself as a shining example to the out- side world, a young town that had grown from unrefined frontier post into a minor metropolis, had found itself building walls against the unseen dangers that could come floating in from the sea. Odessa had gone through the first episode of an internal struggle that would last well into the twentieth century: a conflict between a self-image of openness and grandeur and one of insularity and terror. But there was also a brighter and unexpected side effect. The sadness inevitably produced by thousands of deaths, coupled with a long and deadly winter, brought a new and happier epidemic. City officials noted a marked increase in births in the autumn of 1813.[18]

OF RICHELIEU's several innovations in dealing with the plague, perhaps the one that mattered most to the city's future was the egalitarianism with which even the harshest restrictions on movement and public gatherings were enforced. Surprisingly for the time, Jews were subjected to the same regulations as their Christian neighbors (although infected Jews were treated in a separate surveillance facility and hospital).

In previous instances of the plague, from Provence to Catalonia and from Switzerland to the Rhineland, Jews were usually the scapegoats for outbreaks of infection. They were routinely blamed for a host of imagined transgressions, from their allegedly inadequate hygiene to grand plots aimed at weakening Christian civilization. From the fourteenth century forward, repeated attacks on Jews in western Europe—burnings, beatings, tortures, and exiles—were one of the principal incentives for Jews to migrate to the east, to the borderlands of central Europe and Russia, from the Baltic to the Black Sea, which would eventually become the cultural epicenter of European Jewry. In this particular epidemic, however, Richelieu managed astutely to avoid the frequent and fatal combination of plagues and pogroms—providing an early example of Odessa's place as a refuge for an increasingly diverse community.

In addition to the hundreds of sailors stopping off at Odessa each trading season, the city had begun to attract a mottled collection of individuals seeking their own fortune at the border of sea and steppe. Some of the earliest informal censuses recorded contingents of Greek and Albanian soldiers; Italian, Jewish, Greek, and Bulgarian merchants; runaway Russian serfs; as well as communities of Cossacks. The city was already gaining a reputation as a place in Russia—barely—but decidedly not of it. It was located on a sea that had become, in just a few short decades, "the common domain of the Nations of Europe," wrote Robert Stevens, and Odessa now lay at the center of the "vast speculations" launched by the opening of trade.[19] As the comte de Lagarde noted, "Through beautiful squares planted with trees and crossed with footpaths circulate the Turk, the Greek, the Russian, the Englishman, the Jew, the Armenian, the Frenchman, the Moldovan, the Pole, the Italian, and the German, most of them wearing the costume appropriate to each and speaking different tongues."[20]

As the owners of the major trading houses and with strong family and business connections with the Mediterranean, Italians dominated city life, a recapitulation of their role when Genoese and Venetian trading centers ringed the Black Sea. Italian became the city's lingua franca, lilting through the commercial exchange and wafting up from the docklands. Street signs—another innovation of Richelieu's tenure—were written in both Italian and Russian, a practice that lasted well beyond his days in office.[21] An eight-hundred-seat opera house, established by Richelieu only three years before the plague and designed by Jean-François Thomas de Thomon, one of the great shapers of St. Petersburg, featured a visiting Italian company performing a standard repertoire of classics. The company offered an early-nineteenth-century version of surtitles: a Russian actor would helpfully summarize the libretto for any audience members who happened not to speak Italian.[22] Even the city's ubiquitous carters and petty traders, or *chumaks*, were known to break into choruses of "La donna è mobile"—that is, unless they were singing their own ditties about the glories of the city at the end of the drover trails:

> *I'm makin' my way to Odessa*
> *'Cause in Odessa you can live it up.*

No carryin' sacks of wheat,
No toilin' for the lord and master,
No payin' the poll tax,
No trudgin' behind the plow . . .
They call me *master now!*[23]

Richelieu finally retired his post on a cool Monday in late September of 1814. Vehicles clogged the streets, and well-wishers trailed behind his carriage as it exited the city's environs. It was said at the time that he left Odessa with no more than a small leather trunk and a few days' change of clothes. Unlike administrators in other parts of the empire, he had developed a reputation for modesty and honest dealings, and a supreme aversion to using his position as *gradonachal'nik* for personal gain. He not only built the city but also saw it through its first devastating crisis.

As Richelieu passed the quarantine barrier on his route out of town, his heart was already in his native France. The previous spring a grand coalition of European armies had pushed into the streets of Paris. Napoleon had abdicated as emperor. The Bourbon monarchy, in the person of Louis XVIII, was returned to the throne. The heady thrill of restoration drew Richelieu westward. He eventually translated his family name and his international connections into a new career in service to France. He witnessed Napoleon's escape from exile on Elba, his momentary return to power, and his final defeat at Waterloo. As France's years of crisis wound to a close, he was named prime minister of a country from which he had been absent for most of his adult life. He died in 1822, not yet sixty years old. France and Russia were in positions they had not enjoyed for decades: at peace with each other and with most of their neighbors.

Far to the east, in Odessa, Richelieu had realized the vision first laid out by de Ribas. He had bridged the period from Catherine to Alexander, from the era of exploration and Enlightenment to that of modernity. "Odessa . . . will flourish without me," he wrote to one correspondent several months before his death.[24] As French ships continued to visit the growing port, now recovering from the creeping death and providential arson of 1812–13, a new generation of builders and visitors was making Odessa a vibrant, thriving, and—for one long-suffering husband, his wife, and an exiled poet—supremely romantic corner of the Russian Empire.

CHAPTER 4

The Governor and the Poet

The great modernizer: The statue honoring the duc de Richelieu, which stands at the top of the "Potemkin steps," shown in a late-nineteenth-century photograph. *Author's collection.*

On a fine and sunny Saturday morning in late May of 1828, a huge crowd gathered along Nikolaevsky Boulevard to welcome the duc de Richelieu back to Odessa. The duc himself had died six years earlier, but Odessans were now turning out to witness the installation of a statue in his honor—the first public monument in the entire city—on the tree-lined street running above the harbor.

His immediate successor—Louis Alexandre Andrault, comte de Langéron—had improved on Richelieu's original design for the boulevard, installing trees and pavements for the citizens who regularly gathered each weekend to take in the sea air. Langéron was there among the crowd, but ill health had caused him to give up the leadership of the city several years earlier. Like Richelieu, he had escaped the French Revolution by hiding out in the court of Catherine the Great and had skillfully translated that experience into a lifetime of service to his adopted country. As chief administrator of Odessa and New Russia, he had continued Richelieu's work, most importantly by securing "free port" status for the city, a position that rendered Odessa a gigantic duty-free zone and made it even more of a magnet for foreign commerce.

As Langéron and other dignitaries looked on, a canvas sheet lay draped over the new monument. Its four corners were attached to a short railing at the base of the stone plinth, with the flags of Great Britain, France, Austria, and Russia standing as sentinels. Soldiers from a battalion of the tsar's own Ufa Regiment, resplendent in their colorful uniforms, stood at attention in front of the veiled statue. Facing them were ranks of bespectacled professors and students from the Richelieu Lycée, the city's most prestigious school. Foreign consuls, dressed in formal attire, joined the spectators. Thousands of average Odessans pressed forward expectantly to catch a glimpse of the action.

At around eleven in the morning, a procession began to wend its way from the central cathedral. The local archbishop led a bevy of clergymen, his heavy, embroidered robes trailing in the dust. When the procession arrived at the ceremonial site, an official read out the tsar's charter giving Odessans permission to erect a monument to Richelieu's memory. The archbishop then mounted the rostrum and, in stentorian and ecclesiastical Russian, bestowed blessings on the city and its people.

When he had finished, the canvas was drawn back to reveal a

glistening bronze statue of the duc, dressed in a Roman toga and garlanded with laurel leaves, his right hand extended as if show-ing off the city with a sweep of the arm. The crowd cheered. The troops saluted. A band struck up a martial tune. In the bay, cannons roared from warships drawn up for the occasion. More speeches followed—one in French from Charles Sicard, one of the city's oldest inhabitants, others in Italian and Russian from two learned teachers at the lycée—before a march-past by the Ufa infantrymen and more festive music from the brass band. That evening, anyone walking past the monument found it illuminated by torchlight, the duc's likeness glowing in the darkness.[1]

There were plenty of dignitaries in the crowd that May. But the master of ceremonies, taller than most of the men around him, with soft blue eyes and a round face, was the new governor-general of New Russia. He was a generation younger than de Ribas and Richelieu, a man of trousers and coatees rather than breeches and tricorns, now charged with governing a city that was squarely on the path toward becoming Russia's premier southern metropolis. He was also the first of the crucial figures in Odessa's history since Potemkin to have a Russian name.

––––––––––

MIKHAIL SEMYONOVICH VORONTSOV was born in St. Petersburg in 1782 into a wealthy but recently titled aristocratic family. At the age of only two, he was whisked away to London by his father, who had been appointed Russian ambassador to the Court of St. James. Thus began an association with Britain that lasted the younger Vorontsov's entire life. It also became the source of many jokes about his anglophile ways and cool manner. Leo Tolstoy, in his novella *Hadji Murat*, portrayed him much as he was seen by his contemporaries, as "ambitious, kind and gentle in his manner with inferiors and a subtle courtier in his relations with superiors," with a "vulpine" face and possessing a "subtle and genial mind."[2]

Mikhail's father, Semyon, was a courtly rival of Potemkin's and had been one of the many nobles forced to resign from state service during the brief and turbulent reign of Catherine's son, Paul. This personal familiarity with the caprice of tyranny, combined with a childhood diet of English liberal values and country estate vices, formed much of Vorontsov's character. After graduating from Cambridge, Vorontsov returned to Russia for the coronation of Alexander I and began his own long and distinguished career of state service.

His early experience was a trial by fire, however. As a young man of considerable social standing, he was given a commission in the Preobrazhensky Guards, one of the most illustrious and storied of Russian military units, with origins stretching back to Peter the Great. When he took up his officer's sword, in the late autumn of 1801, the place to be for a young and ambitious lieutenant was the Caucasus, the jumble of mountains on Russia's southern frontier. There, a host of independent kingdoms, clans, and tribal groups formed a buffer between Russia and its rivals, the Ottoman Empire and Persia. The tsar had recently concluded an agreement with the Christian kingdom of Kartli-Kakheti (in modern-day eastern Georgia) that allowed for the kingdom's absorption into the Russian Empire. Vorontsov requested a transfer to the military command in the kingdom's capital, Tiflis. He soon found himself in a delicate set of circumstances.

The royal family of Kartli-Kakheti, although convinced of the need for Russian protection against its Muslim neighbors, was unenthusiastic about full-scale annexation. Other kings and princes in the neighborhood were similarly wary of Russian territorial ambitions masquerading as a desire to protect embattled Christians. Through a combination of skillful diplomacy, persistent cajoling, and sometimes brute force, Russia's commander in the region, Pavel Tsitsianov, finally brought the reluctant Caucasus nobles to heel. Vorontsov's role was relatively minor. He served on a

Portrait of Mikhail Semyonovich, Count Vorontsov (1821)
by Sir Thomas Lawrence. *State Hermitage Museum,
St. Petersburg/The Bridgeman Art Library.*

series of diplomatic missions for his commanding officer and occasionally saw battle in skirmishes against highland raiding parties. But his brief Caucasus sojourn taught him a lesson that he would later take to Odessa: that Russia's empire, like Britain's, was now vaster and more complex—politically, culturally, and religiously—than anyone in St. Petersburg seemed to realize. To administer such a territory required skills more refined and nuanced than storming a citadel during the occasional summer campaign.

Vorontsov was a member of the generation of Russian soldiers and statesmen who were fully removed from the values and strategies of the eighteenth century and who were moving, however uncertainly, into the nineteenth. His performance in the Caucasus immediately recommended him to other commanders. Over the next thirteen years—from 1805 to 1818—Vorontsov found himself on the frontlines of nearly every major military engagement Russia faced: Napoleon's initial thrust against the tsar's ally, the king of Prussia; a new war against the Ottoman Empire; and finally the defense of the Russian heartland after Napoleon's invasion of 1812.

In that conflict, Vorontsov—by now a major general—was a central character. He was present at the decisive Battle of Borodino, sustaining a serious bullet wound to his leg, and at the bloody engagement at Craonne, where he commanded troops arrayed against Napoleon himself. When the French invaders made their forced retreat from Russia, Vorontsov's troops were close on their heels. In March of 1814 he walked at the head of his division down the Champs-Élysées. The following year, the tsar elevated him to the post of commander of the Russian occupation forces in Paris.

For the first time in his career, Vorontsov, now in his midthirties, was entrusted not only with overseeing a military unit in the field but also with administering a distinct and stationary population of thirty thousand men plus their dependents: the occupation army. Over the next three years, he introduced an array of innovations, including the development of a postal system for his corps, a literacy and educational program for his noncommissioned officers and men, and a reform of the existing disciplinary system—previously based on brutal corporal punishment—for unruly soldiers. Just as Richelieu was helping to remake the French government after the disruptions of the Napoleonic era, Vorontsov was helping to reshape Russia's contingent of occupiers. When the occupation ended in late 1818, Vorontsov led his army on the long trek home. He soon returned to Paris to enjoy a period of relaxation after years as a field commander. It was there, at a grand party in the middle of a city just awakening from war and foreign occupation, that he met Elizaveta Branicka.

Lise, as she was generally known, was a member of a family of Polish landowning magnates on her mother's side. Through strategic marriages with the Russian nobility, the family had become wealthy, highly regarded, and supremely well connected in European society. She was the great-niece of Potemkin, and her mother, Countess Alexandra Branicka, had cradled the great prince's head as he wheezed with pneumonia in his final hours.

Lise was a woman who would today be described as handsome rather than beautiful, of finely chiseled, if not delicate, features, graceful and elegant, with blue eyes and raven hair, which she kept swirled in ringlets atop her head. She was rather coquettish by reputation even though she was now well beyond her youth. Her charm and poise, if sometimes too self-regarding, gave her a social stature and desirability that lasted well into her maturity.

At the dangerously old age of twenty-six, a suitable marriage partner had not yet crossed her path—or, more likely, no one had yet met the rigorous standards of her mother, by this time an aged and increasingly avaricious widow. When they met, Vorontsov was immediately smitten, and Lise returned the admiration. The old countess, in turn, was taken with the general, a man old enough to be well established, with an already storied career and trailing a long pedigree of titled and moneyed Russian and British relatives. Lise and Vorontsov were married in a magnificent ceremony in May of 1819.

Vorontsov was now at a turning point. He was comfortable in the salons of Paris and the drawing rooms of London, and he had also served the tsar gallantly on the battlefield. Where should he make his home and plot out the next stage of a well-managed career? He spent the next several years traveling back and forth to Russia, sometimes with Lise in tow, even after the couple had started a family. In the expanse of New Russia, he saw immediately the possibilities for settlement, commerce, and farming. He visited Odessa on the invitation of his friend, the comte de Langéron. The city was booming, and governing it required energy and drive, traits that Langéron himself admitted were not among his virtues. "I do

as little harm as possible," he wrote in a letter to Vorontsov. "I flat-
ter myself always that if there is no longer war I will see you replace
me one day in this post."[3] Through delicate maneuverings at the
tsar's court and in the Russian civil service, Vorontsov scouted the
possibilities for succeeding the fatigued Langéron. To ensure his
livelihood, he used portions of Lise's considerable dowry to purchase immense estates in the south, in Crimea and around Odessa
and Taganrog, a port on the Sea of Azov. In the late spring of 1823
it was official: Vorontsov was to be the governor-general of New
Russia, a title only recently created for the chief administrator. The
Vorontsov family soon decamped to the shores of the Black Sea.

———————

BY THE 1820s, the province of New Russia was dotted with towns
and river ports. New roads had been cut across the steppe. Colonies of German, Bulgarian, and Serbian farmers made the prairie
bloom. It was administered by a generation of talented administrators sent south to tame the frontier and remake the *dikoe pole*, or
the "wild field," as it was known in Russian.

For all these improvements, it was also still a place of exile.
The frontier towns and ports of New Russia, with their masses of
bedraggled peasants recently arrived from the countryside, newly
settled nomadic herders, and Mediterranean and Levantine sailors,
were a far cry from the well-kept streets and urban bustle of the
imperial capitals. They were fitting destinations for political agitators or self-important men of letters who, while not presenting a
direct threat to the power of the tsar, might find their libertinism
and youthful insolence an affront to the powerful classes in St.
Petersburg or Moscow. Such was the case with Alexander Pushkin.

A notorious romantic and a writer of fiery and dyspeptic spirit,
his curly hair fashionably unkempt and a mass of whiskers trailing
down his cheeks, Pushkin was a descendant of Avram Gannibal, an
African who had been reared in the court of Peter the Great and

was later granted landholding rights by the tsar. The official reason for Pushkin's relegation to the south was his transfer from a post in the Ministry of Foreign Affairs to government service helping to oversee the colonization of the southern territories. In reality his journey was a form of internal exile. Already a poet and publicist of some note while still in his late teens, Pushkin pioneered the Russian literary genre that mixed lyrical imagery with political radicalism, cloaking calls for reforming the stifling tsarist autocracy in language infused with romantic suffering. When he emerged as one of the most vocal members of the coterie of young writers and artists that swirled through the salon society of St. Petersburg, he increasingly came under the attention of government censors, who ordered his banishment from the capital in 1820.

Pushkin spent the next three years on the southern plains, near the Caucasus Mountains and in the borderland district of Bessarabia, a land of rolling hills, sunflower fields, and Gypsy encampments. The region fueled his imagination and confirmed his self-image as a passionate outsider—in his own mind, a latter-day Ovid reduced to writing plaintive epistles from the Black Sea. "Accursed city Kishinev! the tongue would tire of berating you," he wrote to one correspondent from the Bessarabian regional seat.[4] By 1823 his frequent requests to be transferred to Odessa had been granted, in large part because of the personal intervention of Vorontsov, who took pity on the poet. He was reassigned to the staff of New Russia's governor-general.

Pushkin's reputation at this stage was decidedly mixed. He had gained some renown as a clever writer, even if he had a habit of stepping over the line of propriety when making impromptu verses at parties or society dinners. He continued to publish in the literary press during his exile, and his southern meanderings added a wisp of orientalism to his work, an oeuvre that was already heavily influenced by the eastern themes and quaint Islamophilia of Lord Byron. Pushkin's longing and lyrical "The Fountain of Bakhchisaray" offered the poet's reflections on the frailty of humanity and empire after viewing a delicately carved fountain in the old palace of the Tatar khan of Crimea, the same residence that had hosted Catherine and Potemkin several decades earlier. His poem "The Captive of the Caucasus," born of his active imagination while viewing the majestic Caucasus Mountains at a distance, became the empire's quintessential literary statement of its own wild south: a land of romantic natives, restless frontiersmen, and exotic beauty.

When Pushkin finally arrived in Odessa in the hot July of 1823, he came with a literary and public celebrity that made the transfer of his exile something of a public event. He was never at a loss for dinner invitations or drinking partners. He was known to the city's substantial number of prostitutes, who were well acquainted with Greek and Italian sailors but rather less famil-iar with poets. He had spent the last three years wandering the empire's far-flung borderlands (albeit in a good deal of luxury) and now found himself sloshing through dust and mud to attend a salon or late-evening supper. "I am again in Odessa and still can-not become accustomed to the European mode of life," he wrote to his brother, Lev, in August.[5]

The city had changed considerably since the time of de Ribas and Richelieu. The population was growing rapidly, on its way to tripling in size by mid-century to nearly 116,000 people. Occupy-ing the site of the old Turkish fortress, a handsome stone palace for the new governor-general would soon rise at one end of Niko-laevsky Boulevard, to be completed by 1830. The state rooms on the ground floor were outfitted with doors, shutters, and chimney pieces from the Mikhailovsky Palace in St. Petersburg, the resi-dence of the late Paul I (and the site of his murder). A billiard hall, a grand dining room, a large salon, and a library were decorated with elegant English furniture, while a separate "Turkish" chamber had a soaring ceiling, gilded fixtures, Persian carpets on the floor, and silk-covered divans arrayed around the walls. A library held the finest private collection of books, pictures, and samples of scientific instruments in the entire empire.[6]

Elsewhere in the town, plastered facades with tile- or iron-covered roofs were going up around a circular plaza, soon to be flanked by a new local museum, public library, and government buildings. Hotels run by Genoese and other foreign entrepreneurs dotted the city. A selection of bars and lesser eating establishments catered to new arrivals. At the height of the commercial season, from April to October, the population could swell by as many as ten thousand people, as laborers, wagon-drivers, Russian and Polish landowners, and foreign merchants descended on the port, which still enjoyed the privilege of free trade with the wider world.[7] Were it not for the exoticism of this transient population, noted an English visitor during Vorontsov's tenure, "Odessa may be said to be Petersburgh in miniature."[8]

Pushkin was still in his early twenties when he moved to Odessa, and he soon began his pursuit—and occasional conquest—of the local notables, married and single, young and old. There was the twenty-seven-year-old Karolina Sobańska, still technically married to a wealthy Odessan businessman but living openly with the commander of military colonies in New Russia—while also working secretly as a government spy to ferret out political radicals. There was Amaliya Riznich, with a pronounced Roman nose and already pregnant when they first met.

Pushkin was a giddy and voluble correspondent on matters of love and sex, gossiping in infantile detail with many of his friends. "I'll be glad to serve you / With my crazy conversation," he wrote to Filipp Wiegel, a closeted gay friend who was serving as a tsarist official in Kishinev. "But, Wiegel,—spare my arse!"[9] But the most telling record of Pushkin's loves during his days in Odessa comes from an unexpected source: his own doodles. In the marginalia of an early draft of his masterpiece *Evgeny Onegin*, a work he began in Bessarabia and continued while working for

Alexander Pushkin. *Prints and Photographs
Division, Library of Congress.*

Vorontsov, tiny portraits of women and men frame the text—
friends, acquaintances, people he saw on the street, and one after
another of his obsessive loves. There, amid an angelic choir of
widows and ingénues, dark-haired foreigners and fine-featured
Russians, is a woman seven years his senior, someone with whose
likeness he decorated the manuscript more often than any
other—Vorontsov's wife, Lise.

WHEN EXACTLY Lise and Pushkin first met is uncertain, but the
small size of Odessa's high society and the necessarily public life
of the governor-general's wife meant that they would have encountered one another at some point early in Pushkin's stay. He had

taken rooms in the Hôtel du Nord, located on Italian Street, but soon moved to another hotel nearer the sea, at the corner of Deribasovskaya and Richelieu streets, where he could take in the fresh air and recuperate after his sojourn in Bessarabia. (A desperate need to breathe the rejuvenating sea air was one of the reasons he had adduced for requesting a transfer to the coast.) From there, he regularly made his way to a calendar of events that packed the long, warm social season.

Lise enjoyed creative socializing, and the galas, balls, and suppers she organized were renowned across the empire. "It was difficult to leave Odessa," complained a contemporary Russian visitor, "since I did not want to absent myself from the company of the count and countess, the likes of which are not to be found in other parts."[10] The grand Vorontsov palace was not yet in existence during Pushkin's time in Odessa, but the later parties that Lise staged there give some sense of the fêtes she probably organized even in lesser quarters.

A visitor to the Vorontsov palace might have descended into the residence's grand salon around nine o'clock in the evening. A band would already be playing as the guests, some masked and others in fancy dress, perhaps in the tunic and trousers of a Russian coachman or the lace apron of a Swiss peasant, turned quadrilles on the parquet floor. Suddenly, a giant sugarloaf might glide onto the dance floor, out of which would pop an old man doing a lively jig. Amid the dancers, dressed in the brocaded and corded coatee of a Hussar cavalryman, was the Countess Vorontsova herself, welcoming the guests who had just arrived from their country estates or from the streets leading off Nikolaevsky Boulevard: General Lev Naryshkin, Vorontsov's cousin, and his wife Olga; her family, the Potockis, the great Polish-Russian landholders; Baron Rainaud, a French hotelier (and Pushkin's landlord); the Shcherbinins and the Blarembergs, the Pushchins and the Raevskys.[11]

With his newfound commercial success and a rebounding reputation—"The Fountain of Bakhchisaray" was on its way to publication, and printers were clamoring for rights to further editions of "The Captive of the Caucasus"—Pushkin's natural swagger only increased. He may have met the countess in the autumn or early winter of 1823, perhaps at a seasonal ball or at one of the governor-general's twice-weekly entertainments, over a session of parlor games or whist. Pushkin fell for her as quickly as Vorontsov had done just a few years earlier.

His affections, by all accounts, were returned. Lise was known to enjoy the flirtatious interactions that even a provincial city such as Odessa had raised to a high art. Pushkin's witticisms and impromptu verses were a striking contrast to Vorontsov's business-like bearing. More important, the governor-general, following established form among Russia's noble class, had himself already taken a mistress, Olga Naryshkina, nearly a decade younger than Lise. Olga was married to a prominent general, but the affair was a public secret.[12]

In the bitter winter of 1823–24, with the edges of the Black Sea encrusted in salty ice and the winds howling down unpaved streets from the flatlands beyond, the poet and the countess developed a relationship that soon became the scandal of Odessa society. The affair was probably consummated in early February, when Vorontsov was away in Kishinev, an encounter that Pushkin noted in the marginalia of the *Evgeny Onegin* manuscript as "soupé chez C. E. W."—"had supper with Countess Elise Woronzoff," using the French initials of her name.

As winter gave way to spring, and with the return of the governor-general to the city, the couple began meeting at a country villa owned by Baron Rainaud, the prominent hotelier. Rainaud had constructed a bathing area in the seaside cliffs bordering his rural estate. The hideaway, detached from the city but still close enough for the two lovers to slip away to throughout the season, produced one of the more plainly erotic of Pushkin's short verses:

Love's refuge is ever filled
With a coolness, murky and damp.
There the waves, unabashed,
Never silence their prolonged roar.[13]

The affair was apparently not the first for Lise. Like many couples of the era, she and her husband had settled into an arrangement that allowed both partners a considerable degree of sexual license. The problem was Pushkin's insistence on flouting a relationship that was intended, by social convention, to remain decorously unspoken. As one of Pushkin's biographers has noted, the poet bent to the common temptation of despising those one has injured.[14] His weapon of choice was the epigram. "Half milord, half shopkeeper" was one quick summary he gave of Vorontsov's character. "Half hero, half ignoramus" was another.

Those ill-considered lines—which circulated widely in several different versions—clearly reflected Pushkin's public attitude toward Vorontsov. It was a careless and dangerous way of behaving. Vorontsov was not only his lover's husband—and by rights deserving of some public respect, even though now a known cuckold—but also Pushkin's boss. After all, the poet's only reason for being in Odessa was to serve on the governor-general's staff. A dismissal without a recommendation for further employment meant that Pushkin would be in genuine exile, wandering about the Russian plains without promise of aid or station, and still prevented from returning to St. Petersburg. But Vorontsov was in a bind too. Since the tsar had banished Pushkin, the sovereign's express permission was necessary to remove him from the governor-general's care. "Deliver me from Pushkin," Vorontsov wrote to the Russian foreign minister, Count Karl Nesselrode, in the spring of 1824. "He may be an excellent fellow and a good poet, but I don't want to have him any longer, either in Odessa or Kishinev."[15]

Suddenly, in one of those miraculous and disastrous occurrences

for which Odessa was already becoming famous, a new calamity descended on the city and provided the vehicle of Vorontsov's
unexpected deliverance: an infestation of locusts. The surrounding countryside was routinely subjected to massive locust attacks,
a nearly annual occurrence that could ruin crops, denude trees, and
eat up fodder intended for cattle and horses. Millions of insects,
their wings clacking and popping overhead, formed a black cloud
that hung like thick smoke over fields and gardens.

Once the locusts had arrived, the options for local citizens were
tragically—and comically—few. The main recourse was to create
enough noise to scare the insects away. One English lady, living
with her merchant husband in a country villa, organized an annual
parade to deal with the pests. First came her husband swinging a
large bell, then the gardener banging on a watering bucket, then the
footmen clanging on shovels, followed by the housemaids striking
pots and kettles, and lastly the children tapping with toasting forks
on tea boards.[16] Even in the city, wrote one visitor upon arriving by
ship, "a fearful battle [was] raging between the inhabitants and the
ruthless enemies of vegetation. Every noisy weapon, from pistol
to a mortar, from kettle-drum to a tin casserole, was rattling like
thunder in the hands of the horrified citizens, for the purpose of
defending their little domains."[17]

Like Richelieu during the plague crisis a decade earlier,
Vorontsov reckoned that more information about the relative size
of each year's locust brood could contribute to devising a better
strategy for dealing with the expected attack. In May, the governor-
general officially ordered Pushkin to proceed through several rural
districts and survey the extent of the locust egg population, assess
the efficacy of efforts to destroy the eggs before they hatched later
in the summer, and offer his conclusions in a written report.

It was a shocking assignment. Pushkin had never penned a single
official document throughout his time in government service. Rus-
tication, to count locust eggs no less, was clearly a calculated rebuff.

Pushkin protested in writing. He was a littérateur of some renown, he said. He was a self-confessed failure as a government official and would make a hash of the job. He had an aneurysm that might pop at any moment. None of that persuaded Vorontsov. Pushkin was soon dispatched on his mission against the tiny invaders.[18]

Vorontsov's move had its desired effect. After a few weeks in the countryside, Pushkin submitted his resignation from the civil service. It was a foolhardy move, but perhaps the only honorable one he could make. He had publicly embarrassed a man of considerable power. Odessan society had turned against him, not for overstepping the bounds of sexual propriety but for doing so in such an ungentlemanly fashion. By the middle of the summer, his fate had been decided. Vorontsov petitioned the central authorities for the poet's removal from Odessa, and the tsar responded favorably.

But the affair and Vorontsov's personal feelings toward Pushkin probably played a secondary role in the governor-general's decision to seek his transfer from Odessa. Given the customary randiness of Odessa's high society, flamboyant adultery and unseemly talk of it were hardly news. The more important of Pushkin's transgressions—one that was as typically Odessan as the promiscuity of the provincial gentry—involved the rumor of revolution.

A FEW YEARS before his arrival in Odessa, Pushkin wrote to a correspondent about a series of "occurrences of importance not only for our land, but for all Europe."[19] In 1814 a secret organization of Greek patriots called Philike Hetairia, or the Society of Friends, had been founded in Odessa. Their goal was to rally the Greek diaspora throughout southeastern Europe and launch a revolt to wrest ancient Christian lands—from Constantinople to the Greek mainland—from the control of the Ottoman Muslims. Odessa provided the ideal environment for hatching revolutionary plans.

It was a city that political radicals could enter with relative ease, located far from other major centers of imperial governance. A climate of social freedom was readily apparent. Public smoking, fashions that bordered on the scandalous, and public discussion of contentious issues from international affairs to taxes were relatively uncommon privileges in St. Petersburg or Moscow. But they were part of normal street life in Odessa. Dozens of secret societies— some quasi-religious such as the Freemasons, others vaguely political and modeled on the Italian Carbonari, still others secret for the sake of being secret—enrolled radical intellectuals, public officials, and sons of noble families.

As a free port, the city attracted more and more ships each year. New political ideas were filling up Odessa's numerous restaurants and drinking establishments just as wheat was filling up the newly constructed silos near the harbor. "A gentleman, with whom I am acquainted calls Odessa the world's end," reported an English visitor in the early 1820s, "it is, certainly, a place by itself—a singular spot—a semi-oriental city."[20] Its very location, far removed from the Russian imperial capitals and looking out on a teetering Ottoman Empire, allowed the city to become a hotbed of political intrigue. Italians seeking to throw off Bourbon kings or establish a constitutional monarchy, Greeks and Romanians desiring an end to Muslim domination, and Russians pushing a reformed version of tsarist autocracy all found haven there.

Philike Hetairia's members were generally disorganized, truculent, and only waveringly loyal, but their underground machinations linked up with geopolitical changes already taking place in the rest of Europe. Farther to the south, patriots in Greece revolted against their Ottoman rulers and declared independence. Soon, other Ottoman dependencies—such as Odessa's immediate neighbors to the west, the Romanian principalities of Moldova and Wallachia— launched their own bids for freedom. In February of 1821, a ragtag army under Alexandros Ypsilantis, a Greek in Russian military service and one of Philike Hetairia's leaders, crossed the Prut River separating Bessarabia from the Ottoman vassal principality of Moldova, seeking to spark a full-scale uprising of Christian peasants—the event that Pushkin referred to as "occurences" of importance to both Russia and Europe. Contemporary observers compared it to Caesar's crossing of the Rubicon, the beginning of what many hoped would be a large-scale uprising of Balkan and Mediterranean Christians against the Muslim empire. Romantics from across Europe flocked to the Greek cause, just as their fathers had moved east to join Catherine's army and navy a generation earlier. Lord Byron—whose work had been an inspiration to Pushkin—died during the Greek war for independence a few years later.

The Greek revolt inaugurated a decade of struggle for the future of southeastern Europe. Greek guerrillas and irregular troops—the *klephts* and *armatoloi*, dressed in their colorful highland garb and wielding scimitars and deadly long muskets—staged small attacks and pitched battles against Ottoman forces throughout the 1820s. Conservative European powers, at first wary of any hint of revolution, gradually sought to manage the Greek crisis through diplomatic overtures to the Ottoman sultan. Russia joined the struggle informally in 1827, helping to destroy an Ottoman-Egyptian fleet in the Mediterranean at the Battle of Navarino. A year later, Russia entered a brief war with the sultan (1828–29) to ensure freedom of shipping on the Black Sea, which had been placed in peril by Ottoman efforts to quell the Balkan rebels.

Odessa was the birthplace of the Greek revolution, and sympathies there were strong. The problem for Russian authorities was that revolution—like locusts and the plague—was not choosy about its host. What had begun as a movement among Greek-speaking soldiers and intellectuals aimed against the Muslim Ottomans could easily infect Russia itself. Mutinies against the tsar were not unknown. The elite Semyonovsky Guards in St. Petersburg had revolted in the fall of 1820 in protest over harsh military discipline. The mutiny was quickly suppressed, but it illustrated the fact that Russia was not immune to the revolutionary feelings circulating throughout Europe. Secret societies such as Philike Hetairia were the chief vector for spreading ideas of liberty and political reform.

Pushkin had long been suspected of flirting with radical ideas, and his sojourn on the southern frontier had only increased his antipathy to the harshest elements of the tsar's policies. Vorontsov was able to use those suspicions to his advantage. In his written complaints to central authorities, he hinted at Pushkin's radical, perhaps even republican, politics—gleaned as much from the reports of provincial gossips as from the writer's own occasional poems in praise of liberty. By the summer of 1824, St. Petersburg had become convinced of the dangers of leaving the poet relatively unsupervised in the hothouse environment of Odessa. Pushkin was to be dismissed from public service, but he still needed to be watched. Otherwise, "making use of his independent position, he will, without doubt, disseminate more and more widely those harmful ideas which he holds and will oblige the authorities to employ against him the most severe measures," wrote Nesselrode to Vorontsov.[21]

Pushkin was to be sent home, to his family's country estate at Mikhailovskoye, in Pskov province, where he would have little opportunity to get into trouble and could be easily invigilated from the capital. On July 29, 1824, he set out on the long journey north, leaving Lise and Odessa forever. Nine months later, Lise gave birth to a daughter, Sophie. Odessa gossips whispered that the child was Pushkin's, a rumor that the poet did little to squelch. After all, their love story would soon be immortalized in other ways, not just in the marginal doodles of the *Evgeny Onegin* manuscript but, in fictionalized and poetic code, in the storyline itself. Like the initially besotted Lise Vorontsova, one of the central characters, Tatyana Larina, ultimately chooses loyalty to her husband over imprudent love. Wisps of Odessa remained in the work of a writer who went on to become Russia's national poet and the supreme architect of the literary Russian language.

For reasons both personal and political, Vorontsov had secured Pushkin's removal from Odessa. But the city's growing reputation for radicalism came close to tarnishing Vorontsov himself. Tsar Alexander I had been a liberal-minded reformer in his early years on the throne. However, the revolutionary swells that seemed to threaten the post-Napoleonic order made him increasingly suspicious of those around him. In December of 1825, during a journey to New Russia, he died suddenly—and heirless—in Taganrog. Rumors flew. Had the tsar been assassinated? Was he really dead? The public mood was tense and the outcome of the imperial succession uncertain. As his body was being transported back to St. Petersburg, Alexander's younger brother Nicholas announced after some delay that he would become tsar, seemingly skipping over the elder brother and next in line to the throne, Constantine.

The uncertainty over the succession—and the public perception that Nicholas was purposefully bypassing Constantine— sparked a rebellion. That icy winter in St. Petersburg, a group of military officers and their sympathizers refused to swear allegiance to Nicholas. On December 14, three thousand mutinous troops massed in Senate Square, arrayed against a far larger number loyal to Nicholas. A few cannon shots dispersed the protestors, leaving scores dead and injured. Sweeping arrests and dismissals followed. Five of the ringleaders—liberal activists and intellectuals known to history as the Decembrists—were eventually hanged.

In Odessa, the echoes of the Decembrist movement were profoundly felt. One of the centers of liberal activism had been Tulchin, a small garrison town to the north of Odessa, where young nobles, regimental officers, and writers exchanged ideas of liberty, social reform, and even an end to the tsarist monarchy. The suspicions of the new tsar, Nicholas I, naturally fell on the city and its governor-general, whose liberal disposition and progressive ideas—formed in English drawing rooms and Cambridge debating clubs—seemed dangerously close to the rebellious thinking of the Decembrists.

Vorontsov was at great pains to demonstrate his personal devotion to the monarch and convince him of New Russia's loyalty. "It is worth noting that in the city of Odessa, about which so much ill has previously been spoken, there is not a single inhabitant nor a single functionary who has had any part in the conspiracy, much less been arrested for it," the count wrote in his memoirs.[22] He traveled to St. Petersburg to pay personal homage to the sovereign. He was so sincere in his professions of loyalty that he was soon appointed to the state tribunal in charge of prosecuting the Decembrist rebels. Vorontsov's career and the city he commanded were delivered from immediate suspicion, but the aroma of rebelliousness was never completely gone. It would linger in Odessa for another century.

VORONTSOV HAD A CHANCE to demonstrate the city's fidelity when the emperor and his family paid a visit in the summer of 1828. Lise, whose skills as a hostess were already celebrated, organized an elaborate garden party on the occasion of the empress's birthday. The site was on the outskirts of Odessa, near the country estate where the royal family was spending part of its time in the south.

A triumphal arch of boughs and rushes was thrown up across the road leading to the estate's gardens. Nearer the sea, a small theater was erected, along with a tent of Turkish draperies held up with spears. A band of regimental lancers provided music, while before the archway stood a detachment of noble girls and young women, all dressed in white summer gowns and grouped according to the color of their hats and ribbons. When the empress arrived, young Sophie Vorontsova—perhaps amid whispers about the girl's alleged father, Pushkin—presented her with a garland of flowers.

The band struck up a tune. The crowd soon shifted to the seashore, where three men stood dressed in armor on the beach. Just

Portrait of Countess Elizabeth (Elizaveta) Vorontsova (ca. 1823) by Pyotr Fyodorovich Sokolov. *Museum of Tropinin and His Contemporaries, Moscow/ The Bridgeman Art Library.*

Sketch thought to represent Lise Vorontsova, from the manuscript of Pushkin's *Evgeny Onegin.*

offshore, Mademoiselle Mariconi, the prima donna of the Odessa opera, was slowly rowed ashore as she sang one of the arias from Rossini's *Tancredi.* Waltzes and quadrilles followed, interspersed with breaks for iced refreshments, as Chinese lanterns illuminated the twisted trees on shore and the yardarms of ships anchored off the coast.[23] Nicholas was so taken with the city that, some time later, he remarked that Odessa should be rightly considered second only to St. Petersburg in its importance to the empire.[24]

The grand frivolity of the imperial visit inaugurated an era in which Odessa was no longer a frontier town but rather the renowned southern counterpart to Russia's northern metropolises.

Under Vorontsov's leadership, Odessa began to acquire the accoutrements of a real city. A near-daily Russian newspaper, *Odessky
vestnik* (Odessa Herald), was launched in 1827, following on from
the earlier French-language biweekly, the *Journal d'Odessa*. A public
library opened in 1830. An experimental steamship service started
in 1828 and would eventually be expanded to connect Odessa to all
the major ports on the Black Sea and beyond. By the early 1840s,
the city had over a hundred schools employing nearly four hundred
teachers and enrolling close to five thousand students, both boys
and girls—not counting the private institutions founded by the
Greek, German, Jewish, and Armenian communities.[25]

From a ship anchored in the quarantine harbor, one could look
up at the well-established city above: the boulevard, the commercial exchange, the classical columns of Vorontsov's palace, the
theater, the green and gold domes of churches. "It was, indeed, a
European town we beheld, full of affluence, movement and gaiety," wrote a French engineer, Xavier Hommaire de Hell, in the late
1830s.[26] The spire of the massive Preobrazhensky Cathedral, the
city's foremost church, was completed in 1837, and four years later
Vorontsov presided over the opening of Odessa's most recognizable landmark: the grand staircase that flows from the upper city
to the port below. The 220 steps and ten landings were designed by
two Russian architects and fashioned in sandstone imported from
Trieste at the exorbitant cost of 800,000 rubles. The staircase was
generally reviled at the time as an "escalier monstre" and a poorly
constructed folly likely to collapse in a few years.[27] Yet crowned by
the statue of Richelieu on Nikolaevsky Boulevard, the steps almost
immediately became the preeminent symbol of the city.

From the bottom, the steps seemed to stretch almost to the sky,
a ladder that gleamed gray-white in the sun. That effect was calculated, for the steps are considerably wider at the bottom than at
the top, giving the sense that the statue of Richelieu is in fact far
larger than it is in reality, an imagined colossus at the head of his

own artificial mountain. From the top, the observer looks down the staircase and sees only the wide landings; from the bottom, the landings disappear entirely, leaving only a formidable flight of steps. Even today—with ten of the original steps now gone to provide for an enlarged port and the entire staircase encased in local granite rather than the original, fragile sandstone—Vorontsov's creation pulls Odessa toward the sea while convincing newcomers of the grandeur of the city on a hill.

Decades later, after Vorontsov had moved beyond New Russia to serve as viceroy in the tumultuous Caucasus, his contributions to the city were still remembered. He died of a stroke while traveling through Odessa in November of 1856. He had just weathered his last crisis, one that had been personally devastating. His two homelands—Russia and Britain—had ended a grinding and inconclusive struggle against each other in the Crimean War, a conflict in which Vorontsov's relatives fought on both sides. The days in which Odessa's founding giants could easily move between multiple worlds were coming to an end. The city was situated in an empire that would later become enamored with the purifying ideals of Christian Orthodoxy, nationality, and autocracy. At the memorial service for Vorontsov, the local archbishop reflected on Odessa's expansion and prominence during the governor-general's tenure in office. "Cherished like a child, she grew above all other cities," he intoned in the soaring Preobrazhensky Cathedral, "she became truly the southern capital of Russia."[28]

CHAPTER 5

"There Is Nothing National about Odessa"

The epicenter of the *maskilim*: Cantor and boys' choir of the Brody synagogue, early 1910s. *From the Archives of the YIVO Institute for Jewish Research, New York.*

*L*ebn vi Got in Odes! went a traditional Yiddish phrase. "To live like God in Odessa!" could be a blessing, a curse, or a jab at the puffed-up pretensions of city folk. Odessa was a magnet for Jews from other parts of eastern Europe and Russia, a place where the social environment was relatively liberal, the weather pleasant, and

97

the business prospects promising. Unlike in many European cities, there was never a distinct "Jewish quarter." Class and wealth, rather than religion or ethnicity, were the determinants of neighborliness. The only time the city ever had a Jewish ghetto was when fascist occupiers created one during the Second World War.

Jewish merchants—six families, according to tradition—were already living in Khadjibey at the time of the Russian conquest, out of a total population of perhaps a few hundred. In the first informal censuses in the 1790s, several hundred Jews were recorded as working there as traders. Within a few years, the principal institutions of Jewish life, such as a synagogue, a burial society, and the Kehillah, or the body in charge of the community's affairs, were in place.[1] Throughout the nineteenth century, the Jewish population grew from under four thousand during Richelieu's tenure as administrator to over seventeen thousand by the 1860s, representing around a quarter of the total number of Odessans. As the city's overall population grew, it also became steadily more Jewish.[2]

The overland trade routes that linked central Europe to the Black Sea created lines of contact that had been traversed by Jews from the Middle Ages forward. This extensive commercial network ran through cities that became the inland partners of the port at Odessa. Cities such as Brody, a major market town to the north, in Galicia, were linked to the sea by the thousands of cattle drovers, cart-drivers, and merchants who, month after month, made the passage across the hills and plains between the heart of Europe and the coast. In the space of just over a century, Odessa's Jewish community became the engine of the city's economic life. By the early 1900s, around two-thirds of the handicraft shops and industrial enterprises, nearly 70 percent of the trading companies, and nearly 90 percent of the grain-trading firms had Jewish proprietors.[3]

Odessa attracted immigrants of all types and creeds, but there were particular reasons for its appeal to Jews. Free-port status opened the docks and quays to ships from throughout the Black

Sea and Mediterranean worlds. That, in turn, provided an essential hub for overland routes to Jewish communities in central Europe. The great centers of Jewish life had emerged in inland cities and villages, from Warsaw to Vilna to the shtetls of western Ukraine. In the Russian Empire, restrictions were placed on Jewish residency and professions. From the late eighteenth century forward, Jews were by and large confined to the so-called Pale of Settlement, a vast swath of territory on the empire's western frontier that included much of modern-day Lithuania, Belarus, eastern Poland, Moldova, and western Ukraine. Jewish migration to other parts of the empire was generally prohibited. Even within the Pale, Jewish sources of income were limited by law to a specific array of jobs, such as tavern-keeping, alcohol distilling, and petty trading. Jews remained a relatively small minority in the Pale, forming just over 12 percent of the total population by the 1890s. But their concentration in a small number of towns and cities made them one of the most visible—and often most easily targeted—ethnic and religious communities in the empire.

Italians and Greeks had seen Odessa as the northern partner of port cities on the Adriatic and Aegean seas, and they remained largely in control of the export businesses until the middle of the nineteenth century. But Jews emerged as the critical middlemen in Odessa's commerce, linking up with peasants, immigrant farmers, and herders in the interior and forming an essential bridge to the large export concerns in the port city. Through their energy and social networks, Odessa became something that none of its early founders, from Potemkin to Vorontsov, could have imagined: the preeminent port of the Yiddish-speaking world. As a frontier city in need of both people and income, Odessa became one of the major urban centers of the Pale system, a modern and dynamic city where Jews could find economic prosperity and a degree of freedom within an otherwise constraining system. While Jews were viewed as competitors to Christian businesses in other corners of the empire—one

of the reasons for legal restrictions on Jewish economic activity—
their business contacts were seen as a boon in the growing city.

In order to conduct business in Odessa, merchants were
required to register for membership in one of three established
guilds. Each guild came with particular privileges, and membership was based on a graduated system of fees. In the middle of the
nineteenth century, members of the first guild were required to pay
an annual fee of 980 silver rubles (about $740 at the time) and, in
return, were allowed to transact any form of business abroad and
with Russia, as well as to operate up to three retail establishments.
Members of the second guild paid the lower fee of 400 silver rubles
(about $300) but were restricted to an annual turnover in their
business of no more than 90,000 rubles. Members of the third
guild paid the lowest fee, just over 100 silver rubles (about $80),
but were further restricted to conducting business within Russia
and not abroad. Foreign merchants, with a few exceptions for those
who had long been established in Odessa, were required to be members of the first guild, while Russian subjects could choose among
the three, depending on their means and the nature of their business activity. Significant numbers of Jews were represented in each
of the three guilds. According to one report from the late 1850s,
twenty-five merchants were registered in the first guild in Odessa,
of whom five were Jews, while fifty-two merchants were inscribed
in the second guild, of whom fifteen were Jews. The real distinction
came in the third guild, where nearly half of the total number of
members—367 of 782—were Jews.[4] Crisscrossing the countryside
and linking up with coreligionists and family members in the other
cities and villages of the Pale, Jews quickly became prominent players in internal Russian commerce to and from Odessa, turning a
deeply restrictive and often oppressive legal system into a vehicle
for economic success.

The raucous business environment in the city, characterized by
immense freedom of commerce and an entrepreneurial spirit, had

an effect on other spheres of life as well. Freedom to trade meant freedom to establish businesses of all sorts—provided one could afford the appropriate guild status—which in turn enabled a certain license in public affairs that was unknown in other parts of the Russian Empire. The libertinism of high society that had been so attractive to Pushkin and his contemporaries had an equivalent in the other elements of Odessa's public life, from the busy quayside to the commercial exchange where deals were hatched and fortunes made. Even public entertainments, such as the theater and opera, provided venues in which different classes and ethnic groups mixed more freely than virtually anywhere else in the tsar's domain.[5]

For all its possibility, however, Odessa had an ambivalent relationship with its own Jewishness. As a young city on the old Turkish frontier, it had none of the great rabbis, learned scholars, or mystical preachers found in other cities and towns. There was no Ba'al Shem Tov, the founder of Hasidism, and no Vilna Gaon, the preeminent scholar of Jewish law. The ways of the shtetl and the insular courts of Hasidic tsadiks, or sages, which made obscure east European villages into sites of learning and pilgrimage, had no equivalent in Odessa. Much of eastern European Jewry looked on the city as a second-rate upstart at best and a den of crooks and apostates at worst. "Everything here is topsy-turvy. It's as if they were trying to make fun of the world," says the wandering beggar Fishke the Lame, a character created by Mendele Moykher-Sforim, the father of modern Yiddish literature. "Your Odessa is not for me."[6] The locus of traditional Judaism lay far to the north, in the Polish-Lithuanian borderlands. Youth and distance kept the city on the margins of traditional Jewish thought and culture.

Yet despite this *goyish* reputation among many Jews, to gentiles Odessa's Jewishness—as one part of its culturally mixed identity— was an obvious and distinctive feature. "I saw here people of every nation," recorded a Russian traveler in the 1830s, "Greeks, Italians, Germans, French, yids (there are a lot of them here), Armenians, and a mass of Ukrainians resting with their oxen and wagons in the squares."[7] As one contemporary French guidebook put it succinctly, "People see the Jews as a collective cabal, and they avoid them like the plague."[8] But Odessa had something that was patently invisible to many of its detractors: a special community of progressive, optimistic, and economically successful Jews who turned out to be the city's signature contribution to Jewish life in the Pale of Settlement and the wider empire.

———————————

THERE IS NO REASON to notice the building on the downhill slope of Zhukovsky Street in the city center. It is overshadowed by the stoic grandeur of the nearby Philharmonic concert hall and dwarfed by the plane trees that arch over the length of Pushkin Street around the corner. But the blue-gray building, its foundations shifting and its plastered facade crumbling away behind a wrought-iron fence, was for a time the major symbol of one of the peculiarities of Jewish life in Odessa. Until it became the Rosa Luxemburg Workers' Club under the Soviets and then a storage facility and archive during the Second World War, it was the principal synagogue of the group known as the *maskilim*.

In the late 1820s the roughly four thousand Jews in Odessa accounted for a little less than 13 percent of the population.[9] Over the next decade, the size and nature of the Jewish community underwent a profound change. Jewish immigrants began to flood into Odessa from other towns and cities in the Pale of Settlement. Business opportunities in the free port, along with the Russian government's lax enforcement of residency restrictions, rendered Odessa a desirable destination for ambitious Jewish traders and merchants. These new arrivals brought new money and energy into the city, but they also carried with them a set of novel ideas: the beliefs, orientations, and cultural mores of the Haskalah, or the Jewish Enlightenment.

The Haskalah movement was spawned by the life and work of Moses Mendelssohn, the famed eighteenth-century German Jewish intellectual. The core of Mendelssohn's thought was that many of the traditional features of Jewish life—from rabbinical authority to social isolation—should be transformed in line with the values of reason, freedom, and progress. Mendelssohn and his followers did not reject all the features of Jewish culture; rather, they sought to modernize and cultivate only those that would enable Jews to become integrated citizens of enlightened polities. They promoted changes in dress, language, relations with non-Jews, and the range of professions through which Jews might find new avenues of achievement, such as agriculture.

In practice, the Haskalah was reformist rather than rejectionist, and many of its outward manifestations were evident in the urban landscape of central and eastern Europe: synagogues that resembled Christian cathedrals, liturgical choirs that used the scales and harmonies of European classical music, and publishing houses that preferred German, Polish, or Russian to Yiddish. In the Pale of Settlement, Mendelssohn's ideas took root after his death in 1786, but the values and practices of the Haskalah created rifts within the Pale's existing Jewish communities. Jews were divided not only among a number of different strands of *maskilim*—the general term for the pious but progressive adherents of the Haskalah—but also among their common opponents: traditionalists, Hasidic Jews, and those who rejected the Haskalah in favor of even more radical assimilation to Russian culture.

Maskilim had made their way to Odessa from other parts of the Pale throughout the first two decades of the nineteenth century, but the new wave of migration brought scores of foreign families, especially Jews from Brody and other parts of Galicia, to the seaport. Like Odessa, Brody was a free city, exempt from most commercial taxes, a status it had been granted when it came under Austrian control after the partition of Poland in 1772. It came to occupy a critical role in the trade between central Europe and the Russian Empire, an effective inland port that negotiated among the Austrian, Prussian, and Russian components of partitioned Poland. After the creation of Odessa, Brody found its natural sea-facing partner. In time, migrants followed the business connections that grew up between the two cities, moving permanently to Odessa and taking advantage of the boom in imports and exports.

Greeks and Italians remained the mainstay of Odessa's trading class, as they had been since the city's founding, but by the 1830s Jews from Brody occupied a central role as middlemen, particularly in agricultural goods. They knew the local producers in the hinterland. They had good relations with drovers and carters. They had an extensive network of friends, relatives, and associates throughout central and eastern Europe, who in turn acted as financiers and wholesalers for the bales, bundles, and barrels that arrived quayside from the Mediterranean. Joachim Tarnopol, one of the city's foremost Haskalah writers and thinkers, described the power wielded by the Brody immigrants: "The people from Brody are normally of an exemplary zeal and energy: they spare no honest measure in honorably making a living and meeting the needs of their families. . . . [T]heir relations with several notable financiers in Europe and their fairness in punctually meeting their obligations allow them to take in the full range of banking operations, and they [thus] render . . . a great utility to the commercial world."[10]

Jews from Brody and its surrounding region were known not only for their business acumen. They were also central proponents of the Haskalah. In short order, they set about the task of creating social institutions in Odessa that re-created and surpassed, in a southern climate, those they had known in Galicia. With the support of the city government, they established a private school teaching biblical subjects as well as Russian, mathematics, geography, and bookkeeping—a style of education ardently opposed by traditionalist Jews in the countryside. Later, they secured funds to build a small synagogue with worship conducted according to the "enlightened" styles already prevalent in central Europe. Permanent seating prevented jostling and overcrowding. Worshippers were enjoined not to speak during the service, prohibiting a practice among traditionalists that *maskilim* found primitive and chaotic. Old music was jettisoned in favor of innovative choral works composed by Nissan Blumenthal, the celebrated cantor who would remain in place until his death in 1903 at the age of ninety-eight. By the 1860s, congregants had raised sufficient funds to erect a second, more elaborate structure, a soaring building of Moorish design that became one of the most prominent public buildings in the city—today the tumble-down structure at the corner of Zhukovsky and Pushkin streets.[11]

As Blumenthal's four-part harmonies echoed through the synagogue on the Sabbath, the Brody *maskilim* could reflect confidently on their place in the city's establishment. Like all Jews, they still faced a host of legal restrictions and social prejudice, even from relatively liberal administrators such as Vorontsov. But within the city's Jewish community, *maskilim* had taken control of local affairs, heading the key committees and public bodies that governed Jewish communal life, literally from *bris* to burial. They had given to the city a distinctly progressive cast, and the reforms they pioneered were catching on throughout the empire. Odessa's Jewish school became the model for wider, state-sponsored experiments in Jewish education. Blumenthal's compositions floated from synagogue to synagogue—many are sung around the world today—while his choir school produced generations of singers and composers. The assertiveness and confidence of merchants, musicians, and religious leaders made the city's growing Jewish community an object of respect and awe, even as it was routinely denigrated by Jewish traditionalists. In time the ways of the *maskilim* evolved even further. Assimilation to Russian language and culture supplanted the orientations of the first generation of Galician Jews, who had looked to pioneering German reformers for inspiration and instruction. The city was already on its way to becoming the great center of modernizing Judaism in the Russian Empire.

"The fires of hell burn around Odessa," went a saying popular among Yiddish-speaking villagers; in some versions, the flames were said to spread for seven miles beyond the city limits, in others for ten or more. But the distant glow was more of an enticement than a warning. Odessa became a place where mixing rather than enforced separation came to define Jewish life. On Saturday evenings, Nikolaevsky Boulevard was filled with Jewish families taking in the sea air, the men dressed in frockcoats and the women in the latest European fashions, before decamping to a café near the Hotel Richelieu.[12] At the opera, Jewish patrons sat next to gentiles or crowded the standing-room area near the stage. A city lodged within the Pale of Settlement—a territory meant to restrict Jews' ability to mix with gentiles—was becoming a crucible in which traditionalists and reformers, Jews and Christians, could occupy the same social space. "It is to foreigners," one commercial report noted succinctly, including most of the city's Jews in that category, "that the town owes its present flourishing condition."[13]

Odessa was New Russia's answer to the shtetl—it was a place where Jews were socially integrated rather than isolated, "enlightened" rather than traditionally minded, and generally optimistic about their ability to convince the Russian state of their social utility. New ordinances provided for a greater Jewish voice in imperial institutions. New educational opportunities were emerging for Jewish youth. From time to time, the Russian state even restricted the wearing of Hasidic kaftans and other distinctive styles of dress, a move generally welcomed by the *maskilim*. As Joachim Tarnopol declared in his confident survey of Jewish life in Odessa in the 1850s, "[T]he flame of civilization ... [has] dissipated the shadows of prejudice and has spread the light."[14] Yet over the next two decades, as Jews moved out of middlemen positions and into the very center of Odessa's economic life, the openness, opportunity, and integration that had originally attracted the *maskilim* were put to the test.

———————

WHEN FOREIGN TRAVELERS ventured across the Eurasian steppe, it was difficult to know which was worse: bouncing along rutted roads in a hired wagon careering along at breakneck speed, or stopping in a fly-blown inn where a meal was little more than moldy bread and rough wine, and one's bed a straw mat covered by a ragged blanket.

It was all the more surprising, then, when travelers came across a small slice of Germany that had been transplanted to the windy flatlands. Small wooden houses were gathered in neat rows around a plain stone church. Doorposts were painted with simple but elegant flower motifs. Blooming flowerboxes decorated the street-facing windows. A visitor was greeted with a friendly but wary *"Guten tag,"* and if he asked for onward directions to another village or city, he should be sure to know its name in German rather than in Russian. "How agreeably was I surprised to see the advanced state of agriculture as we travelled southwards," wrote the wife of a Russian officer not long after Odessa's founding, "and to find this mighty empire, which, I own, judging from its vast extent, I supposed to be thinly peopled, covered with populous villages and waving corn [wheat]."[15] Germans, especially members of the reclusive Mennonite Christian denomination, had been invited by Catherine the Great to set up farms across New Russia shortly after her acquisition of the territory from the Ottomans. Germans brought agricultural skills that were lacking in a frontier peopled mainly by nomads and Cossacks. In turn, they received land, exemption from military service, and ready outlets for their produce in the burgeoning Russian ports along the Black Sea.

Odessa was founded by foreigners in Russian service, and that heritage reproduced itself generation after generation. Niche

industries abounded. If you were a well-to-do merchant, your barber was likely to be an Armenian, your gardener a Bulgarian, your
plasterer a Pole, your carriage driver a Russian, and your nurse-
maid a Ukrainian.[16] "There is nothing national about Odessa,"
recalled one visitor disapprovingly.[17] Some could describe it only by
analogy—as a Russian Florence, a Russian Naples, a Russian Paris,
a Russian Chicago, even a Russian Cincinnati.[18] Others could do no
better than give a litany of the exotic types you might encounter on
the major boulevards, in the docklands, or at the bazaar: the Armenian in his astrakhan hat; the Greek in his blue breeches; the Albanian with fustanella and tall felt hat; the Turk in brimless fez; the
Tatar in pink pelisse or enormous cape; the long-bearded Orthodox priest with his violet robes and gold-headed staff; the schoolboy in the severe uniform of the Richelieu Lycée; the Russian or
Ukrainian woman in an embroidered cloth headdress; the peasant
with his blue calico trousers stuffed into low boots; and the officers of a hundred naval and civilian ranks, brocaded, beribboned,
and festooned.[19] Arriving after a fifty-hour steam journey from
Constantinople in the summer of 1851, the travel writer Edmund
Spencer found a "semi-oriental" city rather than the Russian one
he expected: "Strictly speaking, Odessa cannot be considered a
Russian town with reference to its inhabitants, who are principally
Germans, Italians, Greeks, Jews, Armenians, and a few French and
English; and being a free port, merchants from every part of the
world may be seen wandering about the streets in all the variegated
costumes of Europe and Asia, which adds not a little to the gaiety
and variety of the promenade."[20]

What many observers overlooked was the segmented unity of
the city: the fact that despite its extreme diversity of habits, religion, dress, and profession, there was a growing sense of being
Odessan. Indeed, to be a local, by birth or adoption, was to be an
outsider in whatever particular sense one wanted to define it: a progressive Jew as opposed to a traditionalist; a German farmer on the

far-flung Eurasian steppe rather than the floodplains of northern Europe; a free-holding peasant, working one's own land rather than toiling exclusively for a distant noble landlord; a Greek or Italian, clinging to the same seacoasts once visited by ancient Aegean seamen and medieval Genoese merchants. Over time, the balance of power among all these groups changed. But there was a golden thread that bound Odessa's quiltlike population together, and it was the product that, more than any other, enabled the great boom in Odessa's economy at mid-century. From the 1830s through the 1860s, the grain trade made the city the busiest and most vibrant port in the Russian Empire and transformed the lives of its many diverse communities.

"WHEN GRAIN is in demand, things go well."[21] That was the simple equation once proposed by the duc de Richelieu, and it might have been Odessa's motto for much of the nineteenth century. Until the 1860s, Odessa was the breadbasket for much of the Western world, feeding a hungry European and, increasingly, global market. Foreign consuls sent breathless dispatches to European capitals about fluctuations in the prices of wheat and barley. Foreign ministers contemplated the effects of diplomatic squabbles on the supply of foodstuffs. Only with the discovery of oil farther to the east, in the Russian Caucasus and the Caspian seaport of Baku, was Odessa's chief cash export exceeded by that of a rival Russian city.

Odessa's commercial success lay in its position at the intersection of flatlands and seascape, where the produce of the former could be sent to markets across the latter. But a series of fortunate accidents allowed the city to enhance this natural gift. Talented administrators such as Vorontsov argued for maintaining the free-port status, which was a considerable inducement to foreign and local entrepreneurs. Improvements in the harbor allowed larger ships to enter and lie safely at anchor. The fall-off in plague outbreaks around the Black Sea reduced much of the time that ships, goods, and passengers spent in quarantine. When the Peace of Adrianople was signed between the tsar and sultan in 1829, ending nearly a decade of diplomatic bickering, trade squabbles, and outright war, Russia had secured a historic set of concessions from the Ottomans, including an end to the Ottoman practice of boarding and searching Russian merchant ships. The period of relative peace that followed—from the late 1820s to the early 1850s—provided ease of shipping through the Bosphorus and Dardanelles straits.

The economic results were immense. Grain exports from all the Russian Black Sea ports stood at a yearly average of under two million *chetverts* (a unit of Russian dry measurement equal to 5.77 U.S. bushels) before 1813, but by the 1860s that figure had risen to over

Oxen and wagons filled with sacks of wheat in the port of Odessa, from a nineteenth-century photograph. *Author's collection.*

sixteen million *chetverts*. Over half those exports were coming solely from Odessa.[22] Between the 1830s and 1850s, the annual volume of grain exports to Italian ports more than doubled, while the French were importing ten times as much Odessa grain at the end of that period as at the beginning.[23] After the late 1840s, the easing of restrictive import laws in England and the introduction of hardier wheat varieties in Russia opened new markets for Odessa's produce, well beyond the traditional Mediterranean destinations. By the middle of the century, well over a thousand ships were leaving Odessa each year.[24] The number of British ships sailing into the Black Sea increased sevenfold between the mid-1840s and the early 1850s, with Britain accounting for a third or more of all destinations of vessels exiting the port.[25] Wheat, barley, rye, and other grains filled the holds of long-haul sea vessels flying the flags of most major European powers.

Of all these goods, the queen was wheat. Ninety percent of Russian wheat exports flowed out of the empire's Black Sea ports, and many of the sights, sounds, and smells of Odessa derived from its production and sale.[26] Immense herds of cattle provided manure for fertilizer in the countryside and pulled the thousands of wooden carts that bore the harvested grain from field to storage centers. *Chumak* carters and drovers followed established routes that cut deep ruts across the steppe, converging from the far reaches of Bessarabia, Podolia, and other parts of the western empire. Once in the city, they could deposit their loads in any of hundreds of storage facilities, some of them empty, repurposed stone houses, others elaborate granaries, resplendent with pilasters and pediments, rising on the far side of the ravines that divided the city.[27]

Some carters would return north with cloth, wine, or other imported goods offloaded from merchant vessels in the harbor, while others chose to transform their infrastructure into capital. The dried dung could be collected and sold as fuel to poor families, and the animals could then be given up to slaughter for meat and hides. The sweet smoke of burning, grass-rich manure mingled in the air with the reek of tallow vats and the sharp odor of tanneries, the factories that produced the bricks of processed fat and bundles of unworked leather destined for Turkey, Italy, or France.

With hundreds of thousands of head of livestock coming through the city each harvest season, dust and mud were constant features of Odessan life. Choking, white-yellow clouds, stirred up by hooves and swirled about by the prevailing winds, powdered residents like talcum. Rain turned inches of accumulated limestone grime into impassable sloughs. Carriage drivers were forced to adopt a uniquely Odessan approach to dealing with the provisional swamps of gray mud. Whereas the British drove on the left and the French on the right, one visitor reported, Odessa's coachmen would simply shout out to an oncoming driver, "Go to the left!" or "Go to the right!" depending on the location of the obstacle.[28]

An open, brick-lined drainage system, about two feet deep, ran alongside the major thoroughfares, crossed by occasional foot-bridges and wooden planks. But the rivulets they contained—the wastewater runoff and solid offal of houses and hotels, as well as animal dung and mud from the streets—could gag even the toughest pedestrian.[29] The blooms of acacia trees and oleander fought back with their perfume, but it usually took a change in wind direction, blowing off the plains and toward the sea, to unburden the city of its own stench.

Odessa's distinctive sounds, too, rose up from the wheat trade. The curses of carters correcting a recalcitrant bullock mixed with the lows and screams of cattle from the docklands and slaughter-houses and the brittle pop of old wheat carts being broken up for firewood. Each ox brought its own swarm of flies, buzzing around businessmen inside the Exchange or thumping against the windows of the shops along Pushkin and Richelieu streets. When the *chumaks* came to town, swelling the population by thousands from April to October, hawkers and organ-grinders added to the carnival atmosphere, their calls and tin-pipe tunes filling the squares and avenues. Even in the quieter streets, the Byzantine harmonies of an Orthodox choir or the European chords floating out of the Brody synagogue wafted around the grand buildings whose foundations were built on the grain trade. In the center of town, near the theater and the Hotel Richelieu, café patrons called out for coffee or *kvass*, the beer made from fermented bread, trying to be heard over the rattle of dice boxes, the slap of dominos, and the clink of glasses. "The words 'roubles' and 'grain,' 'grain' and 'roubles,' are, however, to be distinctly heard above all this hubbub," one observer remarked in the late 1830s, "and now and then, 'hides,' 'wool,' 'hemp,' and 'tallow.' "[30]

The wealth that flowed into the city in the middle decades of the nineteenth century enabled the raising of new public buildings and municipal improvements. The city's early builders had required imperial or noble patronage to erect the accoutrements of a real city, but these gave way to publicly funded efforts to address the problems of sanitation, dust, and decay. The soft limestone of which many of the major buildings were constructed was easily scarred by the wind and salt air, giving even newer buildings an ancient and pockmarked appearance—and adding further to the gritty dust circulating through the town. Each year, buildings were refaced and plastered and, bit by bit, streets paved or macadamized, covered with a packed layer of broken stone.

New cultural institutions sprang up to meet the demand of a wealthier and more sophisticated populace. By the middle of the century, Odessa hosted three printing houses, a lithographer, six bookshops, and scores of private clubs, theaters, learned societies, and public and private schools, including the famed Richelieu Lycée, which later served as the foundation for both a *gymnasium* and Novorossiya University. Opera and theater were the main entertainments in a city *"fanatico per la musica,"* as one visitor remarked, with performances by traveling companies as well as the city's own repertory players.[31] One of the city's boosters, the historian Konstantin Smolyaninov, wrote that as of 1851 the city could boast thirty-two churches, of which seventeen were for non-Orthodox Christians; two male and female monasteries; four synagogues; thirty-four Jewish prayer houses; seventy-six public buildings; five public gardens; sixty-five private gardens; 4,463 private houses; 1,619 shops; 564 granaries; forty-seven factories; three boulevards; and forty-nine streets (of which twenty-four were paved).[32]

But the foundations of Odessa's mid-century success were always shaky. Smolyaninov's revealing list showed that shops, granaries, and public buildings far outnumbered factories. Apart from bricks, rope, and some foodstuffs (macaroni, for example) the city produced rather little. It was a center of business — of movement, commerce, and finance — but not of manufacturing. With its wealth coming to a great degree from effective slave labor in the countryside — the dark fruit of Russia's serf-based economy — producers had little incentive to invest in improved agricultural techniques. And since peasants were largely tied to the land, there was no readily available and truly mobile labor force even if Odessans had decided to try their hand at building factories.[33] Dependent on the grain coming from the countryside and the imports coming from the sea, Odessa's fate was also captive to the whims of nature and the fickleness of foreign producers. Locusts, hailstorms, or a lasting drought could destroy the harvest. A devastating dry spell in the middle of Mikhail Vorontsov's tenure as governor-general, in the early 1830s, produced a famine across New Russia, with thousands kept from starvation only by handouts from state reserves.[34]

Even within the city, freshwater was always a scarce resource. Odessa was situated far from a river or other natural source. From the city's earliest days, huge cisterns and reservoirs were required to provide drinking water for livestock; on the outskirts of town, lines of watering troughs stretched deep into the prairie.[35] For humans, too, freshwater was hard to come by and, therefore, expensive.

The main source was a spring situated a few miles from the city, on the seashore and down a steep embankment. A small building was erected over the site, which was guarded by a detachment of Cossacks. The water, gushing out of the surrounding limestone, was collected in barrels and transported to the town. Prices in the 1820s stood at a ruble and a half per barrel, and a household could pay as much as twenty rubles for sufficient freshwater for a week— a substantial sum even for prosperous families.[36] An aqueduct was added later, but it was not until 1873 that a system of piped water carried all the way from the Dniester River began to meet the city's needs.[37] Until then, as Pushkin once quipped, the wine in Odessa was cheaper than the water.

The city learned to live with shocks: a late-season icing of the harbor, which disrupted shipping; a scorching summer or a sudden gust of hail and wind, which thinned livestock herds and flattened wheat or knocked off barley heads; an outbreak of typhus, cholera, or even the plague, which sealed off the city and choked its commercial lifelines; or a sudden shift in the preferences of kings or the tastes of the buying public in a faraway country, which could cause prices to fluctuate wildly and make the Exchange buzz with speculation about world affairs. That was the case in the spring of 1854, when news reached the city that Russia was now suddenly and unexpectedly at war with Odessa's best customer, Great Britain.

––––––––––

ODESSA WAS FOUNDED in war, and war was not always bad for the city. Russia's conflict with Napoleon had enabled it to flourish as an alternative route into the empire for European products and a source of raw materials for a continent strangled by French trade restrictions. The disorders in Greece and the Balkans in the 1820s had produced a new wave of Greek immigration to the city, which enhanced the class of energetic entrepreneurs. But in the 1850s, Odessa was near the center of conflict. For the first time, it was a target not for British shippers and merchants but for British cannons.

The Crimean War was about nothing and about everything. The proximate cause was a dispute between the tsar and the Ottoman sultan over control of the holy places in Jerusalem, specifically which empire should superintend the Church of the Holy Sepulchre: the Islamic power on whose territory the church was situated—the Ottomans—or the Orthodox Christian power that claimed a special religious connection to it—Russia. But the bigger issue concerned the struggle for influence along the borderlands of both empires: in the Caucasus, in the southern Balkans, along the Danube River, and on the Black Sea.

Over the first half of the nineteenth century, Russia had carved out greater control over the old kingdoms and principalities that had once insulated one empire from another. Some—such as the kingdom of Georgia and the Muslim khanates near the Caspian Sea—had been wholly absorbed into the Russian state; others— such as the twin principalities of Moldova and Wallachia north of the Danube River—had periodically been placed under temporary Russian occupation, even though they were still Ottoman vassals. Russia had shown itself to be a consummate meddler in Ottoman affairs, for example, by supporting the Greek uprising that had been launched by Philike Hetairia. Western powers were increasingly concerned. Britain and France had by and large lauded the humanitarian impulse of protecting Christians in the Near East from despotic Muslims. But Russia's habit of provoking Ottoman aggression now seemed part of a strategic plan—perhaps even to resurrect Catherine's aim from the previous century and seize control of the Bosphorus and Dardanelles straits.

When diplomatic overtures to resolve the status of the holy places failed, in July 1853 Russia sent its troops across the Prut River into Moldova and Wallachia, occupying two principalities recognized as Ottoman protectorates. Fearing that Russia would soon

The bombardment of Odessa by British ships during the Crimean War,
April 1854, from a nineteenth-century engraving. *Author's collection.*

cross the Danube—igniting a full-scale revolt among Orthodox
Christians in the Balkans and perhaps even threatening the capital
of Constantinople itself—the sultan ordered military operations to
begin against Russian forces along the river as well as on the Caucasus front. The Ottoman fleet was ordered into the Black Sea to
disrupt Russian shipping and naval activity, and then to winter well
beyond the vulnerable capital, in port at Sinop in the middle of the
sea's southern coast.

The Ottoman ships were safely distant from Constantinople, but
they were closer than ever to the center of Russian naval firepower:
the port and arsenal at Sevastopol, an easy sail from Sinop across the
sea in Crimea. In a surprise attack on the morning of November 30,
1853, Russian ships under the celebrated admiral Pavel Nakhimov
sailed out of Sevastopol and descended on the Ottoman fleet. It was
the last time in European history that wooden-hulled sailing ships
would square off in a major naval engagement, yet it proved to be
an ignominious end to the age of sail. Caught completely off guard,

hemmed in at anchor by the approaching vessels and protected by inferior shore batteries, the Ottoman ships were easy targets. In the space of only an hour, the fleet was destroyed. Some three thousand Ottoman dead floated ashore in the following days, while the Russians reported only thirty-seven men killed in action.[38]

The fear in western Europe was that the uneasy balance around the Black Sea was now upset. Russia would undoubtedly press its advantage against the Ottomans to its logical end, nibbling away at the edges of the empire until the tsar was able to take the real prize, Constantinople, and with it control of the only seaway access between the Mediterranean and the Black Sea. The Ottoman Empire, weak and ineffectual, was a constant inducement to Russian interference. But it was also a strategic necessity to European powers wary of Russian ambitions. Without the sultan in place, there was little to prevent Russia's political and military dominance in the Balkans and the eastern Mediterranean.

After the debacle at Sinop, Britain and France sided with the sultan and declared war on Russia the following March, once the winter storms and unfreezing of Russian ports had enabled naval action. The British, French, and Ottoman expeditionary forces made the Black Sea the locus of their response to Russia's adventure in Sinop, and in September the allies landed on the appendage sticking into the sea, the Crimean Peninsula. Over the next year, allied forces laid siege to the Russian naval base at Sevastopol and to other strategic towns and ports along the Crimean coast, in a series of military engagements—such as the Charge of the Light Brigade—now famous for their bravery and folly. The damp winter, boiling summer, and rampant disease took an enormous toll.

Odessa was near the seat of war, less than two hundred miles from Sevastopol—the same distance that Nakhimov's fleet had covered to stage the surprise attack on Sinop. The city was thus vulnerable to allied ships en route from Constantinople or anchorages along the western coast. And given Odessa's long-standing commercial ties to Britain, part of Russian strategy involved not only trying to defend the city against allied attack but also closing it down to civilian shipping, ensuring that British importers would not continue to profit from the very port their ships were likely to shell.

Once the western allies seemed certain to join the conflict, Tsar Nicholas I imposed a ban on the export of all grain from Russian ports on the Black Sea and the Sea of Azov on any vessel—an effort both to preserve strategic food reserves and to undercut British and French commerce. At the time, a million *chetverts* of grain, nearly six million bushels, were in deposit in Odessa, where they were becoming ready fodder for mice and rats. Merchants had no way of quoting prices for commodities, since trade had ground to an absolute halt. "Transactions have been abated to such a degree as never yet has been experienced at this place," reported the U.S. consul John Ralli.[39]

Soon an even more threatening problem appeared on the horizon: the British and French expeditionary fleet. At the beginning of April, thirty allied warships anchored in the Odessa roadstead. On April 9, 1854, at about four o'clock in the afternoon, the fleet sent a small boat ashore and demanded that all British, French, and Russian commercial ships be surrendered. The local military commander gave no reply. The next morning the fleet opened fire on the artillery batteries ringing the harbor. Little damage was reported, but a city that had been open to the world now had its first experience of war. The allied fleet eventually sailed on to Crimea, where the distant explosions of cannon and mines rattled the windows of Odessa's houses and hotels.[40] Two steamers remained behind to blockade the port and search any neutral ships that might pass by for evidence of munitions.

When the city's inhabitants got a chance to take revenge, they grabbed it. On April 30, 1854, a British steamer, the *Tiger*, ran aground off the coast in a heavy fog. When the retreating mists revealed it the next morning, stuck fast near the shore, the Odessa batteries began firing from atop the cliffs. Most of the 260 men aboard managed to flee the damaged vessel, which soon lowered its flag in surrender. Heavy cannon fire that evening caused it to explode in a spectacular rush of steam and saltwater. The officers and men were taken prisoner, while the guns recovered from the wreck became prized trophies, although some exploded unexpectedly when the Russian army attempted to fire them in salute.[41]

Ships appeared off the coast, passing by en route to Crimea. Grain fields lay fallow. Granaries were empty. Within three years, it was all over. News reached Odessa by telegraph in the first week of April 1856 that Russia and the allies had signed a peace treaty in Paris, ending a brutal war that had left the Russian fleet at the bottom of Sevastopol harbor while accomplishing little of real strategic value for Britain, France, or the Ottomans. The news was relayed to the allied steamers still anchored outside the Odessa harbor. The captains in turn sent a boat ashore and requested permission to salute the Russian flag. Crowds gathered in the port as the ships drew near, the Russian colors hoisted on their mainmasts. They fired a salute, which was returned by the shore batteries, themselves now flying the British flag in gentlemanly reciprocity. Shortly thereafter the blockade was lifted, and the steamers retired from their long duty as unwelcome sentries.[42]

"I confess that I was formerly amongst those who thought that Odessa ought to have been destroyed," wrote a British war veteran on touring the city in 1871, "but now, having visited the place, I am of a different opinion."[43] The civilized ending to the conflict masked the profound changes that the city soon faced. Its status as a free port, suspended during the war, was never restored. The British and French, chastened by the effects of the export ban, were seeking new sources of foodstuffs. The Kansas and Nebraska territories soon competed directly with New Russia for the lion's share of the European grain trade. The grand project to find a southern outlet from the Mediterranean—the Suez Canal—reached com-

pletion in 1869, shifting trade in ways that dampened the significance of the Black Sea. Overland routes from central and southern
Europe to Persia and Central Asia, which had previously had their
trailheads at the Ottoman Black Sea ports, were now displaced by
the easier water route through the Suez.

The wheat business remained important. The average annual
output of cereals probably doubled again before the outbreak of
the First World War.[44] But other Russian ports on the Black and
Caspian seas—Novorossiisk, Batumi, Baku, even Sevastopol,
rebuilt and improved a decade after its destruction by the allies—
were now stepping out from Odessa's shadow and building their
own reputations as centers of trade, industry, and military power.
By 1914 Odessa was still the largest commercial center in the Russian south, but it accounted for less than 20 percent of the value
of goods traded on the Black Sea.[45] Cities such as Nikolaev and
Rostov—both older than Odessa but long eclipsed by their western
neighbor—were catching up.[46]

The Russian Steam Navigation Company, founded not long after
the war's close, used steam technology to enable travel and commerce across the entire sea and tie together its varied ports. By 1860
thirty-five Russian steamships were making regular runs on the sea
and the major rivers, from the Danube to the Dnieper.[47] But railroads
began to reorient trade away from the south, easing the transport of
goods across the empire and toward the busy ports of the Baltic Sea
to the north. Count Vorontsov was gone, and his successors, some
more able than others, never managed to continue the enlightened
governance and privileged status forged by the founding generation
of administrators. The office of governor-general of New Russia was
finally abolished in 1874, replaced with a state administration more
concerned with centralization and rooting out political subversives
than with enhancing Odessa's natural endowments.

Society, too, seemed to be changing in ways unfamiliar to Odessans who had thought of their city as a model of seaside hospitality

and a haven for good-natured libertinism. Serfdom was abolished
in the Russian Empire in 1861, part of a wave of liberalizing reforms
under Tsar Alexander II, who had assumed the throne during the
middle of the Crimean War. But peasant uprisings in the countryside disrupted harvests, and the flight of villagers to the city began
to tax an already groaning municipal administration. The rate of
suicides was up, increasing by nearly a quarter between 1870 and
1890. More people killed themselves in Odessa, relative to the city's
size, than in St. Petersburg or London. More managed to do it with
guns than in any other major city in Russia. The greatest number
of deaths occurred during the spring and summer months, when
flowers filled the city's public parks and warm winds caressed the
shoreline—but when fortunes could also be made or lost, depending on the harvest or the caprice of buyers in Marseille or Livorno.[48]

Public violence was always a part of Odessa's life, but the state
was beginning to play a role in it. In August of 1878 newspapers
reported that the first execution for a political crime in the city's
history—for belonging to a socialist-revolutionary party and for
forming an illegal underground group—had recently been carried
out by firing squad. In the closing decades of the century, Russian
judges would order more hangings in Odessa than in any other
city.[49] Residents used to make jokes about the police; if you were
stuck up to your ankles in the mud-choked streets, the story went,
you could be sure of hitting something solid, since a mounted officer had probably gone in, horse first, before you.[50] Now the humor
took on a darker edge. The tsar's secret police began to see the multilingual and cosmopolitan city as a breeding ground for agitators,
saboteurs, and terrorists—because in large part it was. Odessa was
a natural meeting place for radicals of various persuasions, and the
lax customs regulations and venal culture of port officials meant
that even minimally adept conspirators could smuggle incendiary
books and pamphlets, along with weapons.

After the Crimean War, it was still possible to amass considerable wealth as shipping picked up and trade returned. Many of the buildings rising from the streets and boulevards of the central district—the old banks, trading firms, and hotels that hide their wedding-cake facades behind plane and horse chestnut trees— were products of the continued growth in the city's fortunes. A new drumlike, Italianate opera house, still the first old building visible to ships rounding the headlands on a clear day, opened its doors in 1887 on the site of Richelieu's smaller establishment, which had been destroyed in a fire.

But the mid-century crisis did mark something of a watershed. The era of freewheeling commerce was giving way to a more somber, more turbulent time. The city could no longer take comfort in its being on the sidelines of empire, quietly being itself and making money while the affairs of states and peoples unfolded far from Nikolaevsky Boulevard. Odessans were awakening to the fact that the world mattered to them in ways far removed from wheat prices, the exchange rate for silver rubles, and the new opera premiere.

PART II

The Habitations of Cruelty

CHAPTER 6

Schemes and Shadows

An urban promenade: Richelieu Street, with a view of the Opera,
from a nineteenth-century photograph.
Prints and Photographs Division, Library of Congress.

Lev Bronstein chalked up his earliest lessons about treachery and manipulation to Odessa, especially his classes at St. Paul's School on Uspenskaya Street. St. Paul's was a *realschule*, a secondary school specializing in mathematics, science, and modern languages, rather than history and classical languages as taught in the more traditional, and more prestigious, *gymnasiums*. His parents had sent Bronstein from the family farm in rural Kherson province

127

to Odessa in 1888 to live with a distant relative—a successful Jewish publisher, Moisei Spentzer—and to take advantage of the educational opportunities the city provided.

St. Paul's had been founded by Lutherans, but its teaching staff was a mix of confessions and nationalities, all teaching in Russian and keeping close tabs on their rambunctious charges. "The percentage of freaks among people in general is very considerable, but it is especially high among teachers," Bronstein recalled in his memoirs.[1] He was severely disciplined and suspended on several occasions yet managed to graduate at the top of his class. He took two lessons away from the experience. One was that the city—like the broader empire of which it was a part—was both disorderly and overgoverned, a place at the same time "commercial, multi-racial, loudly colored and noisy" but still "perhaps the most police-ridden city in police-ridden Russia."[2]

The other lesson was that in such a place few people could be trusted. The school's authorities saw Bronstein as the ringleader of a group of thuggish boys habitually engaged in disrupting classes. He was only fingered, though, because one of his associates informed on him. "These were the groups that resulted from that episode," he wrote, "the tale-bearers and the envious at one pole, the frank, courageous boys at the other, and the neutral, vacillating mass in the middle. These three groups never quite disappeared even during the years that followed. I met them again and again in my life, in the most varied of circumstances."[3]

Bronstein left the city in 1896 and rarely returned. But the political gloss he put on his early experiences led him down the path of the professional revolutionary. Not long after leaving Odessa, he joined the life lessons of St. Paul's with the political tenets of Marxism. Soon, he was arrested by the tsarist government as a political agitator and exiled to Siberia. He eventually changed his name and dedicated his life—as Leon Trotsky—to stirring up the "neutral, vacillating mass" he first discovered among the uniformed schoolboys, milling about in their tunics and peaked caps, on Uspenskaya Street.

Odessa has always had two undergrounds, a figurative one explored by the future Trotsky and a literal one of caves and passageways. A labyrinth of catacombs wends through the porous stone on which the city rests. Some of the tunnels are natural, while others have been quarried and carved out over the centuries as storage rooms, places of refuge, and hideouts for everyone from truant schoolchildren to prostitutes, political agitators, and partisan guerrillas. The damp limestone crumbles to the touch in the narrow caves that snake for hundreds of miles under the city and its suburbs.

Drop down any courtyard well, Odessans say, and you will find a side tunnel leading to a hideout or smugglers' den. But Odessa's limestone underworld was a literal representation of a shadow city that existed alongside the real one, above ground and in plain sight. In the final years of the nineteenth century, the city's demimonde— a place of criminality, disease, conspiracy, and revolution—became the source of its signature reputation as well as its enduring ills. Its heart lay a short distance from St. Paul's school, in a neighborhood called Moldavanka.

The district's name is an oblique reference to the Romanian-speaking Moldovans, an ethnic minority that first came into the city as cattle drovers and workmen. According to some sources, the neighborhood predated the founding of Odessa. It first emerged as the temporary quarters of Moldovans who labored to build the Yeni Dünya fortress under the Ottomans. It was later home to Bulgarians, Albanians, Greeks, and others, including sympathizers of Philike Hetairia and refugees who fled the warfare of the 1820s in the Balkans.

By the middle of the nineteenth century, however, Moldavanka held more poor Jews than Moldovans and Bulgarians. It was infamous as a dilapidated den of poverty, cheap booze, and inventive criminality, all set amid the facades of Catholic and Orthodox churches and Jewish synagogues and prayer houses. Aggressive child beggars roamed the streets, past milliners and tailors, tinkers and carters. Yiddish-speaking teenage boys ruled the alleyways at night, looking for a brawl to start or a wedding party to crash. (One of them, Yankele Kulachnik, or "Jake the Fist," later mended his ways and became the great American Yiddish actor Jacob Adler.)[4] The district's Jewish gangsters were known to be kindly neighbors as well as ruthless killers. The police generally stayed away, refraining from pursuing criminals unless they first secured permission from the gangland "kings" who dispensed both justice and cruelty from their leafy courtyards. The line between Moldavanka and the city center— defined by the street known as Staroportofrankovskaya, or Old Free Port Street, the inland boundary of the nineteenth-century duty-free zone—continued to be seen as something of a frontier well into the Soviet era. Even today you know you have moved to the wrong side of the tracks when you cross it—into a big village of acacias and catalpas, where grapevines cover low, tumble-down houses and the street life seems a little rougher than on the wide avenues of the center.

Most sea and river ports have well-earned reputations as havens for shysters, and cities as diverse as Naples, London, and Rio de Janeiro, at various points in their history, developed criminal classes famous for their conniving ways and brutal behavior. But Odessa's underworld produced a collective pride in the seamier side of the city and its immediate outskirts—a way of living woven into the very identity of the city, to outsiders as well as to Odessans themselves. As the nineteenth century raced toward its end, the city's dangerous underworld became one of the deepest and most enduring features of its character. In the alleyways and overcrowded houses, in the wharf area and the dust-choked neighborhoods, Odessa developed the Russian Empire's greatest collection of criminals, delinquents, and creative crooks, men and women who managed to raise the vocation of the lowly *goniff*—an ingenious

Two portraits from the Odessa streets by the photographer
Rudolf Feodorovets, 1860s-70s. *Pavel Khoroshilov Collection,
courtesy of Nic Iljine.*

schemer and artful dodger, in Yiddish—to a profession. Underground Odessa was where some of the city's most distinctive qualities, as well as its most tragic ones, were forged.

WARNINGS ABOUT the wily ways of Odessans go back to the beginning of the city itself. "Having spoken of the productive population
of Odessa, it still remains to say a word about a disagreeable element common to all new towns," reported one of the city's earliest
historians, Gabriel de Castelnau, "that is, the arrival of adventurers
in swarms."[5] Even the comte de Langéron, once he had finished his
tenure as governor-general, complained that the city was congeni-
tally unruly, containing as it did "the dregs of Russia and Europe."[6]

Its natural partner across the sea—Constantinople—was a hub
of illicit commerce. Ottoman officials imposed exorbitant duties

while European governments managed to wrench lopsided commercial privileges from the sultan. Sailors and merchants traveling through the Ottoman capital often found little changed once
they reached the other side of the Black Sea. As one saying went,
cheats learned their profession in Pera—the medieval headquarters of Genoese merchants, situated on the heights overlooking old
Constantinople—but practiced it in Odessa. In both cities, bribes,
baksheeshes, and blandishments could be negotiated in a version of
Italian, a mainstay of the dockside culture of stevedores and ship
captains.

The city's outward prosperity through much of the nineteenth
century was the catalyst for venality and thievery, but the real fuel
of Odessa's *goniff* reputation was its shadow world of deep and
abiding poverty. Beyond the fashionable central streets near Nikolaevsky Boulevard, Odessa harbored shantytowns where Jewish,
Ukrainian, Russian, and other inhabitants plied their trades. Living in overcrowded courtyards or ramshackle huts, they were usually the first and most vulnerable victims of the downturn in the
grain trade or a shift in the exchange rate. The city's population
increased by 3,677 percent from 1800 to the 1890s, a figure astro-
nomically higher than for other rapidly growing imperial cities such
as Moscow, St. Petersburg, Warsaw, and Riga.[7] By the time of the
1897 census—the first truly comprehensive population count in the
empire's history—just over 400,000 people were crammed into
the old central district and the close-in neighborhoods of Peresyp
to the north, Slobodka-Romanovka to the northwest, and Moldavanka to the west. That figure would swell beyond 650,000 by the
First World War.

With the magnetic pull of paying jobs in the port, many people
broke their formal ties to the countryside but dragged along with
them many of the ways of the village. "Could we even grace with
the name of town the place where we then were and the streets we
beheld?" asked a French traveler in 1838. "It was a great open space

without houses, filled with carts, and oxen rolling in the dust, in company with a mob of Russian and Polish peasants, all sleeping together in the sun."[8] In fact, the alleged contrasts between Odessa and the most backward parts of the Pale of Settlement could often be superficial. In the shtetl, a beggar eats his crust of bread in gloom, quipped the Yiddish writer Mendele Moykher-Sforim, but in Odessa he eats the same crust to the music of a hurdy-gurdy.[9]

Early on, the city developed the central trait that visitors to the developing world know today: the extreme costliness of poor-quality service. Public conveyance might be accomplished in a closed carriage, but more often travelers were required to make their way through the dust and mud on a horse-drawn droshky, a rough contraption consisting of little more than four wheels joined by a leather-covered board.[10] Even then, the passenger might find that the driver had charged a multiple of the normal rate.[11] When he arrived at his hotel, an establishment guidebooks might describe as decent and fashionable would require that guests provide their own linen and bedding, offering only a room and an empty bedstead at an exorbitant rate.[12] Still, the constant stream of visitors to the city—as seamen, *chumaks*, runaway serfs, European travelers, and summering Russian nobles—helped knit its many districts and social classes into an economy of hierarchical dependence, despite their mixed origins and transient habits.

In the late 1890s, the American consul in Odessa reported one emblematic instance of Odessa's reputation as an oddball haven, the case of a man known as Whirlwind. A Lakota Sioux by origin, Whirlwind—the apparent translation of his given name, Hampa—arrived in Odessa in unusual circumstances. He had been part of a traveling Wild West show on tour through the Russian Empire, an Indian whose job was to be routinely chased around arenas by a herd of American cowboys. His career was proceeding well, enabled by the new steamship connections that ran between the major Black Sea ports and the Russian susceptibility to the alien allure of cowboys and Indians. But after seven years on the road, things began to sour. The availability of cheap vodka took its toll. When the company stopped for a performance in Sevastopol, Whirlwind was discharged for drunkenness, left penniless and utterly alone.

Whirlwind's plight came to the attention of the British consul in Sevastopol, who took pity on the destitute performer and paid for his passage to Odessa, a city with a well-established American consulate that would be able to look after its "ward," as the American consul later described him. (As an Indian, Whirlwind was not considered a full citizen of the United States but was nevertheless entitled to protection and consular services while abroad.) With the consulate's help, he scraped together enough money to have a new costume made. One imagines the American diplomat and the washed-up circus performer from America's Great Plains sweating inside a stifling shop in Moldavanka, trying to explain to a Jewish tailor what an Indian costume was supposed to look like.[13] This in turn allowed Whirlwind to secure employment with a small entertainment show in Odessa, presumably reprising his old warrior role on a much smaller stage.

The consul, Thomas P. Heenan, requested reimbursement for the $7.50 it cost to deal with the case. Heenan couldn't shake the sense that he had been cheated. He had gone out of his way to help someone who wasn't even a real American, he implied in his letters to his superiors, and Whirlwind would probably disappear into the city's underworld, drunk again. But being taken advantage of, in one form or another, was an expected outcome in Odessa— especially among the mass of lower-middle-class workers and traders who would have been the main audience for Whirlwind's Wild West entertainments.

————————

FROM THE PERSPECTIVE of the tsarist state, Russian society was divided into identifiable and highly regulated "estates," or *sosloviya* in Russian. Membership could be fluid, at least across several generations, and in many cases one's estate was never as predetermined or immutable as one's sex or eye color. But it was still a fundamental part of a Russian subject's social identity. In contrast to what Marxists would identify as "class," an individual's estate membership had little to do with his or her place in the hierarchy of economic production, much less with wealth or income. Like for the impoverished nobles in the works of Tolstoy or Chekhov, estate status was part of one's birthright, the genetic code of Russian society as a whole, not a reflection of economic power. When the state came to sort and categorize its own citizens, the labels that presented themselves in the late nineteenth century were clear: nobles, clergy, military, civil servants, peasants, and a group known as the *meshchane*—by far the largest estate in Odessa.

The *meshchane*—a word that might be translated as the petty bourgeoisie—were the large group of semi-skilled workers, tradesmen, shopkeepers, and Russian subjects caught between the castes of large-scale landowners and their former serfs living in grinding poverty in the close-in suburbs. They eked out a living on the fringes of Odessa's trading economy, vulnerable to the pendulum swings of commerce and the periodic blights afflicting agriculture. Unlike the wealthiest members of society, they had little recourse when times were hard, other than to join the day laborers hanging around the docks or hoping to pick up a job as a porter at one of the city's bazaars. Unlike their peasant neighbors, they had few real connections to the countryside that might allow them to weather economic fluctuations in town. Already by the middle of the nineteenth century, Odessa was largely a city of these vulnerable *meshchane*. In 1858 the nobility comprised 3 percent of the city's population, merchants nearly 5 percent, foreigners (that is, people who were not Russian subjects) just over 4 percent, peasants nearly 4 percent, and the military under 7 percent. The remainder—nearly 70 percent of the city's total—were *meshchane*.[14]

With a transient foreign population and a constant stream of newcomers arriving by ship and overland carriage—far more than in the empire's twin capitals, St. Petersburg and Moscow—Odessa was ripe for the kind of swindles, trickery, and palm-greasing that helped ease the economic burden of the petty bourgeoisie. When visitors complained of the hotelier who charged extra for bedding, the cobbler who charged twice to repair the same shoe, or the droshky driver who charged different rates for the same ride, it was the city's huge estate of *meshchane* who were the makers of the city's reputation. They could be found in virtually any profession. In 1892 over half the city's 607 prostitutes reported that they were *meshchane* by estate.[15]

Odessa's reputation was self-reinforcing. If it was the *meshchane* who were the foundation of the city's culture of self-confident thievery, it was the same group that, by and large, loved to read, hear, and tell stories about their own exploits. Between the twilight of the nineteenth century and the dawn of the twentieth, a wealth of true-crime reportage filled the city's panoply of Russian-language broadsheets and tabloids. It was a convenient fiction among upper-class Odessans that criminality was bred in the lower-class periphery, in places such as Moldavanka, and readers were treated to regular portrayals of life among the unhygienic and morally corrupt poor of these districts. But in reality the city's thievish reputation depended on criminals' talents for infiltrating and parroting the upwardly aspirant, if not upwardly mobile, petty bourgeoisie.

The criminal class included an intricate array of specialized professions. Some were defined by the area of the city in which they worked: the rough and tumble port district; the central Boulevard district atop the cliffs; the southern dacha-filled suburbs of Maly, Sredny, and Bolshoi Fontan; or the sparse industrial reaches of the north and northwest. Others were known for the days on which they worked, such as the weekenders who targeted the crowds that filled Deribasovskaya on Saturdays and Sundays. Still others were infamous for their creative disguises. One Ekaterina Ratsinskaya passed herself off as a cook for a wealthy family—only to show up at one of the local bazaars with 300 rubles' worth of jewelry she had spirited away from her employer by expertly picking the lock on a chest of drawers.[16] A person dressed up in gentlemanly attire might hit the most popular theaters and restaurants—the main theater on Langéron Street known simply as the Opera, the New Theater, or cafés near Alexandrovsky Park—as part of a well-turned-out gang of thieves who put their marks at ease before expertly slipping their hands into the pocket of the unwary.[17] A kind passerby who flicked the dust off a neighbor's frock coat could also lift his wallet. A respectable lady browsing in a luxury-goods store could turn out to be a resourceful shoplifter casing the joint.[18]

Other criminals were more creative. One P. Zhukov, "a coffee lover," as a local newspaper called him, took employment with the trendy Fanconi café only to make off with thirty pounds of freshly roasted beans, for which he was sentenced to three months' jail time.[19] In the central districts of the city, there were stories of nighttime assignations and ingenious cons. Women threw vitriol in the faces of their cheating husbands. Men claimed to be wealthy in order to ingratiate themselves with the best families, only to abscond with their silver. Attractive young prostitutes, pretending to be bored but respectable housewives, sought the intimacy of leading businessmen—and then used the affair to blackmail their unsuspecting johns. A well-dressed gentleman might express a deep interest in a woman whose marital prospects seemed dim. He would return week after week, eventually popping the question and settling down for a life of bliss—until he ran off with whatever money she brought into the marriage.[20]

In the city's newspapers, tales of criminal mischief competed with more pedestrian accounts of neighborly disputes and everyday disturbances. A September 1894 issue of *Odessky listok* (Odessa Folio), one of the city's more sober Russian-language dailies, carried the story of a small-time criminal syndicate run by the male-female team of Nikolai Yerginov and Aksina Oleinikova, probably Russians or Ukrainians by ethnicity. Their racket was selling stolen chickens to a middleman, Blum Goldberg, presumably Jewish, who claimed to be oblivious to the birds' origin. In court, Yerginov and Oleinikova put forward a classic crook's defense: that it was all a terrible misunderstanding, and that the chickens had been part of the estate of Yerginov's late, lamented father. The judge didn't buy the explanation, however, and Yerginov—a repeat offender, as it turned out—was given a year and a half in jail, while his female accomplice and Goldberg were set free.[21]

Another issue carried news of eighteen-year-old Olga Popik, the daughter of an Odessa *meshchanin* who had fallen in love with a wandering sailor, Mikhail Filipenko. When Popik became pregnant with Filipenko's child, the sailor made a quick getaway, marrying another woman shortly before Popik's baby was due. At the end of

The popular Fanconi café on Catherine Street, ca. 1913, from a contemporary postcard. *Courtesy of Nic Iljine.*

her term and distressed by news of the sailor's marriage, Popik stole away to a ravine running down to the sea and there gave birth to a baby girl. Passersby discovered the child's body some time later. Popik was put on trial for murder. The young woman, frightened and alone, had smashed the child's head with a rock.[22]

Stories such as these, repeated in their hundreds in the local press and in café-table conversations, reinforced Odessa's image as a haven for larceny and sensational crime. But they also contributed to the persistent view among outsiders that the city's real sin was its blatant *arrivisme*—the shallow, crass, impatient, and fly-by-night tendencies that passed for strivers' virtues. Like the ambitious middle class everywhere, Odessa's *meshchane* became practiced in spinning merits out of fate: celebrating pragmatism; reveling in melancholy; making their own distinctive patois out of the Italian, Greek, Yiddish, and Russian that tumbled out of doorways and courtyards; and trying, in an often unpolished and comical way, to turn fleeting trickster talents into something more permanent and profitable. "Experienced, shrewd, a trickster, a manipulator, a maneuverer, a man of ingenuity, a screamer, an exaggerator, a speculator" was how Vladimir Jabotinsky described the archetypical Odessan, labels that he intended as compliments.[23] Even disease was something the city's social classes learned to embrace.

SINCE RICHELIEU'S DAY, Odessa struggled to fend off and manage infectious illnesses. Five separate outbreaks of plague devastated the city between the 1790s and the 1830s.[24] Even as the threat of plague declined—in part because of improved enforcement of quarantine restrictions, in part because of the waning of the disease in the Ottoman ports across the Black Sea—other diseases such as typhus, cholera, and smallpox appeared with fatal regularity. Yet despite the frequent recurrence of serious disease, Odessans usually displayed a certain reticence to trade freedom for safety. "Your aim, young lady, is to inoculate smallpox, and with God's help, you are inoculating it," says a Jewish almshouse elder to a needle-wielding doctor in a story by Isaac Babel. "Our aim is to live out our life, not torture it!"[25] In several senses, locals usually found disease to be a useful, if not always desirable, companion, especially when the Russian state was involved.

The effort by captains and passengers to evade quarantine restrictions was a fact of life on the Black Sea, as certain as the circular migration of fish around the coast or the coming of violent storms in the winter. Already in the 1790s, Russian officials were complaining that ship captains routinely spent forty to sixty days making the easy journey from Constantinople to the north coast, a trip that should have taken no more than eight days under sail. The sluggish pace meant that goods rarely got to their destination with any rapidity, but it also ensured that those goods would be exempt from inspection or confiscation since they had been at sea long enough for any plague symptoms in passengers and crew to become manifest.[26] That was a boon for asymptomatic passengers, but infected goods could still make their way easily into port, which in many cases guaranteed the spread of disease beyond the docklands.

When the city government began to improve the quarantine system during Vorontsov's time as governor-general, the goal was to create a model of modern efficiency, a real barrier against the leap-frogging of sickness around the Black Sea ports and into the Russian heartland. The experience of going through the quarantine usually left a rather different impression, however.

The process started in the harbor. Ship captains were ordered to fly red flags if signs of plague had been noted on board or yellow flags for those effecting quarantine and thus off limits to new passengers. When a new ship arrived, a public health officer would row out from the quay and, bobbing along shipside, take charge of any mail the captain or passengers might have for delivery. To prevent any direct contact with potentially infected newcomers, the official would extend a long pair of iron tongs, using them to pick up the mail from the deck before securing it in an iron box and rowing away. The letters would then be fumigated at the quarantine facility, usually with sulfur dioxide to eliminate any disease-carrying insects, and delivered to their recipients the next morning.[27]

After a day or so, passengers could be disembarked on the long mole, or built-up breakwater, that defined the so-called quarantine harbor. Each passenger was rowed ashore separately and placed in the charge of a uniformed soldier, with rifle in hand and bayonet fixed, who in turn conducted the passenger to the custom house at the end of the pier. Once there, the passenger's travel documents were checked by a team of officials seated behind an iron railing. A doctor carried out a preliminary examination from behind a similar barrier, requesting that the passenger punch himself smartly under the arms and in the groin. The telltale sign of the plague—inflamed pustules over the lymph nodes—would presumably be easily discovered if the passenger winced in pain, while the examining physician avoided any direct contact with the potentially infected.

Once a passenger had been deemed disease-free, he was escorted, again under guard, to the lazaretto, the central quarantine facility that housed passengers during their period of observation, usually fourteen days. Situated on high ground, the lazaretto featured a large enclosure, perhaps twenty acres, of lawns and gravel pathways. Fronting on the sea was a row of buildings with separate apartments, each with a small courtyard and a few acacias. There, passengers were assigned to their quarters, at which point they were asked to strip naked and surrender their clothes in exchange for a flannel gown, underwear, stockings, and a woolen cap, all provided by the quarantine authorities. Their personal effects were taken to a separate chamber, where they were hung and fumigated for twenty-four hours. The central rule in the quarantine was to avoid contact with other passengers. Armed guards, usually old soldiers working for food and whatever gratuities might come their

way, followed passengers on their walks along the lazaretto's pathways. If they witnessed contact between two passengers, the quarantine clock would start over again, with both passengers cooling
their heels for another fourteen days.

This was the way things were supposed to go, and sometimes
the system worked as it was intended. The food was decent and the
surroundings pleasant enough, especially when the acacias were in
bloom in midsummer. Already by the 1830s the lazaretto was said to
rival the one at Marseille, which since the eighteenth century had
been the outstanding model for port quarantine systems around
the world.[28] The city's health did improve over time, and despite
periodic outbreaks of the plague, Odessa was never again threatened with the wholesale destruction that had loomed in Richelieu's
day. But with so many rules to be observed, and so many foreign
travelers spending so much time in enforced isolation, sooner or
later Odessans were bound to discover ways of making money. In
fact, the business of disease came to play significant and unexpected roles in Odessa's public life.

In a city where rule-flouting was a form of art, the quarantine
system was ripe for abuse. Some travelers avoided quarantine altogether if they were willing to pay sufficient bribes. Others had their
time in quarantine reduced or received the privilege of making periodic forays into town, so long as they returned at night. For those
without cash or connections, the wait could seem interminable,
which probably explained the carvings—names, initials, and other
graffiti—that reportedly covered the wood-paneled walls of the
customs office.[29] For those consigned to the lazaretto for the full
stay, there were plenty of other opportunities to be relieved of cash.
The café and restaurant, as the only sources of sustenance, charged
whatever rates they wished. Captains and seamen, along with passengers, whiled away the hours at the billiard table, losing money to
the more experienced guards or lazaretto staff in the process.

The supply of food in the lazaretto was contracted to a private firm, a way of saving money for the usually strapped city govern-ment. The contractor would buy up foodstuffs in the town and suburbs, which would then be passed on, at a considerable markup, to passengers effecting the required quarantine. With passengers confined to the lazaretto for two weeks and the contractor enjoying a monopoly on supplies during that period, the opportunities for enrichment were enormous. The contract was so coveted, in fact, that the government eventually decided to limit the length of the contract to six years, with a requirement that a new firm be brought in at the end of that period.

The term-limited contract opened up avenues for creative busi-nessmen to propose exceptions to the rule. One particularly enter-prising firm came up with the novel idea of taking over the operation of the opera house—often a money-losing operation but critical to Odessans' civic pride—if the government would waive the contract limit. That produced an odd codependence of etiology and enter-tainment. The quality of entertainment during any particular season usually depended on the virulence of the plague on the other side of the Black Sea. When disease was raging in the Ottoman ports and passengers were subjected to the maximum quarantine in Odessa, revenue flooded into the lazaretto—and provided plenty of funds for scheduling serious talent: the soaring soprano of a renowned diva, a new work by Rossini, the output of an up-and-coming playwright, or the offerings of a promising but itinerant composer. When Franz Liszt gave a series of piano concerts in Odessa in 1847 or when Niko-lai Gogol sat through a run of his new play, *The Inspector-General*, they probably had little idea that their work was funded in large part by the wildly successful business of disease.[30]

No one was more familiar with the creative and destructive power of sickness than Ilya Mechnikov, a professor at Novorossiya Uni-versity and the city's foremost contributor to the science of infection. Mechnikov's Odessa years were the most turbulent of his long and eventful life. It was in a despondent decade in his adopted city that he first formulated the theories of infectious disease and cell behavior that became his life's work. He eventually went far beyond the old port, settling at the Pasteur Institute in Paris, becoming its deputy director, and garnering a string of accolades from scholarly academies in St. Petersburg, London, and Rome. In 1908 Mechnikov received the Nobel Prize in Physiology or Medicine (shared with the German researcher Paul Ehrlich) for his work on immunity, specifically the idea that some cells have the natural ability to destroy microbes. Today when Odessa students walk along Pasteur Street, into a tree-shaded courtyard and through the dingy yellow facade of the city's main institution of higher learning, they are entering a place that now carries his name: the Odessa National "I. I. Mechnikov" University.

Ilya Mechnikov—known after his move to Paris as Élie Metchnikoff—was born in May 1845 on the estate of Panasovka in the province of Kharkov in eastern Ukraine.[31] The family fold was modest but hospitably appointed, an oasis on the flat expanse of steppe that surrounded it. One side of the family was descended from a branch of Moldovan nobles who, fleeing the advancing Ottoman armies, had found refuge in the domain of Peter the Great. The other side, Mechnikov's maternal line, was Jewish. While he was studying at the local lycée, the loan of a microscope sparked his passion for scientific research. After earning a university degree at Kharkov and publishing regularly in biology journals, he settled down to an academic position at Novorossiya University in Odessa, where the sea breezes and the good Italian opera were major attractions.

A researcher with a growing scientific reputation, Mechnikov traveled frequently to St. Petersburg, where he was thrown into the center of Russian scholarly life, as well as the social world of learned societies and the Russian Academy. Before long he was introduced to a young woman of good breeding, Lyudmila, whose chief virtue was her ability to assuage his natural melancholy. "She is not bad-looking, but that is all," he wrote to his mother in Kharkov. "[E]ven though I have dark previsions for the future (as you know, I am not given to seeing life through rose-colored glasses), I cannot help thinking that by living with Lussia I should become calmer, at least for a fairly long time."[32] Closer to the truth was the fact that Mechnikov found some diversion from his own dark introspection by caring for Lyudmila. Chronic bronchitis, probably the early stages of tuberculosis, struck her on their wedding day. She had to be carried to the church in a chair.

Their new life together was mainly spent apart, he in St. Petersburg and Odessa, she in Switzerland and Portugal, hoping to find some relief for her fluid-filled lungs. In the winter of 1873, during a break between two of his lectures, he received a letter from his sister-in-law saying that Lyudmila was nearly gone and that if he wished to see her again, he should come as quickly as possible to Madeira, where she was convalescing in the archipelago off the Portuguese coast. By the time he arrived—after a grueling journey across the breadth of Europe—she was only a shell, bedridden and morphine-dazed. She lasted only a few days longer.

On the return journey to Russia, his despair was obvious. He destroyed the scientific papers he had been working on. By the time he reached Geneva, he had downed a vial of morphine. He was saved by his own enthusiasm for death: the huge dose induced vomiting, which expelled most of the drug before it could be absorbed.

Surviving both his wife and his own botched suicide, Mechnikov redoubled his commitment to work. He took on new research projects on evolution and adaptation. He organized an anthropological expedition among the steppe nomads of Kalmykia along the Caspian Sea. To earn extra income, he took on tutoring jobs in Odessa, including for the children of the noisy neighbors who lived in the apartment one floor above his own. In time he grew attracted to one of the young girls in the family, Olga. In February of 1875 the wide-eyed teenager, still a schoolgirl and more passionate about art and the theater than science and nature, married the pale and gloomy professor.

Olga soon discovered that her new husband was a knotted skein. He was given to sudden, furious outbursts. An unexpected noise — a barking dog or a mewing cat—would unnerve him. He would fly into a rage if confronted with a difficult problem, no matter how frivolous. But he had reasons beyond his own mercurial nature for worrying about his own life and career.

Mechnikov was living through a time of immense change in Odessa and the empire. Students at the university were calling for better teaching and greater attention to science and the applied arts. Underground circles, from liberal to socialist and revolutionary, were thriving. Disturbances in the wider empire—village uprisings after the emancipation of the serfs in 1861, a failed rebellion in Poland in 1863—were causing the tsarist government to fear that any calls for reform were masks for revolutionary agitation.

Public disturbances pitted some of Odessa's citizens against others: locals against newcomers, liberals against conservatives, young students against older professors, and nearly everyone against Jewish shopkeepers and merchants. A pogrom left stores ransacked and houses in Moldavanka razed. When a bomb-throwing terrorist assassinated Tsar Alexander II in March of 1881, Mechnikov fell into another deep depression, convinced that the political troubles spawned by the killing would surely reach Odessa and the university, which was already rent by student activism and the appointment of reactionary administrators.

Throughout his bouts with depression, with his classes canceled or the university closed, with crowds running through the streets and Olga periodically ill from typhus, and faced with a weak heart and failing eyesight, Mechnikov managed to proceed with the research that eventually made him famous. The problem

Ilya Mechnikov (right) with Leo Tolstoy in 1909, a year after Mechnikov received the Nobel Prize. *Prints and Photographs Division, Library of Congress.*

that concerned him was the body's response to crisis. His contemporaries, Louis Pasteur and Robert Koch, had begun to refine the germ theory of disease, the idea that small organisms such as bacteria—not the imponderable workings of a cold draft or a swampy miasma—were the true causes of infection and transmission for many diseases.

Mechnikov's insight, obtained from early experiments on the regenerative power of starfish, was that cells can fight foreign agents introduced into the body. Cells rush to the infected site,

surrounding the invading matter and consuming it, a process easily observed under a microscope. Phenomena that had previously
been seen as by-products of infection—white pus around a wound,
say—were actually evidence of the body's healing process. He gave
that process the name "phagocytosis." Immunity, he reckoned,
was simply the ability of an organism to deploy phagocytes against
invaders. Inflammation was not only a problem but also a sign of
the body's own desperate attempt at a cure. The award of the Nobel
Prize marked Mechnikov's research as fundamental to the way sci-
entists think about disease and the human body's reaction to it, a
theory of immune response covering everything from a splinter to
the bubonic plague.

Mechnikov's reputation did not survive his fame, however. In
books and public lectures, he promoted the idea that "intestinal
putrefaction" was the real cause of aging, senility, and premature
death. He railed against the large intestine, that den of rotting
waste that sends its poisons coursing through the neighboring
organs. He stopped short of advocating its prophylactic removal,
eventually settling on the ingestion of yogurt, teeming with benefi-
cent bacteria, as the key to health. From his own experience, he
reasoned that a pessimistic outlook could enhance the putrefaction in the gut, which is why he urged his audiences to look on the
sunny side or, as he called his system of optimistic philosophy and
yogurt-eating, "orthobiosis." Until his death in 1916, he remained
fascinated by medical cases in which surgeons had managed to
create an artificial anus and thus bypass the maleficent intestine.
The pathbreaking scientist died peacefully, at Pasteur's institute in
Paris, as an eccentric quack.[33]

It doesn't take too much imagination to see the troubled professor, faced with deep personal loss and witnessing the evasion
of public health regulations in the busy seaport, having the first
inkling of a revolutionary idea: that like the old soldiers working for tips in the lazaretto, or the venal quarantine officials find-

ing ways of fleecing a ship's captain, or the administrators at the opera house giddily planning a new season after news of a plague outbreak in Constantinople, sometimes the true vanguard in fighting disease is the body's own remarkable ability to turn threats into opportunities.

But if these peculiar skills had allowed Odessa's citizens to build a multicultural and often tolerant boomtown, they were weakening in the closing decades of the nineteenth century. "The thought of Odessa always brings on very bitter feelings in me," Mechnikov wrote to a correspondent shortly after he and Olga began their long sojourn abroad.[34] The crowds that filled the streets were no longer the gay and colorful masses that had enchanted travelers earlier in the century. Cudgels and banners, mobs and shouts, the sound of breaking glass and rapid footfalls on the granite pavers were now familiar sights and sounds. Mechnikov's family had converted to Christianity two generations earlier, and given his mother's Jewish roots, he might have sensed the chill descending over the city. Between the lecture hall and the laboratory, he had witnessed the opening salvos of Odessa's long and brutish war on its own Jewishness. The city had embarked on a new century of self-loathing that would test the harder virtue that the city's founders, like Mechnikov's energetic phagocytes, had tried to cultivate: the struggle to consume difference without being destroyed by it.

CHAPTER 7

Blood and Vengeance

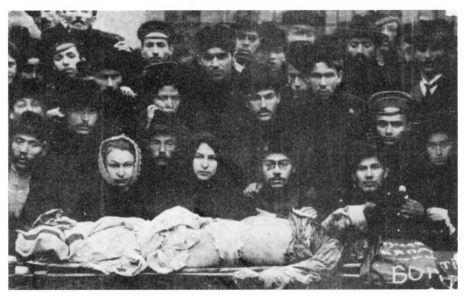

Heroes and martyrs: Members of a Jewish self-defense group posing with the body of a comrade, one of the victims of the violence of 1905. *From the Archives of the YIVO Institute for Jewish Research, New York.*

" [E] very year at Passover the Greeks beat up the Jews and robbed them," recalled the actor Jacob Adler, who spent his childhood in Odessa.[1] Riots and rough-ups involving Jews and Christians were recurring, if not constant, features of the city's social life, much as they were in virtually any European city with a Jewish minority. Odessans were as susceptible as any Russian subjects to the persistent antisemitic myths that dogged Jews throughout the Pale of Settlement and beyond, from collective responsibility for the death of Christ to the grotesque idea that the recipe for matzo required the blood of Christian children. When violence occurred, pervasive cultural antisemitism was only the catalyst for more pedestrian causes. Significant riots erupted in 1821 and 1859, mainly involving Greek residents who blamed Jews for a host of imagined crimes, from aiding the Turks in their battles with Greek revolutionaries to conspiring against Greek merchants in the grain trade.

By Ilya Mechnikov's day, the optimism of the old *maskilim* was still high. Jewish newspapers—including *Razsvet* (Dawn), established in 1860 as the first Russian-language Jewish periodical in the entire empire—carried stories of worldly success and progress. Some were even confident enough to air controversies and disputes internal to the community—such as the tension between assimilation and tradition—in their pages. Yet several new features of city life exacerbated the uneasy relations between Jews and Christians, eventually turning Odessa into the site of the first large-scale pogroms in modern Russian history.

The city's population was exploding, tripling in the second half of the nineteenth century. Newly freed Russian and Ukrainian peasants and the growing number of workers in the mills and metal shops of the city's suburbs—often young, male, and single—found themselves in a city where Jews were confident of their social status and economic might. Jewish firms accounted for well over half the total income from the grain trade.[2] However, the city's great industrial concerns—the Weinstein flour mill, the Zelberschmidt and Goldberg noodle factory, the Brodsky sugar refinery—were rarely the outright targets of violence. It was rather the small-time Jewish traders and shopkeepers, the local merchants and tailors, whose stores were vandalized and houses burned whenever riots flared.

Jews did not dominate Odessa's economic life overall, given the city's reliance on shipping and agricultural output, areas in which Christian proprietors and producers still held pride of place. But their role tended to be public, prominent, and precisely in those spheres where they and Odessa's newer immigrants were in most direct contact. Given state-imposed restrictions on landownership and access to particular professions, Jews were naturally concentrated in the roles still open to them by law and convention. By the beginning of the 1880s, Jews accounted for two-thirds of the city's registered merchants and traders, nearly three-fourths of the innkeepers and proprietors of public houses, and two-thirds of veterinarians and pharmacists. By contrast Christians made up over 80 percent of the city's workers, including some three-fourths of the workforce employed in Jewish-owned factories.[3]

When carters had a sick cow, when petty traders haggled over the price of a bolt of imported cloth, and when working men sought to combat the winter chill with a bottle of vodka, they were in intimate interaction with their Jewish neighbors. But in a context of rising Russian nationalism and the state's growing fear of political subversives, this familiarity bred the opposite of fellow-feeling. "The common remark therefore is that 'Everything is in the hands of the Jews,'" the U.S. consul reported to Washington.[4]

The spark for violence could be minimal. In April of 1871, on Orthodox Easter Sunday, a group of Jewish boys was said to have insulted Greek Christians attending religious services outside an Orthodox church. Words were exchanged, and the two crowds threw rocks and punches. As word of the scuffle spread, Russian workmen joined in, chasing the Jewish boys through the streets and lobbing rocks at the windows of synagogues. Organized crowds—perhaps as many as twenty thousand men—soon formed throughout the city and launched a systematic attack on Jewish taverns, grocers, ironmongers, jewelers, pottery shops, and dry goods stores, destroying what they could not loot. Jewish printing presses were wrecked, and all the windows of the Brody synagogue were shattered.[5] After three days of chaos, six people had been killed, nearly two dozen wounded, and hundreds of businesses and homes damaged or destroyed. Infantry and mounted lancers were called in to restore order. Artillery was deployed in the streets, and the police and military arrested some fifteen hundred people.[6]

The basic conditions that facilitated public violence only grew over the next decade. More peasants arrived from the old noble estates, bringing with them a repertoire of mob activism and an unwavering faith in the pronouncements of Orthodox priests. The *meshchane* were declining as a percentage of the population and disappearing as the bedrock of urban life. Student radicals took advantage of the relatively easy access to books and periodicals of several political persuasions—nationalist, liberal, socialist, and anarchist—and formed underground circles dedicated to remaking the empire in accordance with their own political and social programs.

The Russian state, always wary of Odessa's openness, also began to develop its own program for managing social change and disorder. Police surveillance increased. Public administration swung between robust local control and harsh centralization. When violence returned in the spring of 1881—student riots and another pogrom in response to the assassination of Alexander II—state institutions sought to use the chaos for their own ends, intervening to halt the violence only when rioters threatened more than Jewish shops and homes. The next year, new imperial ordinances, the infamous May Laws, placed harsh restrictions on Jewish property ownership, residence, work schedules, and participation in city government. The laws were a sop thrown to the radical Russian nationalist groups that had directed anti-Jewish mobs throughout the southern empire, and they now signaled the state's clear retreat from the relative liberalism of the previous twenty years.

Violence was not new, but the state's acceding to it, even facilitating and rewarding it, in large part was. Anti-Jewish violence in Odessa established a template of accepted explanations and a menu of official responses that were replicated throughout the empire over the next two decades. The term we now use in

English for these events—pogroms—is itself of Russian vintage (although anti-Jewish violence at the time was usually described euphemistically as "riots" or "disturbances"). It derives from *grom*, the Russian word for thunder, as if attacks on Jews had a natural, perhaps even heavenly, source. When violence occurred, the theory went, it was because Christians were simply fed up with Jewish treachery and venality. The state could justifiably, even productively, step aside when Jews got what was coming to them, reserving real intervention until the outpouring of gentile discontent threatened the general public order. The historical evidence now suggests that the central Russian government had little direct role in organizing the pogrom-makers, but regional and local officials were at least complicit by their own inaction.[7]

A city in which Jews had managed to reach the heights of commerce, even moving into the realm of city administration, was closing down around them. The confidence of the old *maskilim* wavered. Jewish choices were now limited but clear. Some left altogether, creating the same brief dip in the Jewish percentage of the population that had occurred after the violence of the early 1870s—one of the periodic waves of emigration to western Europe and the United States that would continue for the next century.[8] Others formed self-defense organizations, storing up knives, pistols, and determination to fend off the next round of bloodletting and in the process providing yet further targets for police agents and informers.

Still others found answers in ideologies of liberation and revolutionary change, sober political faiths and utopian movements that would soon be labeled Zionism and Russian social-democracy. For both Jews and Christians, schools and the local university became informal training grounds for a new generation of young men and women who saw "revolutionist" as a profession, from famous dissenters such as Leon Trotsky to lesser-known exponents of radical philosophy and political action. One of the clearest expressions of the pathways available to Jews—and indeed to many non-Jewish

Odessans—comes from a work that probably has the truest claim
to being the great Odessa novel.

———————

The Five, the work of the Odessa journalist and Zionist leader
Vladimir Jabotinsky, was written in Russian in 1935 and published
in Paris the next year. It was translated into Hebrew in the 1940s
but only made it into English—the first translation into any Western language—in 2005.[9] The novel looks back on a much earlier
time, the transition from the nineteenth to the twentieth century,
and Odessa's long march away from the cosmopolitan ideals in
which its reputation was grounded. It contains poetic descriptions
of early-twentieth-century Odessa, with nostalgia-tinged portraits
of its streets and smells, its characters and passions.

The story lines are multiple and disjointed, but the main arc
follows the lives of a group of successful, Russian-speaking Jews,
the Milgrom family and their associates. The Milgroms might be
superficially described as assimilated Jews, inhabiting a Russian cultural space and thriving in a city that they considered fully their
own. They sit in a box at the opera. The mother, Anna Mikhailovna,
floats above a shifting array of intellectuals and artists, a society
matron of the first order. The father, Ignats Albertovich, com-
mands a grain emporium whose fortunes run from the Dnieper
River to the Mediterranean. The family's five children have an
infinity of choices in life: to read Nietzsche like Marko or the Torah
like Torik; to take on the trappings of a nihilist and troubled revolutionary like Lika; to skip school and slum it with cardsharps and
crooks like Seryozha; or to be the toast of Odessa society like the
coquettish and unattainable Marusya, the Milgrom's scandalously
modern daughter whose only limit with the boys, she says, is her
diaphragm.

Yet the idea of assimilation—implying a fixed identity that
morphs into something else—barely figures into their self-image.

They wear their religious heritage lightly. They see themselves as having nothing in common with the shtetl Jews who filter into the city during harvest season. Zionism holds little appeal. They are Russian in most senses of the term—most senses, that is, except the one that came to matter most: the ability to negotiate their path through a society increasingly divided along national lines. Odessa was a club of nationalities, says the novel's narrator, a place of "good-natured fraternization" where the city's "eight or ten tribes" managed to get along. But in their homes, they lived apart. "Poles visited and invited other Poles, Russians invited Russians, Jews, other Jews; exceptions were encountered relatively infrequently, but we had yet to wonder why this was so, unconsciously considering it simply an indication of temporary oversight, and the Babylonian diversity of our common forum, as a symbol of a splendid tomorrow."[10]

Like the city itself, the Milgroms found themselves living in a world of tissue paper and crystal, beautiful, delicate, and unspeakably fragile. In an era of political radicalization, Lika is expelled from school and sent off to a two-year exile for seditious activity. Marko puts down Nietzsche and joins a Jewish self-defense organization in the back streets of Moldavanka. Torik, the conscientious student and good Jew who pores over Hebrew textbooks, makes plans to convert to Christianity. Seryozha, the fun-loving hedonist, has acid splashed in his face by a cuckolded husband. Even for Marusya, the perpetual tease, things end badly. In the novel's climax, she performs a shocking act of self-sacrifice. Now married and with children, she heats milk on the stove for her young son, who is playing in the hallway of their country house. In a moment of carelessness, she allows the fire to lick the sleeve of her housecoat. Seconds later, engulfed in flames, Marusya struggles to the kitchen door and throws the latch from the inside, preventing her son from opening it. He remains safely in the hall while his mother burns to death only inches away. Half of Odessa attended her funeral.

The Five has many messages. Decay holds more interest than flourishing. Pride is the essence of human agency. Rebellion against misfortune may seem the logical and heroic option, but pride reinforces the power of the sufferer. Even though it was written more than a quarter century after the period it describes, the novel has a freshness that makes it a powerful characterization of the city's travails. Odessans spent their history learning to laugh at one another, the narrator says, and this was the crucial skill that enabled its many tribes to live together, more or less.

But joie de vivre and jokester skills were only a weak kind of social glue. In times of trouble, the novel asks, what resources did this urban society really have at its disposal other than shrugged shoulders and comic relief? Gentle, early-evening strolls were cut short or abandoned. People now hurried along, drawing themselves into the shadows. "They'd always cursed each other as rogues or idiots, and had sometimes even fought," the narrator says of Odessa's major ethnic communities, "but in all my memory there'd never been any authentic, ferocious hostility. Now all this had changed. The first sign of benevolence among men had disappeared—that is, the southern custom of considering the street as your home."[11]

―――――――――

THE FIVE is a novel about a family, closed and ultimately tragic. But the Milgroms were also living in the middle of the most widespread and destructive public violence the city had yet seen, a series of events that would later seal Odessa's place in the Soviet Union's pantheon of revolution. The events of 1905—especially the brief workers' demonstration in St. Petersburg in January of that year—are now thought of as the first throes of revolutionary change, the beginning of the short march toward October of 1917, the rise of the Bolsheviks, and the coming of the Soviet Union. At the time, however, things were never that clear. Anarchy only seems like revolution after the revolutionary power wins. The tsarist state enacted a series of reforms in response to the uprising—such as forming an elected legislature with real power, the State Duma—but they were short-lived. On the ground across the Russian Empire, the violence of the opening years of the twentieth century looked either devastating or mildly troublesome, depending on one's social standing, business interests, political engagement, and ethnic or religious affiliation.

On the imperial periphery, violence took different forms. In the Caucasus region, anarchic street fights between Armenians and Muslims torched entire villages, brought down a forest of oil derricks, and mangled the pipelines that had made the city of Baku one of the empire's premier boomtowns. In villages and cities across the old Pale of Settlement, rolling pogroms decimated Jewish communities and spurred others to action. Already in 1903 a bloody pogrom in the city of Kishinev left dozens dead and drew international attention to the plight of Jews in Russia. Jewish self-defense units expanded to counter Russian nationalist thugs, whose bloody work was often abetted by local police and Cossack cavalry.

Odessa in 1905: "A demonstration of revolutionists," a photograph from the *Illustrated London News*, November 18, 1905. *Author's collection.*

In Odessa a concatenation of factors led to its own version of 1905, producing the deadliest and most notorious pogrom in Russian history. Worker dissatisfaction was growing. A range of underground socialist and anarchist groups were finding ways of taking advantage of it. Trade unions, mutual aid societies, and workers' cooperatives channeled discontent and provided information and resources for industrial activism. Police surveillance and official paranoia were growing apace. Strikes and occasional mob violence ramped up in the 1890s and early 1900s as the city's growing working class discovered its own power.

Odessa also experienced the one war that it could neither weather nor turn to a profit. On the other side of the empire, tensions were growing between Russia and Japan for dominance in northeast Asia. The Russian navy had made repeated shows of strength in the region, leasing port facilities in Manchuria and threatening Japan's role as power broker in China and Korea. In January of 1904, the Japanese navy launched a surprise attack on Russian forces stationed at Port Arthur. The two ambitious empires declared war, and the war ministry of Tsar Nicholas II rushed to build up sufficient land and sea forces to counter the Japanese. The results were disastrous. Russian forces, undersupplied and overstretched, lost one battle after another. Nicholas was finally forced to sue for peace.

The effects on Odessa were profound. The city had been the primary grain supplier to the Russian Far East, as well as a key trading center for manufactured goods being shipped to the Pacific. The blockade of Russian holdings by the Japanese navy dried up some of the city's major overseas markets. Grain exports were cut in half, and exports overall fell by more than a third. A credit crunch followed, with manufacturing businesses declaring bankruptcy and trading firms closing their doors.[12]

Odessans had more reason than ever to take to the streets. They were joined by the mass of soldiers and sailors who had arrived in the city by train, waiting to be loaded onto ships for the long journey into the Mediterranean, through the Suez Canal, and toward what they knew to be the growing calamity in the Far East. With thousands of men now idle, thefts, burglaries, and general public disorder increased. To augment the number of men available for wartime service, the tsar pardoned prison inmates who had not been involved in violent crimes, releasing some two hundred people from the Odessa jail. "It will therefore be readily understood why the outlook . . . is not reassuring," reported the U.S. consul, Thomas P. Heenan.[13]

By the summer of 1905, discontent was at a boil. Worker activism and strikes turned violent. Barricades filled the streets, and bomb-throwing anarchists attacked police and military units dispatched to quell the unrest. In mid-June crowds descended on the port, looting warehouses and engaging in pitched battles with police. Hundreds lay dead in the streets, the victims of random bullets, raging waterfront fires, and targeted attacks by the authorities on underground political movements and their sympathizers. The arrival in the harbor of a mutinous battleship, the *Potemkin*, spurred on the street fighters. But after sitting ominously in port and then lobbing a few ill-placed shells, the *Potemkin* sailed on to Romania and eventual surrender.

A lull followed the "June days," but disorder returned in the fall, this time in the form of massive attacks on Jews. Antisemitic rumors had blamed Jewish self-defense organizations for the June violence, and the tsarist authorities certainly saw Jewish activists as key instigators of strikes and even of revolutionary agitation aimed at overthrowing the government. A scuffle between Jews and Russians near Moldavanka led to mass marches designed to support the tsar against perceived Jewish revolution. By mid-October the marches had escalated to attacks on Jewish homes and businesses. Those who were willing to pay police reportedly received protection from the crowds.[14]

In contrast to earlier pogroms, there was now a coordinated response by the self-defense organizations that had already tested their mettle in June. Running battles filled the grid of streets in the city center. Political organizations claimed that revolution was in the air. Others sought revenge for past pogroms and riots. But self-defense groups were no match for the crowds that descended indiscriminately on Jewish shops, homes, and synagogues. Even in response to the most brutal acts of violence—the killing of women and children, torture, rape, and mutilation—the city authorities did little, claiming that the size of the disturbances proved impossible to control. Police discipline had broken down, but the attitudes of municipal authorities against Jews were clear: the self-defense organizations were part of the problem, and they were now getting their just deserts. "The position of the Hebrew element of the population is one of great danger, in my estimation, as great bitterness exists against them on account of recent events," wrote Heenan. "The peasantry in many parts of the province are reported to be robbing, stealing, and even worse and telegrams have been received here begging for help. Taking it all and all I think I may safely suggest that the times are out of joint."[15]

The red flags of revolt sometimes fluttered in the sea breeze. Crowds hailed the news from St. Petersburg that the tsar had granted the empire its first ever elected parliament. "Here in the great commercial city of southern Russia," wrote the correspondent for the *Chicago Daily News*, "there was a gloom, silence and abandon that spelled revolution, disorder and economic disaster."[16] But for people in the middle of these events, they had the look not of political change but of a nightmarish circus that upended all the city had built. Odessa's civilized core seemed to have withered and blown out to sea. As Lyubov Girs, the wife of a senior city official, noted in her diary, "Jewish pogroms are breaking out. [The Jews] have organized and armed themselves, and they are going so far as to shoot out of windows at the Russians. On Deribasovskaya Street all the Jewish stores have been smashed and the goods looted, and the riff-raff and their wives are strutting about in expensive clothes, boots, and fur coats. . . . The Jews on our street grabbed a dog and hung a label on his tail that said 'Nicholas II.' "[17]

In the end, perhaps three hundred Jews and another hundred non-Jews fell victim to the violence of October, adding to hundreds of people, both Jewish and Christian, killed the previous June. Odessans had never seen violence of this scale and scope. A score of different causes and motivations were braided together over more than a year of disturbances, street fights, and large-scale confrontations. Political activism, drunkenness, boredom, fear, tit-for-tat attacks, and the religiously inspired antisemitism of the workers

Odessa in 1905: "A rough funeral: conveying bodies of Jewish victims from the hospital to the cemetery," a photograph from the *Illustrated London News*, November 18, 1905. *Author's collection.*

and peasants who ringed the city center all came together to produce Odessa's descent into chaos.

It was a series of events that touched the heart of the business
and administrative classes, groups that had to a degree been exempt
from the routine violence that had previously afflicted the docklands, Moldavanka, and some of the inner suburbs. Overall, the
toll from assassinations, bomb blasts, shoot-outs, and mob attacks
between February 1905 and May 1906 in the wider Odessa region
was staggering: the dead included thirteen provincial governors
and mayors, thirty police captains and senior officers of the gendarmerie, twenty-nine bankers and leading businessmen, fifty-four
factory owners, 471 other police officers, and 257 local constables,
in all some 1,273 deaths that the Russian state attributed to "terrorist acts"—not counting the hundreds of ordinary citizens killed or
injured over the same period.[18]

IT IS HARD TO KNOW when you find yourself in the middle of history. Most Odessans of the day, like the characters in *The Five*, were
not living in a prologue or an aftermath but rather in the uncertain
present. After all, a decade before the unrest, around the time of
Odessa's centennial in 1894, the city was still full of unparalleled
cultural promise—for both gentiles and Jews—despite the earlier
pogroms and tightening government repression.

Odessans, for example, had celebrated their city's birthday with
commemorative albums, military parades, endless speeches, and
solemn masses, all overseen by the long-serving, barrel-chested
mayor Grigory Marazli. More than 1,500 people could crowd
into the gilded interior of the opera house that, for nearly twenty
years, had stood regally at the top of Richelieu Street. After a show,
patrons could stroll down Langéron or Catherine Street, both
flanked by new buildings decorated with classical columns or florid
baroque reliefs, and enjoy a coffee or flavored ices at the Fanconi

or Robinat café. For those with the right credentials, private associations such as the exclusive Odessa Club—earlier known as the English Club—offered drinks, dining, and foreign newspapers.

Citizens with more specific interests might seek membership in the Black Sea Yacht Club, the New Russian Society for the Encouragement of Horse Breeding, the New Russian Society of Hunting Enthusiasts, or the Odessa Society of Amateur Velocipedists. The reading public could find books at several libraries and reading halls, or purchase their own volumes at one of the city's eighteen bookstores. Visitors might find lodging at any of twelve first-class hotels and countless private houses and small inns. They could stroll among the curious statues and engravings displayed in the museum of the Imperial Odessan Society of History and Antiquities, or lose themselves in the green expanse of Alexandrovsky Park. When they had had enough of the city, they could take the regular train service to anywhere in the empire or Europe, or board one of the dozens of steamships making daily runs to the other Russian ports on the Black Sea or weekly excursions to Constantinople.[19]

It was hardly a golden age for the city. The grain trade had fallen off, and Odessa's relative importance in the empire and the wider world was already in decline. But a snapshot of the individual lives being played out in the city's modest homes and courtyards reveals a wealth of talent and imagination—some of it belonging to native Odessans but most connected with people who passed through the city while making their reputations elsewhere. The Yiddish writer Sholem Aleichem was living near the park. He later became the celebrated creator of Tevye the Dairyman and, after a move to the United States, the masterful codifier of what we now think of as shtetl culture. Simon Dubnow, the distinguished historian of Russian Jewry, was holding court in his flat in Bazaar Street. Leon Pinsker, one of the early prophets of what would come to be called Zionism, was dying in his rooms on Richelieu Street. A few blocks away, the register of the Preobrazhensky Cathedral recorded the christening of one Anna Gorenko. She later resurrected an old family name, Akhmatova, as her nom de plume. A few blocks farther to the west, in Moldavanka, the warehouse-owner Emmanuel Babel was celebrating the birth of his son, Isaac.

For Jews, a wide array of ideologies, political programs, and social networks spread themselves through the city like melons offered at the bazaar. The Odessa branch of the Society for the Propagation of Enlightenment among the Jews of Russia worked to forward the values of the *maskilim*, including the use of the Russian language. The Society for the Support of Jewish Farmers and Artisans in Syria and Palestine—known informally as the "Odessa Committee" and for a time the only legal Zionist organization in Russia—supported Jews who opted to begin new lives as farmers in Ottoman-ruled Palestine, at least until the Ottomans began restricting Jewish immigration.

The promise and horror of Odessa in the decade separating 1894 from 1905 seem deeply contradictory. How could a city generally satisfied with its easy cosmopolitanism fall so speedily into communal chaos? Many Odessans—especially Jews—seemed to be swimming against a swelling tide. "Assimilation begins precisely with the relaxation of old prejudices," says one of the characters in *The Five*, "but a prejudice is a sacred thing; . . . Perhaps the genuine meaning of morality . . . consists of prejudices."[20] That was the novel's essential point. The growing exclusion of Jews from Russian civic life was not merely a result of their neighbors' biases. For the author of *The Five* and its thinly veiled narrator, Vladimir Jabotinsky, exclusion, self-awareness, and pride in one's own cultural peculiarities were crucial dimensions of what Jewishness ought to be. In his day, Odessa seemed to confirm the view that national identity was the atomic unit of human society. The veneers offered by assimilation, imperialism, and cosmopolitanism could not disguise the age-old yearning for nations to express their own unique genius. Jews, Poles, Russians, and Greeks might bump up against each other on Deribasovskaya, but everyday civility was not the same thing as commonality of interest or ambition. In the end, this particular way of thinking about nationality was both the antithesis and the product of everything Jabotinsky's native city claimed to be.

NEARLY A THOUSAND MILES away from Odessa, the Israeli port of Acre contains an old prison famous for housing heretics. Originally constructed during the Crusader era, the imposing Acre fortress was a place where the Knights Templar could hide away their infidel captives. Successive Arab and Ottoman rulers used it to stash the rebellious, the unorthodox, and the merely inconvenient. The nineteenth-century religious leader Bahá'u'lláh, founder of the Bahá'í faith, was shoved into a dingy cell by Ottoman authorities for preaching the revolutionary idea that all religions are part of a divine and progressive revelation. Almost a century later, the new political power in the city—the British mandate authorities in Palestine—found the prison an equally serviceable place to keep one of the most troublesome Odessans of the era, the novelist, journalist, and activist Vladimir Jabotinsky, Zionism's archetypical champion as well as its most controversial dissenter. His storied career—from Odessa to Palestine to an early death in the United States—reveals a great deal about the political eddies that swirled around his hometown in the transition from the nineteenth century to the twentieth.

If political activism was drowsing in the 1890s, as Jabotinsky once said about his young adulthood, it awoke in 1905. Russian extremist groups such as the Black Hundreds had been active throughout the empire's southern borderlands for years. To those were added Ukrainian organizations seeking everything from cultural autonomy to outright independence for Ukrainian-speaking peasants and town-dwellers. Socialism, too, had adherents who interpreted Marxism in forms ranging from the gradualist and democratic to the revolutionary and demagogic.

This milieu helped shape Vladimir Jabotinsky as a Russian-speaker, a Jew, and a particular brand of Zionist. He was born on October 5, 1880, the son of a successful shipper. His father died before Jabotinsky's first birthday, and the family immediately experienced a downsizing of means and ambition. His mother opened a small stationery shop, with the family taking up residence in rooms behind the main store. A family of merchants became, almost overnight, a family of shopkeepers, and Jabotinsky became one of the vehicles of his mother's determination to restore the family to its previous social standing. She was insistent that he be allowed to devote time to his studies rather than bring in needed money by learning a trade.[21]

Jabotinsky was born into an era in which opportunity was in shorter supply than it had been earlier in the century, especially for Jews. A *numerus clausus*, or anti-Jewish quota, was introduced for Russian educational institutions around the time he was preparing to enter high school. After several rounds of entrance examinations and many denials, he was finally admitted to the storied Richelieu *gymnasium*—a school at which his contemporary, Trotsky, never managed to gain a place—only to find that plenty of other Jews had managed to skirt the restrictions and ensure a slot on the student roster. Families that had taken for granted their ability to be vaguely Jewish by religion, Russian by language and culture, and unshakably bourgeois by class now found themselves battling a new wave of prejudice.

In his classroom, Jabotinsky was arrayed in a row with the other nine Jews in his group of thirty students, contentedly separate but friendly with his Polish, Greek, Armenian, and Moldovan neighbors. He was a self-confessedly poor student and spent more time enjoying Odessa's beaches and racing through Alexandrovsky Park than completing his lessons. When the *gymnasium* agreed to offer classes in Judaism, only a third of his Jewish classmates signed up. "The extent of my liberalism was that I forgot to get a haircut," he wrote.[22] He later considered his laziness at least partly providential. Had he continued through school, gone on to university, and then taken up a legal career, he might eventually have been killed—like so many other bourgeois lawyers—by the Bolsheviks. Foolishness, he wrote, "is one of the most successful ways of living like a human being."[23] After much begging and persuading, he convinced his mother to allow him to travel abroad as a correspondent for a liberal-leaning newspaper, *Odessky listok*, the same daily broadsheet that repeated salacious stories of criminal mischief and courtroom dramas. He had already achieved some success in placing his articles in the local press, and in the spring of 1898 he left to become the paper's correspondent in Switzerland.

The trip there, by train through Galicia, introduced Jabotinsky to the varieties of Jewishness that had been largely hidden to him in Odessa. "I had not seen either the side-curls or the *kapota* [traditional black coat]," he recalled, "nor such wretched poverty. Nor had I seen grey-bearded, old and respected Jews, taking off their hats when they spoke to the gentile 'squire' in the street."[24] Combined with his exposure to European ideas, first in Bern and later in Rome—socialism and nihilism, aesthetic abandon and nationalism—his time abroad sharpened his intellect and his pen. Jabotinsky was becoming a well-known journalist, a young man interpreting Europe for a city deeply insecure about its own European identity, and also something of a public intellectual. Odessans gobbled up the incisive and stylish prose of a writer who signed his pieces with the Italian pen name "Altalena."

Shockingly articulate, undereducated but erudite, with thick-rimmed glasses fronting a handsome and chiseled face, Jabotinsky shaped himself into a writer typical of Russia's unsettled fin de siècle: someone for whom poetry, short stories, newspaper columns, translations, and novels were all products of a single artistic vocation, that of the socially engaged littérateur. At this stage, Jabotinsky's worldview, if he had one at all, was a jumble: vague cosmopolitanism, warmed-over romanticism, a love of all things Italian, and a Zionism of convenience, based on the idea that Jews deserved their own homeland in Palestine—somehow and someday. He was, in other words, representative of his age and class, someone largely untouched by either traditional or Haskalah Judaism, even if his cultural references and personal opportunities owed a great deal to both, and a man confident in his Russian cultural identity.

Jabotinsky returned to Odessa in 1901 as a literary columnist and cultural commentator for another popular newspaper, the liberal *Odesskye novosti* (Odessa News). Jewish intellectuals in the city were torn by the same debates that occupied their counterparts in other parts of Russia and Europe: between the universal values of the old Haskalah and the more particular demands of Zionism, between Jewish identity as largely cultural or religious, and between Zionism as the desire for a homeland anywhere or the struggle for a homeland specifically in Palestine. A gifted orator, with a knack for cutting and effective satire, Jabotinsky became one of the most energetic members of the city's vibrant and contentious intelligentsia—a group that included the influential journalist Ben-Ami, the Yiddish writers Mendele Moykher-Sforim and Sholem Aleichem, the theorist of cultural Zionism Ahad Ha'am, and the group's polestar, Simon Dubnow.

Dubnow later recalled a literary salon in April of 1903 at which Jabotinsky enraptured the public with his analysis of the Jewish condition. This wraith of a nation would end its hauntings and wanderings, he said, only when it was able to create its own government on its own land, just as another Odessan, the pamphleteer and Zionist precursor Leon Pinsker, had earlier prophesied. During a break in the session, Dubnow stepped outside to find the attendees talking excitedly about news that had just drifted into the city. Refugees were arriving in Odessa from the countryside with stories of new attacks to the north.[25] Jabotinsky had been giving his speech precisely at the time of the event that helped shape Zionism as an international project: the brutal killing of dozens of Jews by Russian nationalists in the Bessarabian capital of Kishinev.

"The beginning of my Zionist activity is connected with two influences," Jabotinsky wrote. "Italian opera and the idea of self-defense."[26] The throw-away line was typical Jabotinskian prose: too cute but more than a little true. The brand of Jewish nationalism he eventually adopted owed a great deal to the Risorgimento variety he had imbibed in Rome—the idea of a divided people becoming conscious of their underlying unity and then seeking the statehood long denied them. He later met one of his early mentors, the Odessa Zionist S. D. Salzman, during an Italian opera at the Odessa theater.

But it was the rise of self-defense organizations that gave life to his ideas about Jewish identity and territory. While Jewish groups had begun to arm themselves after the violence of 1881, in the wake of Kishinev self-defense became the logical response to a Russian state whose local officials seemed to facilitate the work of pogrom-makers. Jabotinsky recalled walking to Moldavanka—perhaps the first time the bourgeois intellectual had ever deigned to visit the down-and-out neighborhood—and finding himself in a large apartment filled with revolvers, crowbars, and kitchen knives. The next time around, Jews would fight back.

Jabotinsky insisted that the 1903 Kishinev pogrom in no sense transformed his worldview. He had been a Zionist before, during his years abroad, and he remained one after. But the political context was different. Kishinev was a major battle in Russia's underground war against its own Jews, one that would extend through the Odessa pogrom of 1905 and to the serial violence of the First World

War and Russian civil war. What had changed were the options available to Jews like Jabotinsky who rejected the paths of revolutionary or democratic socialism. If the Russian state were now complicit in blocking the ability of Jews to live peacefully in the empire—if the imperial authorities, in other words, had become vehicles of a raw and primitive form of Russian nationalism—then perhaps the rift between Russians and Jews was something more than a matter of religion or heritage. Jews were a nation like any other, deeply divided and only semiconscious perhaps, but one that could be awakened to its own destiny. Pride and prejudice were the building blocks of other forms of nationalism—a theme that runs through *The Five* and Jabotinsky's other creative work—and they could naturally be expected to serve the same function for Jews as well. Jews might even find some way of cooperating with the erstwhile pogrom-makers: the latter wanted Jews gone; the former simply needed someplace to go.

Jabotinsky's career as a professional Zionist now gained steam. He served as a delegate to the Sixth Zionist Congress in Basel in the summer of 1903, the last one attended by political Zionism's founder, Theodor Herzl. When he returned to Russia, he left Odessa and settled in St. Petersburg, but still traveled widely as a speaker and newspaper correspondent. With the outbreak of the First World War, Jabotinsky moved abroad and joined British forces fighting to defeat the Ottoman Empire. He helped organize the Zion Mule Corps and several battalions of the 38th Royal Fusiliers, a volunteer force known as the Jewish Legion, that saw action at Gallipoli and in Palestine. He remained in Palestine after the war, during the period of the British mandate, and took on the role of activist, leading the Haganah, or clandestine Jewish military organization. When local Arabs attacked the Jewish quarter in Jerusalem in April of 1920—seemingly repeating the same springtime violence that Jabotinsky had known in Russia—the British blamed the Haganah for provocations. Jabotinsky was arrested and later found himself a prisoner in the Acre fortress, his Russian first name exchanged for a Hebrew one, Ze'ev.

His military activities and imprisonment for the Zionist cause gave Jabotinsky a fame that is now remembered mainly as infamy. An international outcry led to his release from Acre, but fault lines between Jabotinsky and other Zionists quickly widened. He broke with the mainstream Zionist movement not long after his release, founding what came to be called "revisionist Zionism": the right-wing, antisocialist, militaristic, and uncompromising commitment to a Jewish homeland on both banks of the Jordan River. It rested on a belief in the fundamental incompatibility between Jewish and Arab territorial aspirations.

In a series of articles in 1923, he put forward the concept of an "iron wall" separating Arabs and Jews. Arab populations were unlikely to acquiesce to Jewish settlement, nor were the two peoples likely to come to a voluntary and amicable compromise, he believed. The two national movements were at base irreconcilable, and the only way Jews could survive in their own land would be to create an unbreakable wall of military force to discourage Arab aggression and protect Jewish claims.[27] Jabotinsky died before any of these goals could be realized. He collapsed from a heart attack in upstate New York while on a speaking and fundraising tour in the summer of 1940. But he had lived long enough to see the storm clouds gathering. He accurately predicted the coming cataclysm, a genocide that would destroy Jewish culture in Europe and make the homeland in Palestine a reality.

Today, Jabotinsky's views sit uneasily with a tradition that sees the establishment of the Jewish state in 1948 as the end point of a united people's journey from near destruction to triumph. There is a prominent street named in his honor in Jerusalem, but while the Israeli political right continues to see Jabotinsky's writings as prescient, his reputation pales beside those of other Zionists and Israeli statesmen such as Chaim Weizmann and David Ben-Gurion.

Israeli Prime Minister Ariel Sharon gives a speech next to a
photograph of the spiritual founding father of Israel's political right,
Vladimir Ze'ev Jabotinsky, during a Likud Party convention in
Tel Aviv, August 2004. *Pedro Ugarte/AFP/Getty Images.*

His own maximalist stance on most political issues and his biting
denunciations of other Zionists as weak-willed and deluded led
Ben-Gurion to label him "Vladimir Hitler."

Jabotinsky was the founder of a youth organization, Betar,
whose principles and aesthetics still bear more resemblance to
those of European right-wing extremists than to the grassroots
socialism of the kibbutz. In his early writings he was maddeningly
inconsistent in his beliefs. In his correspondence he remained solic-
itous, petulant, and overly concerned with slights and grievances.
His choice of allies swung from the principled to the opportunis-
tic to the plainly bizarre. Zionism and Italian fascism had much in
common, he wrote to Benito Mussolini in 1922, and "the movement
that you represent and your personality interest me greatly."[28]

Ultimately Jabotinsky's contribution—if it can be called
that—was to champion the Zionist cause while also pedestrianiz-

ing it. The central tenet of his thought was the concept of *hadar*, a Hebrew word signifying respect and self-esteem—something he believed was absent among both black-coated shtetl Jews and their "enlightened" coreligionists. Inculcating *hadar* was simply to bring to Jewish communities the actively "national" way of being that Italians knew as *italianità* and Germans as *Deutschtum*: a prideful commitment to embodying the essence of one's race, ethnicity, or nationality. In this regard, there was nothing peculiar about the fact of Jewish nationalism, he believed, other than that it had long been crushed by empires and denied by Jews themselves, who turned to traditional religion, cultural assimilation, or naive socialism as second-best alternatives to their own frustrated national ambitions. "I learned how to be a Zionist from the Gentiles," he wrote in 1934. Zionism was not about finding consolation or a "moral prop" to support an afflicted people, much less about realizing a providential plan. The idea of being the chosen of God was the opiate of the masses, an obstacle to Jewish nationalism rather than its divine essence. Creating a Jewish homeland was the natural political outcome of Jewish nationhood, no different in principle from the aim pursued by other European national movements.[29]

It is not hard to see the particular influence of his Odessan surroundings in Jabotinsky's nationalist philosophy. If every other group in Odessa had sooner or later found their highest cultural expression in nationalism and independence—the Greeks in the 1820s, the Italians in the 1860s, and the Ukrainians and Russians who sought something similar as the old empire faltered—why should Jews be any different? The only thing that distinguished them from their neighbors, he felt, was a matter of commitment: their general unwillingness to struggle against other legitimate nationalist movements whose goals happened to be opposed to those of Jews. Jabotinsky was in this sense a "cosmopolitan ultranationalist," as one of his biographers put it.[30] He believed in national groups as the core species of world society. Survival of the fittest was the basic mechanism that determined which ones ended up with their own nation-states.

This narrative fits awkwardly with the claim to uniqueness that undergirds most versions of national origins and destiny, including the Jewish one. But Jabotinsky's brand of Zionism became far more powerful than its author's relative obscurity might today suggest. The Israeli state he envisioned has moved away from the old socialist version of Zionism on which it was founded. Large-scale privatization has diminished social equality and changed the social contract between citizens and government. New waves of immigration have brought Jews, especially from Russia, who have little direct memory of the European nationalisms that victimized their great-grandparents or of the democratic socialism that inspired them. A real "iron wall" in Jerusalem now reinforces Jabotinsky's metaphorical one.

After two Palestinian uprisings, suicide bombers in Jerusalem restaurants, the expansion of West Bank settlements, and the virtual disappearance of the Israeli political left, Israel has in many ways remade itself in Jabotinsky's image. Revisionism has become the new mainstream. The state has retreated from the more ambitious social agenda of earlier decades to the basic concern that Jabotinsky hoped would define it—security. "Everything begins in Odessa," says the narrator in the biographical film shown at the Jabotinsky Institute in Tel Aviv, the museum and research center that preserves Jabotinsky's personal archive. It does, indeed. The Israel of the twenty-first century—a state that defines itself in exclusively national terms and in which disparities between rich and poor have diminished old commitments to social equality—embodies many of the ideals that Jabotinsky picked from the crumbling cosmopolitanism of his old hometown.

CHAPTER 8

New World

Massacre on the steps: The famous baby carriage scene from
Sergei Eisenstein's 1925 film *Battleship Potemkin. Goskino/The Kobal Collection.*

Sailors and firemen were on strike for much of 1906 and 1907.
Grain carters followed suit in 1910. Underground groups,
although infiltrated by police informants, attracted party members
and sympathizers in the port district and industrial suburbs, with
political programs that ran from socialist to anarchist.

Shipping picked up after the end of the disastrous Russo-
Japanese war but was hit again by the outbreak of a brief conflict

between Italy and the Ottomans in 1911 and two wars in the Balkans in 1912 and 1913. When the Russian Empire entered the First World War in 1914, the city's merchants had already lost entire fortunes in overseas commerce. The Ottomans' decision to join as a German ally—a move that impeded traffic through the Bosphorus and Dardanelles straits—effectively brought business to a halt. With little to do and less to lose, stevedores and seamen, emboldened by ready supplies of vodka, contributed to the general malaise by regularly smashing heads as well as windows.

During the war the city lay near the geographical intersection of Europe's old empires—Russian, Ottoman, and Austro-Hungarian—and of the new kingdoms, nation-states, and nationalities that were quickly spiraling away from their control. The city's three largest ethnic groups—Russians at 39 percent, Jews at 36 percent, and Ukrainians at 17 percent—were ready audiences for political entrepreneurs marketing radically different visions of the future.

Odessans found themselves on multiple front lines: between Jews and their tormentors, between Ukrainian nationalists and their tsarist opponents, between radical Marxists and the forces of autocracy. But it was hard to tell which events heralded major changes and which might blow away with the next northeasterly wind. A visiting American physician observed in October of 1917 that all the ships in the harbor were suddenly flying red flags. "No one seems to know why, as we have not heard of any Naval Victory, nor is it a special holiday."[1] The doctor was witnessing Odessa's version of the Bolshevik Revolution. Yet even that turned out to be of passing importance, at least in the short term.

Faced with horrible conditions on the battlefield and political revolutions in the imperial capitals, the Russian army collapsed over the course of 1917. Soldiers faded back into the civilian population, formed armed gangs and pitiful bands of beggars, or coalesced into the armies that eventually drew up on opposite sides of the Russian civil war—the Whites who remained loyal to the old order and the Reds committed to the ideals of revolution. The Central powers made plans to rush through the door that now opened on the eastern front. To block Germany, Turkey, or Austria-Hungary from gobbling up Russia's industrial and shipping centers, the Entente powers divvied up responsibility for occupying portions of the old empire. British troops were dispatched to the east, to the Caucasus region, to secure control of the strategic oil fields of Baku. In Odessa a disheveled army of French colonial forces—composed in part of North African troops outfitted in colorful pantaloons and woolen great coats—marched down Nikolaevsky Boulevard and instituted a hasty and ill-planned military rule.

This effort in prophylactic occupation was short-lived. Despite the French declaration of martial law, the city remained in near anarchy, with hungry refugees raiding shops and people sometimes being killed in the street for their overcoats.[2] French sailors, subjected to harsh treatment aboard the republic's own vessels, heeded the Bolshevik call to soldiers and seamen to unite against capitalist oppression. The French fleet anchored in the Black Sea briefly raised the red flag of Communism alongside the tricolor.[3] With French forces in disarray, Russian units now loyal to the new Bolshevik government marched into Odessa and claimed it for the revolution. Yet that effort, too, proved to be temporary. By the late summer of 1919, the anti-Bolshevik Volunteer Army, commanded by the famed White general Anton Denikin, pushed out the Bolsheviks and launched a campaign against suspected Red sympathizers.

The tide soon turned against the White armies across the former empire. Denikin's forces fled in the face of a new offensive by Bolshevik troops. As the Bolshevik army made its final entry into Odessa in February of 1920, tens of thousands of refugees crowded with their baggage near the ice-choked harbor, seeking passage aboard the few merchant vessels and Allied warships that remained in the bay. Commander Gordon Ellyson, in charge of the U.S. naval detachment sent to evacuate Americans from the city, reported scenes of pathos and horror. A woman made her way through the crowds with a baby carriage, looking for the husband and child from whom she had been separated in the scramble. Another woman lugged a gilt-edged mirror. A man stumbled to the ships carrying only a banjo with no strings, while his partner struggled under the weight of a small church organ strapped to his back. Sailors strained to hoist an automobile aboard a Greek vessel before the ping of rifle shots from Bolshevik snipers convinced them to abandon the project.

Crowds surged ahead, slipping on the ice-covered docks and trying to stuff themselves aboard small launches. Some were thrown overboard or beaten back by panicked sailors trying to keep their own craft from capsizing. Meanwhile, gunfire echoed throughout the city as the remaining shore-side defenders fired potshots at Bolshevik advance parties. Now and then, the thundering thirteen-and-a-half-inch guns of the British battleship *Ajax*, anchored in the inner harbor, sent shells hurtling toward Bolshevik positions. Within days, the last defenders—bits of the Volunteer Army, Ukrainian irregulars, and Allied soldiers and seamen—had left the city for good.[4]

After the departure of the Whites, the city was a place of burned buildings and refugees. Average urban-dwellers tried to make sense of the power shifts that seemed to occur from month to month. "Miles of houses still await reconstruction," noted a visitor nearly a decade after the war had ended. "Their blackened walls stick up like decayed teeth against the brilliant blue of the sky, and in the suburbs of the city are whole streets, empty, plundered, dead."[5] The march of armies across the defunct empire had put millions to flight, emptying villages and bringing agricultural production to a halt. Jewish inhabitants of the old Pale of Settlement were targeted by all sides, from tsarist units who blamed them for the Red menace, to Ukrainians seeking an independent Ukrainian state, to Bolshevik cavalry who requisitioned grain, goods, and animals at will.

A remarkable snapshot of the chaos of this period—and its particular effect on the region's Jews—is provided by a survey conducted in Odessa in the summer of 1921.[6] With the Bolsheviks now squarely in charge, activists from the Jewish Public Committee for Aiding the Victims of Pogroms, an independent social organization headquartered in Moscow, conducted a survey of Jewish refugees resident in the city. They posted fliers in Russian and Yiddish requesting that Jews register voluntarily at one of ten bureaus set up in the center and on the outskirts of town. Since registering was also a way of receiving aid channeled through the committee from Jewish communities abroad, there was an incentive for Jews to present themselves to be counted. Interviewers collected a wealth of information about families and individuals based on oral testimony. When interviewers had reason to be suspicious about someone's story, they recorded no information unless the person could provide proof, such as showing up with all of their children in tow or producing an official document to confirm residence or employment. The result was a sophisticated sociological record of civilian suffering at the end of the Russian civil war.

Capturing and holding the city had been a strategic goal of the Austro-Hungarians, French, Ukrainians (in several factions), Whites, and Bolsheviks. But given that individuals and families drifted into the city from a relatively limited region—mainly the southern Ukrainian provinces of Kiev, Odessa, Podolia, and Nikolaev—the scale of Jewish displacement and death across the former Pale of Settlement is all the more evident. The committee counted 12,037 Jewish refugees, of whom 9,042 were currently resident in Odessa. Another 1,801 were registered by family members as still living in their home towns and villages; 1,194 were named as deceased. Just under a third had lost at least one family member in a pogrom, around 44 percent of them losing one or both parents. Most often, it had been the fathers, but many had seen their mothers killed as well. Families were still sizable, however, with the average respondent reporting five family members still living. The vast majority of victims were adults, but nearly 17 percent of families had lost someone under the age of sixteen.

Pogrom survivors came from all professions and social classes. Students, traders, business owners, clerks, teachers, and port workers comprised the majority. But the single largest group—nearly 31 percent—were housewives, probably a reflection of the disproportionate targeting of men in pogroms and the wider civil war, with women left as the head of household. (Not surprisingly, two-thirds of the registered dead were men.) With families and entire villages on the move on foot and by oxcart, covering hundreds of miles to reach relatives or the assumed safety of a city; with Cossack detachments, Red and White armies, and ordinary bandits roaming the countryside; and with a history of organized anti-Jewish violence across the western empire stretching back a half century or more, it was no surprise that people reported what amounted to serial victimhood. More than half the respondents said that they had lived through three or more events that they classed as pogroms.

The survey provides a unique, microscopic view of displacement and violence, but it pales in comparison to what we know overall about refugees and death during this period. By the summer of 1917, over seven million people had been displaced in European Russia. The majority were probably what would now be called ethnic Russians, but minority groups—always suspected of loyalty to some enemy power—were explicitly targeted by invading armies, bandits, and the many independent military groups that formed amid war and revolution. In all the cities of the western empire, refugees arrived from the countryside seeking food and a modicum of shelter, adding to the mass of homeless wanderers that had emerged already during the disorders of 1905.[7]

The survey captured a vital change in the city's Jewish population, however. The community—some 125,000 people in the last tsarist-era census—had been as diverse as any other in the city in

terms of profession and social class. But if there was a typical Odessan Jew, at least the kind revealed by censuses rather than by the
antisemitic imaginings of Russian nationalists, it was the lower-
middle-class businessman working as a merchant, petty trader,
innkeeper, or small factory owner, making a living in an economic
landscape that was both uncertain and at times actively hostile.
Russians, Ukrainians, and Germans had nearly as many of their
number living as peasants on Odessa's outskirts as they did working
in urban-based professions on the docks and the industrial periphery. But Jews, far more than the Christians with whom they shared
the city, were the quintessential urban community. By the 1890s
over 95 percent of Jews were classed as petty bourgeois by estate —
the old category of *meshchane* into which they had rapidly moved
over the course of that century.[8]

Yet after nearly two decades of upheaval, from the primor-
dial violence of 1905 through the First World War and the rolling
pogroms of the Russian civil war, that individual was largely gone.
Now the prototypical Jew was likely to be a housewife and widow
who had brought her children from the countryside after some terrible act of violence, and had experienced even more horrors along
the way. That was one of the people whom Odessa's greatest writer,
Isaac Babel, was working to describe at the time.

WHILE VLADIMIR JABOTINSKY was busy trying to create a fighting
force for Palestine, his fellow Odessan was sitting on a horse in a
Cossack cavalry regiment. It was an unlikely place for a Jew, to say
the least. But Isaac Babel made a habit of being in the wrong place
at the right time.

Babel was born in June of 1894 in Moldavanka, to middle-class
Jewish parents. Round-faced and bespectacled, with a hairline
that quickly lost out to an expansive and furrowed brow, he was
steeped in the classics of European literature, as well as in the

ancient traditions of Talmudic reasoning and argumentation. The family survived the 1905 pogrom only because of the intervention of Christian neighbors, who hid several family members from the mobs that roamed the empty streets. Babel's grandfather, however, was among the victims.

Babel's ambitions were those of many Jewish men in Odessa: to complete his education and then go into one of the few fields open to him, such as business, journalism, or the vague but vital vocation known as the intelligentsia. Anti-Jewish quotas in many educational institutions, including the local university, blocked Babel's admission. He enrolled instead in a technical school in Kiev. From there, he eventually moved to Petrograd, using his Odessa wiles to avoid the police since he lacked a residency permit. He soon embarked on a modest career as a writer of short stories and essays.

Petrograd was a city in ferment. More than a decade earlier, while Odessa was being terrorized by anti-Jewish gangs, the city had been the site of a failed uprising that nevertheless managed to wrench some liberalizing concessions from Tsar Nicholas II. Babel found himself swept up in the political fervor that swirled around the imperial capital, its name now changed, through the passions of war, from the overly Germanic "Sankt-Peterburg." He had come under the patronage of the major leftist writer and editor Maxim Gorky, who published a few of his early stories. With that entrée into the world of underground socialists and surreptitious printing presses, Babel became part of the earliest generation of the Bolshevik intelligentsia.

But his true introduction to the realities of revolutionary life came from the Cossacks. After the Bolshevik Revolution of October 1917, the former Russian Empire remained divided between supporters of the new government and their many opponents. For the next four years, the territory of the old empire was scarred by mobile warfare among a host of rival factions—Reds, Whites, nationalists, and local peasants intent mainly on protecting their homes and fields from marauders.

Babel was an early version of an embedded journalist. He was assigned to the detachment of Semyon Budenny, the legendary commander of Cossack cavalry fighting on the Bolshevik side in the western borderlands of the defunct empire. He was technically a correspondent for the horse troops' in-house newspaper, *Krasny kavalerist* (Red Cavalryman), assigned to report on the daily life of soldiers fighting for Soviet power against the forces of imperialism and reaction. But the casual violence of irregular warfare—with villages burned and peasants displaced, often with little justification except the boredom of the soldiers who did the burning and displacing—found expression in what would become Babel's greatest literary achievement: the short-story collection *Red Cavalry*, first published in 1926.

"Babel tells old wives' tales, fumbles in old women's secondhand underwear, narrates in a horror-stricken old woman's voice how a hungry Red Army soldier took a chicken and a loaf of bread; he invents things that never happened, and throws dirt at the best Communist commanders. He fantasizes and simply lies."[9] That was the unequivocal judgment of Budenny himself, the enabling muse of Babel's most creative period as a writer in the terrifying transition from tsarism to Bolshevism. The old cavalryman was right in one sense. It was precisely the gossip and garbage of the civil war experience—an appreciation for which he had cultivated in the muddy streets and steamy courtyards of Moldavanka—that Babel transformed into stories of delicate insight.

The characters who populate the stories are pastiches of people he met in the cavalry ranks and in the villages and shtetls far to the north of his hometown. But many are also versions of Babel himself, people swept up in purposeless violence, spinning in the middle of a revolution that threatened to burn itself out before anything great could be achieved. There is old Gedali, the Jewish pawnbroker, who would gladly trade the message of Bolshevism for "an International of good people." There is the unpredictable and empty-hearted platoon commander Afonka Bida, ruthless in his prosecution of the war but oddly sentimental about his horse.

Over time the stories' first-person narrator—a writer like Babel—finds his own heart callused and bruised by the experience of war. Churches and synagogues are smashed. People are run down on horseback. Looted clothes and valuables produce military units that look less like an army and more like a wandering, apocalyptic carnival. The narrator is as drawn to the broad chests and studied swagger of the Cossacks as he is repelled by their actions, a horrified witness unable to turn his eyes away from the atrocity.

Babel was a man of the borderlands who spent his early life moving between worlds: Jewish and Russian, tsarist and Bolshevik, army and artistic. At the end of the civil war, he returned off and on to Odessa, where he worked on another of his major literary works, the series of short-stories later collected as *Odessa Tales*, a riveting evocation of the crooks, schemers, prostitutes, and bent cops of Jewish Moldavanka. The stories are still a magnificent introduction to the cavaliers of the city's criminal underworld, people who are merciless when exploiting an easy mark or punishing a rival, but who can also be disarmingly nice to old women and charming to romantic interests. Today, Babel's writing is often approached through his Odessa stories, but to do so is to risk mistaking dark elegies for exercises in light nostalgia. Where *Red Cavalry* was a work of searing reportage, a fictional version of experiences that were still fresh and raw when they were published, the *Odessa Tales* is one of twilight recollection. The Odessa that he evoked had already faded into history.

One of Babel's lasting legacies is the fact that when people think of Odessa, it is fictional characters—not the real-life builders of the city—who come most readily to mind. The mobster kingpin Benya Krik is the archetypal inhabitant of this imaginary city. He becomes "king" of Moldavanka by extorting money from business owners and bringing a kind of rough justice to the more disorderly thugs who run the neighborhood. He is the kind of person who can be kind to widows and cruel to subordinates who disappoint, and do it all in a chocolate-colored jacket, cream pants, and raspberry ankle boots, seated behind the wheel of a red car whose horn plays the opening march from *Pagliacci*.

Benya's Odessa—that is, Babel's—is something of a community, one built on theft, prostitution, and murder, but a community nevertheless. There is a kind of honor among thieves, and no one knew its contours better than a writer from the city's most squalid and storied neighborhood, a place that its inhabitants—like the windswept and gritty port as a whole—saw as home. In the stories, it is sometimes hard to tell whether Babel is writing with a smile or a sneer. "Moldavanka, our generous mother," he wrote in one passage, "a life crowded with suckling babies, drying rags, and conjugal nights filled with big-city chic and soldierly tirelessness."[10] But that was precisely the point. You didn't quite get Odessa unless it drew you in and repelled you at the same time.

People like Benya Krik were already passing from the scene by the time Babel first put pen to paper, and that is one of the central messages of the *Odessa Tales*. In one of the later stories, "Froim Grach," which was not published until long after Babel's death, an old gangland boss who claimed to control a criminal army of "forty-thousand Odessa thugs" is executed at the hands of the Cheka, the Bolshevik secret police. "You're killing off all the lions!" the boss says minutes before his death. "And you know what you'll be left with if you keep it up! You'll be left with shit!"[11]

Babel understood that his characters had finite lives. He was writing both about an imperial Odessa that used to exist and about another kind of city, a Soviet one, that was in the process of becoming. In one of the screenplays he wrote based on the Odessa stories, for the 1926 silent film *Benya Krik*, the kingpin himself falls prey to Soviet power. The gangster king of Moldavanka ends up as just another bandit. He is shot by Bolshevik authorities, one more remnant of the old regime erased in the creation of the new order.

If Babel's Benya Krik was a transitional figure in the making of Soviet Odessa, new characters were rushing in to take his place. Their essential qualities were flexibility and an ability to bend their necks to the overwhelming power of the state. Benya had the old tsarist police on the run (or, more frequently, on the take) and ruled his neighborhood with little regard for the niceties of formal law. His successors knew how to deal with the new power, softly and carefully, without the bluster and bravado of Benya's generation. Other fictional characters emerged as the instantly recognizable Odessans of the new era. The writing team of Ilya Ilf and Evgeny Petrov created one of the most memorable, the essential entrepreneur of the easy deal, Ostap Bender—fast-talking, self-assured, and just Jewish enough to be acceptable to Russian readers. Unlike Benya, however, Ostap always shaved his schemes to fit within the confines of the law. "I'm no cherub. I don't have wings. But I do honor the legislative code," he says in Ilf and Petrov's picaresque novel *The Golden Calf* (1931).

That might well have been Odessa's informal motto after the advent of Soviet power. Good-natured criminality, a southern sense of laissez-aller, and a secular, modernized version of Jewishness were part of the city's heritage. To it were added the universal aspirations of Soviet Communism, the cult of the worker, and a talent for bending one's ambitions to the dictates of an overweening state. The core visual representation of this new world was created by a director who made Odessa into the unlikely birthplace of revolution and turned Vorontsov's "monstrous staircase" into a piece of film history.

———————

A FOREIGN DIPLOMAT who traveled by car all the way from Moscow in the 1930s reported that, beyond Kiev, roads reduced to earthen tracks and short stretches of rough, granite-paved highway. Small hotels were available along the route, but they were invariably swarming with flies. It was easy to lose your way because of the lack of signage, and even locals seemed uncertain about how to reach the sea.

When he arrived in Odessa, he was told there were no rooms available in the grand old Hotel London, one of the main buildings along the seaward heights—at least until he displayed his diplomatic passport and demanded accommodation. The only things that made the diplomat feel he was in a remotely well-connected city were the small group of American tourists he found complaining loudly in the hotel's restaurant and the fact that nearly everyone he met in the city, on his reckoning, was Jewish.[12]

What he missed was that Odessa was already being transformed, root and branch, from an imperial city into a new, Soviet one. Shortly after the Bolshevik conquest, old streets were renamed in honor of heroes of the revolution and civil war. Imperial symbols were pulled down and replaced with the hammer and sickle. The opera house staged spectacles lionizing the workers' triumph over tsarist oppression. The bodies of Count and Countess Vorontsov were exhumed from their crypts in Preobrazhensky Cathedral and removed to a local cemetery. The cathedral was then razed and its marble facings used to outfit a nearby school, the old god of tsarist tradition and hierarchy now unfit for an era of progress and egalitarianism. As the site of one of the iconic episodes in the Bolshevik Revolution's own prehistory—the disorders of 1905—Odessa occupied a special place in the emerging mythmaking of the Soviet state.

Today it is almost impossible to separate our understanding of 1905 from the way in which the events were mythologized twenty years later. All of the key images, in fact, come from the skillful hands of one man, Sergei Eisenstein, the master of early Soviet cinematography. Through his 1925 silent film *Battleship Potemkin*, Odessa became the tocsin that heralded the coming of revolution, ground zero for the emergence of triumphant Bolshevism, and by extension the truest birthplace of the Soviet Union.

In late June of 1905, the tsar's steel-hulled battleship *Potemkin*—named for the great eighteenth-century prince and field marshal—had left port in Crimea to engage in firing exercises in the Black Sea. Conditions on board were dire. The beating of naval conscripts by noncommissioned officers was common. Food was in short supply. When a ration of meat was found to be crawling with maggots, the crew refused to eat and gathered on the quarterdeck to display their disgust.

Beyond that point, however, Eisenstein's version of events departed from history. In his film, a contingent of marines is called out to restore order. The sailors rush to their fellow crewmen and urge them not to shoot. The marines hesitate, and a rebellion is born. The mutineers run through the ship, grabbing everyone on board with officers' insignia on their summer uniforms. Some try to hide below decks or plead with the sailors to stand down. Others are thrown overboard. The *Potemkin* then sets sail for Odessa. From the topmast, the red flag of freedom waves in place of the naval ensign.

In the city, workers, peasants, and seamen gather on the cliffs and in the docklands. The body of the mutiny's ringleader, shot by a treacherous officer, is placed on the quayside, an informal lying in state for a martyr of the revolution. Among the starched collars and felt hats of the bourgeois onlookers, a provocateur yells out, *"Bei zhidov!"*—"Let's bash the yids!"—the battle cry of pogrom-makers since the 1870s. But the citizens refuse to respond to this diversion. Fighting the capitalist and imperialist oppressor, not beating up on their fellow citizens, is hailed as the common task of the emboldened masses. The mutiny has become a revolution.

All of this, however, was a work of purposive imagination. The real *Potemkin* mutiny ended with a whimper rather than a bang. The seamen steamed hopefully into Odessa but lost their nerve once

Two makers of modern Odessa: Isaac Babel (left) and Sergei Eisenstein (right), ca. 1935. *Russian Museum of Cinema/Abamedia.*

the ship arrived. They failed to take advantage of a general strike then in progress in the city. Public protests that had filled the tree-lined streets soon fizzled, and the city's revolutionaries slunk back into the shadows. The crew issued periodic proclamations to the workers of the world to join with them against the evils of tsarist autocracy, but in the end, even the crew's enthusiasm waned. The mutineers sailed down the coast to the Romanian city of Constanţa, where they surrendered to Romanian authorities. Some of them were arrested and sent back to Russia, where they were tried and hanged. Others remained behind and made new lives abroad. Until the late 1980s, visitors to a small fish-and-chips shop in Dublin could hear the proprietor, an old veteran named Ivan

Beshoff, regale them with memories of the revolt that paved the way for a revolution.

Sergei Eisenstein was only twenty-seven when he created his version of the *Potemkin* events. Short and compact, with a large head and a shock of wild, clownlike hair that retreated behind his substantial brow, he was not from Odessa. But he was part of Babel's generation, the group of artists and intellectuals who drew inspiration from the revolutionary élan of the Soviet 1920s, an era when novelty in art, literature, theater, and virtually every aspect of social and cultural life was not only tolerated but encouraged.

Like Babel, Eisenstein had served with the Red Army during the civil war and, in 1921, began work as a set painter for Proletkult, the "proletarian culture" movement that became the epicenter of artistic experimentation in the early Bolshevik state. A year later he was made director of the First Moscow Workers' Theater and soon began exploring film. In his first full-length feature, *Strike* (1925), he experimented with the montages that became his filmic signature. In time, as a prominent proponent of the use of film not only as entertainment but as a form of political education, Eisenstein emerged as the dean of Soviet filmmakers and the master of the earliest video imagery of Soviet power. Even today, his staged scenes of revolutionary workers and reactionary soldiers are routinely misinterpreted, by Western audiences as well as by Russians, as "documentaries" of Russia's multiple revolutions.

Battleship Potemkin became one of his preeminent pieces and certainly one of the most copied works in film history. It was commissioned by the Central Committee of the Communist Party of the Soviet Union for the twentieth anniversary of the 1905 revolution, but by the time Eisenstein began the project, the end of the anniversary year was only a few months away. He and a vast team worked in Odessa and other parts of the Black Sea region for weeks, using the Hotel London as their base. To save time and money, they scraped together archival footage that could be used in place of new film. (The shots of tsarist ships steaming ominously toward the valiant mutineers are actually old images of the U.S. Navy on maneuvers, the giveaway being a small American flag visible in one scene.) In a mad rush at the end of the year, Eisenstein cut down some fifteen thousand meters of film into a running time of around seventy minutes.[13] "The fetters of space and the claws of time held our excessive and greedy fantasy in check," he later wrote, surely with little inkling of the lasting success produced by just over three months of scenario writing, set design, shooting, and editing.[14]

What Eisenstein injected into the story was its single most memorable—and in large part imaginary—element: the slaughter on the Odessa steps. Eisenstein's genius was to place the steps at the center of his film, a scene that he called in his memoirs "the very core of the film's organic substance and general structure."[15] Ranks of soldiers and Cossacks fire on the striking workers. When a Cossack strikes a woman across the face with his cavalry saber, we know exactly what has happened in that gruesome and shocking scene, even though the director never shows the sword making contact with her upturned face; the woman simply turns her gouged eye full-on to the camera. In the climactic sequence, a baby carriage teeters on the edge of the staircase then slides horrifically down the granite cataract.

In reality, there was no popular memory of a "massacre on the steps" as the centerpiece of the violence of 1905. The major shooting occurred elsewhere in the city and involved not only the military but also a whole series of self-protection units organized by city neighborhoods to guard against bandits and the inciters of pogroms. The idea for the scene may have come from an illustration of the staircase that Eisenstein found in a contemporary French magazine while doing background research for the film in Moscow.[16] In Eisenstein's retelling, the single bloodiest event of 1905—the murder of hundreds of Jews—faded into the background. Through the film, Odessa was transformed from a place where Jews had been killed in the streets to a city remembered for working-class solidarity and opposition to the tsar's arbitrary rule. It was, to say the least, a heroic act of misremembering.

When Soviet audiences viewed the silent film, they were witnessing the birth of their own country—a revolutionary nation that looked back to the heroes and martyrs of 1905. By the time the film was released in 1925, the Soviet Union had succeeded the Russian Empire as the de facto ruler of much of the Black Sea coastline, including Odessa. Yet it was a country without a history. Its ideology proclaimed youth and rejection of the past as the hallmarks of a new social and political order. Even its founder—Lenin—lay dead, his legacy uncertain and a host of former courtiers now vying for power. The *Potemkin* mutiny, in Eisenstein's talented hands, became the Old Testament of the Bolshevik Revolution, a series of events that presaged the triumphant changes of October 1917.

One of the last places *Battleship Potemkin* was shown was in Odessa itself. It had played at the Bolshoi Theatre and the First Sovkino Cinema in Moscow in December of 1925 and January of 1926, and when the American film stars Douglas Fairbanks and Mary Pickford saw it during a visit to the Soviet Union that summer, they hastened its release abroad.[17] Charlie Chaplin pronounced it the best film in the world.[18] It soon played to packed houses in Atlantic City, New Jersey, before arriving in Odessa later in the year. The film had been taken for a dry documentary elsewhere in the Soviet Union and had been screened to half-full houses. But in Odessa it was an instant hit—and also an instant scandal.

A local citizen claimed to have been a participant in the events on board the original *Potemkin* and brought a court case against Eisenstein, demanding a cut of the royalties for having his personal story stolen by the famous director. When he was questioned on the matter, the old sailor maintained that he had been aboard ship at a critical stage in the rebellion, when a group of seamen were draped with a tarpaulin in preparation for their execution as mutineers. The case was soon dismissed. As Eisenstein pointed out, the tarpaulin scene had been solely the product of directorial creativity—an artistic representation of a collective blindfold being draped across the condemned heroes. No such event had taken place.[19]

Eisenstein's filmic techniques are often stunning in their originality and effectiveness. He decomposes images into their component parts. He moves between one image and another to create a visual metaphor, such as the famous comparison between men and maggots in the dark larder of the battleship. He uses multiple, staccato shots to indicate a single event, rather than recording the action as one fluid set of movements by the actors. The director was clear on the connections among technique, art, and politics. *Battleship Potemkin* was part of a new era in filmmaking, he believed, an age of "the new psychologism" in art that would focus on audience reaction as the central measure of worth and influence.[20]

As Eisenstein recalled in an interview not long after the film's release, the power of the images, not their historical veracity, was the real worth of his creation. "Take the scene in *Potemkin* where the Cossacks slowly, deliberately, walk down the Odessa steps firing into the masses," he said. "By consciously combining the element of legs, steps, blood, people, we produce an impression. Of what kind? The spectator does not imagine himself at the Odessa wharf in 1905. But as the soldiers' boots press forward he physically recoils. He tries to get out of the range of the bullets. As the baby carriage goes over the side of the mole he holds on to his cinema chair. He does not want to fall into the water."[21] Imagery, lighting, camera angle, and editing were all intended to provoke a discrete emotional response in the viewer, and these effects could be calculated with almost scientific precision. The impact on the filmgoer, not the verisimilitude of image and action, were the hallmarks of a film's success, even when dealing with historical topics. "By 'film' I understand tendentiousness and nothing else," he wrote blankly.[22]

Battleship Potemkin is arguably the single most important cultural artifact in Odessa's modern history—a piece of art that did more than any other to encapsulate the city's own image of itself and the way in which it would be remembered for generations to come. If portside hucksters and the mélange of East and West had impressed visitors for much of the nineteenth century, Eisenstein's staging of the *Potemkin* affair came to define the city in the twentieth. Eisenstein included all the basic elements of the incident that were passed down from the participants themselves, such as the crew's refusal to eat rancid meat as the impetus for the mutiny. But he added the heroic gloss that turned Odessa into the avant-garde of revolutionary change, providing a usable prehistory for the Bolshevik Revolution and, by extension, for the new Soviet state.

But that is also why the film has so little to do with Odessa itself. The steps were there, of course, but other images were not. In one sequence, a stone lion seems to lift itself from its plinth, like the working masses of the Russian Empire rising against their capitalist oppressors. Eisenstein composed the scene from separate shots of several statues, each in a different pose from prone to standing. Visitors to Odessa still look in vain for the restless lion, however. The original statues are actually hundreds of miles away, at Count Vorontsov's old summer palace in Crimea.

———

FOR A TIME, Isaac Babel lived in an ornate apartment building not far from the old Brody and Glavnaya synagogues. Today the commemorative plaque is easy to miss beside the plate-glass window of the Bang and Olufsen store that occupies the ground floor. Until recently there was no plaque at all, and the obscurity was intentional.

For most of the Soviet period, Babel's fate remained a mystery, a secret guarded by generations of bureaucrats. The full story only became available once Mikhail Gorbachev's policy of glasnost began to shine light on the blackest corners of Soviet history. A special investigation revealed what even Babel's close associates had never known in detail. He had been arrested as an enemy of the people in May of 1939 and tortured at the notorious Lubyanka prison in Moscow, the dungeon of the People's Commissariat of Internal Affairs, or NKVD, the predecessor of the KGB. Babel's arrest was part of the massive purge of artists and writers that accompanied the broader self-immolation of Soviet society in the 1930s, Joseph Stalin's campaign to reengineer society and root out supposed enemies. The official Soviet story was that Babel had died in 1941 while serving a sentence, bizarrely, for spying for France and Austria. It later emerged that he had already been shot in January of 1940, one of many Soviet artists who fell during Stalin's terror.

Not long before his arrest, Babel had been living in Moscow. He was at the center of Soviet artistic life, even if his output had been modest compared to that of many of his contemporary writers. He had celebrated the birth of a daughter with his longtime companion, Antonina Pirozhkova. (His estranged wife and elder daughter, Yevgenia and Nathalie, had been living safely in Paris for more than a decade, after Yevgenia had emigrated from Odessa in the mid-1920s.) Sergei Eisenstein, a friend of Babel's and always a flamboyant jokester, arrived to welcome the new baby with a child's chamber pot filled with a bouquet of violets.[23] But within two years, Babel's friends and family were left bewildered and paralyzed at the prison door. "I'll be waiting for you," said Pirozhkova as she accompanied Babel and his captors to the Lubyanka. "It will be as if you've gone to Odessa . . . only there won't be any letters."[24] His manuscripts had been scattered and burned by the police.

Babel's fate was emblematic. His hometown had long been a city of arrivals—of grain carts from the steppe, immigrants from the hinterlands, and ships from faraway ports. Even the influx of refugees, seeking safe haven as empires and governments crumbled around them, enlivened Odessa's social scene. The poet and prose stylist Ivan Bunin came to the city after the Bolshevik takeover in Moscow; he became part of the circle of the Odessa writer and memoirist Valentin Kataev, later to emerge as one of the shining lights of early Soviet literature. Russia's preeminent silent film star, the young and almond-eyed Vera Kholodnaya, fled the Bolshevik takeover in Moscow only to die in Odessa in the late winter of 1919. Wailing crowds of mourners elbowed their way into the Preobrazhensky Cathedral and surely dwarfed any public meeting called by Whites or Reds. "In those days, anyone who was anyone could be seen on the streets of Odessa," wrote the memoirist and historian Saul Borovoi about growing up in the city. "First-class actors lit up the stages; the most popular journalists and writers filled the pages of Odessa's newspapers; the most renowned politicians and scholars appeared before crowds of listeners."[25]

After the revolution, however, Odessa seemed mainly a place of departure. Chaim Bialik, the great pioneer of Hebrew poetry, left in 1921, hounded by Bolshevik authorities for his allegedly "chauvinistic" views on national identity. Eight years later, Leon Trotsky—the old schoolboy from St. Paul's who had gone from revolutionary prophet to disgraced enemy of Stalin—boarded the steamer *Ilyich* in the dead of winter, an ice-breaker clearing the way through the frozen harbor. The city he had known as a child was the last bit of Russia he ever saw. As a major cultural center, with long-standing ties to Western forms of art and music, Odessa was an obvious target for labeling as a den of spies and wreckers. The university, founded originally by Richelieu as a haven for scholars on the imperial frontier, was denuded of professors thought to harbor views unfriendly to the Soviet state. Writers who had taken refuge on the seaside as a balm to the imagination were targets of vicious state campaigns against dilettantism and formalism in literature. In the era of Stalin, a hundred Babels, lesser known but similarly products of Odessa's vibrant cultural scene, fell from grace and ended up in prison camps, or worse. According to official statistics, at least 19,361 Odessans—peasants, workers, intellectuals, soldiers, and government officials—were arrested from 1937 to 1941 and charged with a host of crimes, from sabotaging the economy to spying for foreign powers. A third of them were shot.[26]

Yet the makings of the new "Old Odessa," celebrated by Babel and mythologized by Eisenstein, were already in place. It reached its apogee after the Second World War. Odessa eventually became, as it had never quite been before, a real somewhere, a place that average Soviet citizens understood as having a distinct identity, its own brand of nostalgia, and a permanent station in the pantheon of beloved and heroic Soviet cities. The Odessa steps would come to be called the "Potemkin steps"—not after Catherine's imperial partner and one of the city's founders, nor even after the mutinous battleship, but rather after Eisenstein's film.

When later filmgoers saw the staircase in *Battleship Potemkin*, they were not looking at history but past it, into the realm of creative and usable myth. Brave revolutionaries, good-natured *goniffs*, and comic schlemiels defined a city at the center of the Soviet Union's "Red Riviera," as close as that classless society could come to a Mediterranean playground for holiday-making workers and Communist Party bosses. The arresting irony is that much of this happened only after the city's most distinctive community—its Jews—had been brutally erased.

CHAPTER 9

The Fields of Transnistria

The murderous professor: Gheorghe Alexianu (center), governor of
Romanian-occupied Transnistria, at work in his office in the former palace
of Count Mikhail Vorontsov, ca. 1941. Behind him is a portrait of Romania's
wartime leader, Ion Antonescu. *From the journal* Transnistria,
courtesy of the State Archive of the Odessa Region.

Everything changed the day Stalin's secret police decided to
blow up their own headquarters. The multistory building
across from the entrance to Alexandrovsky Park was well known
to average Odessans. It was a place best avoided. People who were

called there for a conversation with the NKVD sometimes never returned.

At 5:35 on the afternoon of October 22, 1941, a massive explosion leveled the building's right wing and damaged adjacent structures. Plenty of people had reason to celebrate. Not only was the ominous headquarters now gone, but under the rubble lay representatives of the army and security forces of Romania, the Nazi ally that had taken control of the city just a week earlier. The commander of the occupation troops, General Ion Glogojanu, was killed, along with eighty-eight other military and civilian personnel, including a number of German naval officers. The cause was determined to be a remote-controlled or time-activated mine, probably planted by NKVD agents once the Romanian military staff had selected the building as their headquarters a few days before the blast.[1]

The building had been swept for explosives once before, and intelligence officers had warned of the likelihood of sabotage.[2] In fact, exactly the same thing had happened to the German headquarters in Kiev only a few weeks earlier. The Kiev explosion prompted one of the most notorious massacres of the Second World War, the shooting of more than thirty-three thousand Jews by German SS and Ukrainian guards in the ravine at Babi Yar.[3] Odessa now followed suit. As the bodies of army personnel were being pulled from the debris, officers sent repeated telegrams to central command detailing the destruction as well as the brutal response that was already being carried out. "I have taken steps to hang Jews and Communists in public squares in Odessa," reported General Constantin Trestioreanu, Glogojanu's successor as head of the 10th Infantry Division and commanding officer in Odessa.[4] It was the beginning of the devastation of Odessa's Jewish community.

In one of the least-known episodes of the Holocaust, at least 220,000 Jews were killed in or en route to a string of ghettos and concentration camps established in portions of Soviet Ukraine and overseen by the Romanian state.[5] Some of the victims came from the city of Odessa and its hinterlands; many more were from other territories Romania conquered when it joined the Germans in invading the Soviet Union in 1941. The Romanian zone of occupation, located between the Dniester and Southern Bug rivers, was known officially as Transnistria, the equivalent of other administrative units established as part of the Nazi "New Order" in eastern Europe, from the General Government in Poland to the Reich Commissariat Ukraine. The horrors in Transnistria and its capital city, Odessa, had analogs in the more extensive and well-documented atrocities committed in the infamous death camps of occupied Europe and at the hands of the German military, local police, and Einsatzgruppen, the notorious mobile killing squads of the Reich.

But the twist was that this brutal episode of Holocaust-era genocide occurred outside the territories held by Germany. The major perpetrators were not the leather-coated battalions of the Waffen-SS, nor were the atrocities committed at purpose-built industrial killing facilities such as Auschwitz. Responsibility for the Holocaust in Odessa and Transnistria rested squarely with Romania, the only country during the Second World War besides Nazi Germany to administer a major Soviet city. By the end of the war, the Romanians had largely emptied Odessa of what remained of its Jewish population. One of Europe's greatest centers of Jewish life and culture had become, in the language of the Nazis, almost wholly *judenrein*.

The fortunes of the city and its inhabitants were uncertain at the outset and dangerously predictable as the war wound on. A host of wrenching decisions—whether and when to evacuate, when and how to make peace with the occupying troops, whether to report to the newly established ghetto—determined the difference between victimization and survival. The unmaking of the city's enormous Jewish community—a third of the city's population by the outbreak of the Second World War—depended equally on the decisions of a small number of Romanian officials, whose own dark stories became entwined with the history of the city they briefly controlled.

WHEN ROMANIA entered the Second World War, there was little doubt as to where its sympathies would lie. The country's ruler, the capricious King Carol II, had already declared a royal dictatorship, suppressed political parties, and organized a youth movement of arm-raising loyalists based on Mussolini's legions. Romanian society, too, had responded to the stirrings of the far right across Europe. The country had spawned its own indigenous fascist movement, the Iron Guard, which combined Orthodox Christian radicalism with seething antisemitism and a millenarian cult of death.

These developments formed the background to the rise of Ion Antonescu, the person who took the title of *conducător*—the Romanian equivalent of führer—and ruled both Romania and its occupied territories throughout the war. Stately and soldierly, with the martial bearing of an old war veteran and conservative patriot, Antonescu had little time for the enthusiasms of his sovereign, Carol, or the rug-biting nationalism of the Iron Guard. In fact, he might never have come to power had it not been for the peculiar strategic circumstances in which the Romanian state found itself by the 1940s. The key issue was real estate.

During the First World War, Romania had sided with the Allies, and the reward for being among the winners was the acquisition of new territories at the postwar peace conferences. Among the lands newly attached to the Romanian state was a province, Bessarabia, that had previously belonged to Russia. (Bessarabia's regional capital was Kishinev, the site of the infamous pogrom of 1903.) The Russian Empire's successor, the Soviet Union, never fully accepted these territorial losses, and underground Communist propagandists worked to whip up local populations against their new Romanian rulers. Bolshevik-inspired uprisings in Bessarabia fizzled or were suppressed by the Romanian military, gendarmerie, and secret police.

The Soviets eventually embarked on a new plan for wrenching Bessarabia away from the Romanian kingdom. Under the secret terms of a nonaggression treaty with Nazi Germany—the Molotov-Ribbentrop Pact of 1939—the Soviet Union arranged for Bessarabia to be apportioned to Moscow's sphere of interest. The borderlands of eastern Europe were now effectively carved into fascist and Communist realms. In June of 1940, Stalin acted on the terms of the accord and demanded the immediate annexation of Romanian territory. King Carol, devastated by the ultimatum and more concerned with romantic trysts than the affairs of state, had little choice but to acquiesce. The Romanian army withdrew in disgrace behind its new frontiers, just as further territories—a slice of Transylvania in the north and a section of the Black Sea coastline— were grabbed by Romania's other neighbors, Hungary and Bulgaria. Carol, shame-faced and politically spent, abdicated in favor of his son, Mihai.

Antonescu soon stepped onto the stage. The new Romanian king was still in his teens, and Antonescu emerged as the older, more capable guardian of state interests. A lifelong soldier and former war minister, Antonescu had flirted with the Iron Guard in the 1930s and shared some of the movement's ideals, including its deep antisemitism. But even liberal politicians saw him as the one person with the stature and authority to lead the country out of the crisis created by Soviet-German rapprochement. He soon replaced Carol's old royal dictatorship with a military one, a "National Legionary State" that drew on the message and symbolism of the Iron Guard (even though the uncontrollable movement itself was eventually outlawed). In November of 1940, Antonescu met Hitler for the first time in Berlin and, as the leader of a smaller and embattled state now seeking protection from the very country that had helped carve up Romanian territory earlier in the year, committed Romania to the German cause.

Romania had been a friend of Britain, France, and Russia in the First World War, but the calculation of national interest was different this time around. When Germany reneged on the terms of its nonaggression pact and invaded the Soviet Union on June 22, 1941, Romanians joined the Nazi armies trudging eastward, hoping to recover the provinces that Stalin had grabbed exactly a year earlier. The military operation was widely popular with average Romanians, who saw the Soviet "rape" of Bessarabia and other districts as a crime that demanded revenge. German armies, trailed by their Romanian, Hungarian, and Italian allies, surrounded and then cut off the major cities of the western Soviet Union in grand pincer movements. The Red Army, stunned at the attack, collapsed before the invading forces. In the north, Lithuania, Latvia, and Belorussia came under Nazi control within a week. Soviet forces had been pushed out of western Ukraine in a week more.

As a major port, Odessa was an object of Axis strategic planning as well as a prize difficult for the Soviet forces to give up. It was one of the few Soviet cities to experience aerial bombardment on the first night of the invasion. By late summer of 1941, the city was effectively cut off, surrounded by the German 11th Army and the Romanian 4th Army, with only the sea as a means of supply and escape. For over two months, the city lay under siege, enduring daily artillery barrages from the Axis lines and responding with nightly counterattacks from Red Army defenders.

The situation might have remained in stalemate had German forces not continued their lightning advance to the north and east, overrunning Kiev and pressuring the Soviet naval base at Sevastopol. Faced with the prospect of massive losses in the Soviet heartland, the Red Army took the decision to abandon Odessa and fall back to the east. The Romanians, by prior agreement with the

Germans, became the first forces officially to enter the city in mid-October, in creaking transport trucks and on loping horses, to find the port wrecked and a population only a fraction of its prewar size.

––––––––––––

ESTIMATES VARY as to how many Jews in the western borderlands of the Soviet Union managed to escape before the advancing Axis armies. Just over five million Jews resided in the former Pale of Settlement at the time, and anywhere from several hundred thousand to over a million may have followed the retreating Soviet army eastward.[6] The 1926 Soviet census, the last reliable one conducted before the war, counted just over 433,000 people in Odessa, of whom around 158,000 were Jews. But there may have been as many as 233,000 Jews living in Odessa on the eve of the Axis invasion, as refugees flooded into the city to escape the German and Romanian armies.[7]

The Soviet evacuation of the city through the summer and early fall of 1941 removed perhaps a third or more of Odessa's population, a group that may have contained an overrepresentation of Jews given the professions that had priority for removal: clerks, administrative personnel, doctors, and others. On one estimate, 80,000 to 90,000 Jews remained in the city when the siege finally succeeded in routing the Red Army, that is, still roughly a quarter of the city's total inhabitants.[8] In the late autumn of 1941, the mayor of Odessa estimated the figure at 50,000—out of a remaining city population of perhaps 300,000—probably as accurate a number as one can find at the start of Odessa's Holocaust.[9]

For many Jews—as well as their non-Jewish neighbors—how to respond to the invasion was an excruciating conundrum. In retrospect, the decision to stay in one's own apartment and ride out the conflict was a gigantic mistake. But home had a magnetic pull, even in a time of growing danger. In a worldly and strategically impor-

tant port such as Odessa—which lay directly in the path of the
invaders—Jews still had little inkling of the atrocities already being
committed elsewhere, especially in occupied Poland and Belorussia.
After all, the Soviet Union had signed a peace pact with the Nazis
close to two years earlier, and Stalin's propaganda machine had
worked assiduously to portray Germans in the best-possible light.

After June of 1941, as refugees began arriving in the city from
the countryside, the stories of burned villages and on-the-spot
shootings might have seemed too fanciful to believe. For many
families, banking on the devil they didn't know rather than the one
that was painfully familiar must have seemed the smarter choice.
Plenty of people had personal memories of the anti-Jewish violence of 1905; a few could even remember the pogrom of 1871 or
1881. Given the choice between abandoning a home and property
to another round of looting by one's neighbors in Odessa or staying
put and dealing with the new occupiers, the latter was not an obviously ludicrous option. "Under the Germans, it's going to be very,
very bad for us. We'll suffer. We'll live with humiliation," a friend
said to the memoirist Saul Borovoi. "But to become a refugee—
that means certain death."[10]

Even when evacuations from Odessa began, people still had
to negotiate the shoals of Soviet bureaucracy. In the countryside,
villagers could load up the oxcart and head eastward, but for city-
dwellers there were only three options: hike out by foot; try to find
a truck or train that was not already packed with military personnel, which required a special ticket; or seek a berth aboard evacuation ships leaving from the harbor, which also required a special
pass that gave priority to Communist Party officials and state
administrators.

Those who managed to get out of the city safely were faced with
the prospect of finding shelter, remaking their lives and professions, and reuniting family members separated in the flight from
the Axis armies. Some ended up as far afield as Uzbekistan and

other parts of Central Asia. Displaced and parentless children were enrolled in specially constructed orphanages. Adults were assigned to refugee camps and shared housing with comrades from other occupied and besieged Soviet cities, conditions that lasted for the next four years or more. The evacuees made the best of their plight. Writers exchanged drafts over scarce cigarettes and vodka. Scholars read papers on obscure themes before learned audiences drawn from across the Soviet Union. Directors crafted documentaries and melodramas—which is why so many Soviet movies of the era feature the Tashkent Film Studios in the title sequences, an unlikely Soviet Hollywood constructed amid Muslim domes and minarets on the Central Asian plains.[11] It was the beginning of the creation of an urban diaspora that carried the values, culture, and proclivities of Odessa throughout the Soviet Union and beyond.

But in the late summer and autumn of 1941, Odessans were making monumental decisions about staying or leaving with little knowledge of what lay ahead, either in the city itself or in some unknown resettlement facility. One Holocaust survivor, Boris Kalika, recalled being dragged down to the port by his mother to catch a Soviet ship. Crowds pushed toward the docks. Luggage lay in piles on the quay. In the melee twelve-year-old Boris, small and frightened, was separated from his mother and sister. He eventually tired of searching for his family and simply walked back to his apartment building, where he remained, in the care of Russian neighbors, until the occupying forces rounded up the city's Jews later in the year. He was briefly interned in the Odessa ghetto and was moved out of the city toward a Romanian-built camp at Domanevka. Lithe and golden-haired, he managed to slip away from the guards and survived the rest of the war by going from village to village, portraying himself as a Russian orphan. It was only after the war had ended and the Romanian troops withdrew that he was at last reunited in Odessa with his mother, who had spent the war years as a refugee in the Soviet east. His sister, however, had

died in uncertain circumstances during the chaotic evacuation of
the city in 1941.[12]

———————

KILLING JEWS was not a primary goal of the Romanian soldiers and
gendarmes as they headed east, but it was a side project pursued
with some of the zeal, if none of the organization, of the Wehrmacht and Waffen-SS. Antonescu's government had enacted a
range of antisemitic laws in Romania, and murderous rampages had
already taken place there, most infamously a pogrom and forced
deportation in the northeastern city of Iaşi that left thousands
dead. But there were no large-scale removals of Jews from Romania
proper to the death camps overseen by Reich officials. Antonescu
eventually rebuffed German pressure to deport the country's large
Jewish community, and at his postwar trial he still maintained that
his actions had always been intended to save Romanian Jews, not to
massacre them. But Romania's actions in the reannexed Bessarabia,
as well as farther east in the occupied territory of Transnistria, were
another matter entirely.

Systematic attacks on Jews had already occurred in the city
from the first hours of the occupation. The German Einsatzgruppe
D, especially its subunit Sonderkommando 11b, entered Odessa
with Romanian forces in mid-October.[13] Prominent Jewish community leaders were murdered, and Jews were ordered to register
with the local authorities, presumably to provide lists of names and
addresses for future operations.[14] But the bombing of the military
headquarters unleashed a new and less regulated round of violence.
Mass hangings and large-scale shootings took place throughout the
city and the suburbs, initiated by the occupation forces and then
expressly ordered by Ion Antonescu himself.

From October 22 forward, Antonescu sent telegrams that
detailed a clear course of action. Two hundred "Communists" were
to be killed for every dead Romanian or German officer and one

hundred for every ordinary soldier. All "Communists" in Odessa were to be made hostages, as well as "a member of each Jewish family," all of whom were to be killed in the event of a second major terrorist incident.[15] In a further elaboration, Antonescu gave a checklist of measures:

1. Execution of all Jews from Bessarabia who have sought refuge in Odessa.

2. All individuals who fall under the stipulations of October 23, 1941 [ordering the killing of "Communists"], not yet executed and the others who can be added thereto will be placed inside a building that will be mined and detonated. This action will take place on the day of the burial of the victims [of the headquarters bombing].

3. This order will be destroyed after being read.

A handwritten version of the order survived. Subsequent communication with command headquarters confirmed that the order had been carried out.[16]

The use of the general term "Communists," as well as the particular antipathy toward Bessarabian Jews, reflected one of the critical dimensions of Romania's policy in Odessa and elsewhere: the lines between Communist, Jew, partisan, refugee, and simple inconvenience were hazy and often nonexistent. The orders issued by the occupation authorities were at times grotesquely vague. On October 23, Trestioreanu instructed the units under his command to hang "at least 100 Jews" each—presumably with full permission to hang even more.[17] These actions were always known by the Romanians as *represalii*—reprisals—and they were aimed almost exclusively at Jews. The intended targets, of course, were Soviet agents, partisans, and their sympathizers, but those were categories difficult if not impossible to assess with any clarity.

Being a Jew became a surrogate for being an enemy of the state,

and certainly was a category easier to identify from personal documents, public records, and routine intelligence-gathering from
neighbors and coworkers. Ease of bureaucratic identification,
combined with the deeper antisemitic equation of Jews with social
undesirables and hidden enemies, was the driver of Romania's policy. For Antonescu and his subordinates, the occupying troops were
simply using lethal force to respond to pervasive partisan activity
and discourage Odessans from engaging in further underground
attacks. If it was relatively easy to survive the war as a Jew inside
Romania, Jews in the occupied lands were placed in a very different
category—that of Russian-speaker, crypto-Communist, and likely
subversive.

The scale of these operations was staggering. Besides the hangings and indiscriminate shootings immediately after the explosion, thousands of Jews were rounded up by Romanian security
forces with the assistance of SS units and executed in the port, in
military buildings on the outskirts of the city, and in sheds in the
nearby settlement of Dalnik. The poles supporting overhead elec-
tric lines that serviced the city's trolley system were used as makeshift gallows, with lines of bodies stretching out into the suburbs.[18]
Meanwhile, SS Sonderkommando 11b was given the task of finding
Jews who might still be hiding in the city and dispatching them to
Romanian killing squads outside town.[19] Mass shootings with rifles
and machine guns, immolations with blazing oil and gas, and the
bombing of buildings packed with Jewish citizens—precisely the
ghoulish symbolism Antonescu had ordered—were carried out in
the weeks following the bombing. "The chaos and the horrifying
sights that followed cannot be described," noted a contemporary
account. "Wounded people burning alive, women with their hair
aflame coming out through the roof or through openings in the
burning storehouses in a crazed search for salvation."[20] Estimates
based on witness reports, postwar trials, and limited survivor testimonies give a figure of at least twenty-five thousand people killed

in Odessa and Dalnik during this period—that is, perhaps around a third of all Jews who were living in the city when it came under Romanian control.[21]

These massacres were carried out according to written orders passed down the Romanian chain of command. As such they were part of the "Holocaust by bullets," as one historian has called it— the mass murder of civilians in ditches, old buildings, and tank traps across Ukraine and other parts of the western Soviet Union. That was the way in which millions of Jews and others experienced the war, even though this version of the Holocaust is usually over-shadowed by the impersonal, mechanized killing in death camps such as Auschwitz.[22] The Romanians did not create extermination facilities, but they did construct an array of camps and ghettos in Transnistria to which the remainder of Odessa's Jews—and many other Jews and Roma (Gypsies) from Bessarabia and Transnistria itself—were eventually sent.

As WITH MUCH of Romanian policy, the confinement of Odessa's Jews to a ghetto was an inconsistent and disorganized process— a fact that produced horrific cruelties as well as possibilities for escape or evasion. Some Jews were forcibly moved to the Slobodka neighborhood, just beyond the city center, as massacres were winding to a close. Some were allowed to return to their homes, but soon men and boys were required to report to the local prison, with a sweep throughout the city picking up any who had not reg-istered. Then, in mid-November of 1941, officials in Transnistria ordered all Jews to report to a hastily arranged ghetto. The policy was only loosely enforced. Soon women, children, and the elderly were allowed to return to their homes, many of which had already been ransacked or seized by their neighbors.[23] It was also possible for men to sneak back into other parts of the city (the ghetto was a neighborhood of houses and apartment buildings, not a walled enclosure) and for other Odessans to visit them there or in other detention facilities. One secret agent reported to Romanian authorities how easy it was to take food to a Jewish neighbor in the municipal prison, whereas that would have been impossible, she said, under Stalin.[24]

The full confinement to the Slobodka ghetto seems to have come later in Odessa than in other parts of Transnistria. Before the late summer of 1941, Romania's practice had been to kill Jews on the spot or to deport them to the east, across the Bug River into German-occupied Ukraine. But the resulting chaos—with disorderly columns of Jews being pushed across the river and then back again by German soldiers unprepared to handle the influx—was meant to be squelched by an agreement signed on August 30, which formally awarded Romania control of Transnistria. The agreement set out Romania's responsibility for dealing with Jews on what was now defined as its own territory. Jews were to be "concentrated in labor camps and required to work" until military operations ceased, at which point they would be "evacuated" to the German-controlled east.[25] In Odessa the creation of the ghetto was probably a matter of timing: with the bombing of the headquarters and mass killings that followed, it took months from the time of the initial invasion for the authorities to devise concrete plans. In mid-December Antonescu gave the order definitively imprisoning Odessa's Jews in the ghetto—the first time in history that Jews were fully restricted from living in whatever part of the city they could afford.

The ghettoization policy was the first step toward the relatively quick removal of the city's remaining Jews. Many had already been deported in October and November, making the long trek to villages and camps farther inland, where thousands were shot by local police or later died of malnutrition and typhus. Acting pursuant to Antonescu's instructions, the civilian governor of Transnistria issued the command on January 2, 1942—Order No. 35—that sealed the fate of Odessa's Jews. They would be expelled from the ghetto and relocated to the districts of Berezovka and Ochakov, to the north and east of Odessa; their goods would be turned over to the state and sold; and they would be subject to a regime of forced labor.[26]

The removal began on January 10. The mass exodus was conducted on foot and in horse-drawn carts, between ranks of jeering soldiers and local Odessans, in temperatures below freezing. Those who fell behind or tried to run were shot on the spot. The bodies of the dead lined the streets.[27] The orders were executed by units of the Romanian army and gendarmes, who reported regularly on the progress of their work. It took months to empty the ghetto, not only because of the transport required to move the tens of thousands of people now living in Slobodka, but also because of the numerous sweeps that were required to make sure that no Jews were left. Even weeks into the removals, Jewish Odessans were still to be found hiding in houses, especially in attics or crawl spaces.[28] Romanian soldiers sometimes had difficulty overcoming their own fear, disgust, and sympathy, according to official reports. To buck them up, the military command required each soldier to sign a personal declaration confirming that he had read and understood the orders prohibiting fraternization with Jews.[29]

Yet the conditions of atrocity, scarcity, and survival created alliances of necessity. The fates of Sergeant Nicolae Tănase and Vera Sepel, for example, were intertwined in the weeks preceding the elimination of the ghetto. Tănase was a sergeant assigned to the headquarters of the Romanian 38th Infantry, which gave him ready access to supplies of food, clothing, and fuel. Sepel was a Jew. But for a few months in late 1941 and early 1942, they made something of a life together. He visited her on multiple occasions. He may even have set up a home with her in a modest apartment somewhere in the city.

When the authorities ordered all Jews deported from Odessa, Tănase and Sepel hatched a plan to get her out. The sergeant used his military connections to arrange travel documents that would allow her to board a train bound westward, for Romania. Sending her to the west—into the heartland of the Nazi ally that now controlled the city—seems a bizarre mode of escape, but it made sense at the time. Jews were routinely harassed there and pogroms had taken place. But Jews were less likely to be slaughtered or deported en masse. In Romania, she might even be able to blend into the local population, her Jewish identity undetected.

The lovers were taking a huge chance. Jews were restricted from riding Romanian trains without express permission from the government, so Sepel's documents probably included false identity papers that would have masked her Jewish surname. On the evening of January 10, as Tănase's fellow soldiers were herding Jews from the newly established ghetto, he met Sepel at the city's main station. He had come prepared with two street maps, perhaps as a way of finding a backup escape route should the initial plan fail. They waited on the platform for the night train to Buzău, a quiet provincial town in the foothills of the Carpathian Mountains, on the other side of the old Soviet-Romanian border.

They never made the train. At eight o'clock that evening, the pair raised the suspicion of a ticket collector, perhaps an old station agent who had served with professional zeal under Soviets and now Romanians. The travel documents, bearing the seal of the commander of the 38th Infantry, were identified as forgeries. Both the Romanian sergeant and the Jewish escapee were taken into military custody. A few weeks later, on February 3, 1942, Sergeant Nicolae Tănase was court-martialed and sentenced to three years' imprisonment for "falsifying the documents of a Jew," plus five further years for "attempting to remove a Jew from internment in the ghetto." Vera Nikolaevna Sepel was sentenced to five years' imprisonment for attempting to escape the ghetto and evade deportation from Odessa.[30]

Their fates after that point are unknown. If she remained in detention after her arrest and sentencing, Sepel was probably removed the following March when the Odessa prison was emptied of Jewish inmates. After that, she may have died somewhere inland of typhus or of exposure, or at the hands of a Ukrainian policeman or German militiaman. If she were able to convince her captors that she was really from the Romania heartland rather than occupied Odessa, she might have survived the war. Perhaps she was eventually expatriated to Romania with a new name and a new identity, just as the sergeant had intended.

The deportations that Tănase and Sepel sought to evade—or "evacuations," in the terminology that Romanian authorities adopted from the Germans—were formally concluded months later, on April 11, 1942. The summary report from the prefect of the Odessa region stated that 32,643 Jews had been "counted and evacuated." Another 847 were found dead in the ghetto or killed in the process of removal. A further 548 (including pregnant women) were still located in the ghetto hospital but were scheduled for transport to the facilities in Berezovka district as soon as they were movable. A new survey was conducted to identify any remaining Jews in the city and to find a way of disposing of the property confiscated from the deportees.[31]

Things would get worse in the countryside. Widespread disease such as typhus, systematic killings by Romanian gendarmes and police units recruited from among local ethnic German populations, and the inhuman sanitary conditions in Transnistria's numerous camps and ghettos—in places known by their Ukrainian names such as Berezovka, Bogdanovka, and Domanevka—claimed tens of thousands of lives. For those who survived, Transnistrian officials, acting on the authority of Antonescu, imposed what amounted to a system of slave labor, decreeing in December of 1943 that all Jews between the ages of twelve and sixty would be required to work in several specified jobs, from collecting eggs to staffing abattoirs. Odessa, however, was to remain a city almost wholly free of Jews. No work assignments were to be made in the city without the express permission of the government's senior civilian administrator.[32]

By the spring of 1942, as the acacias were budding and flowers opening in the parks, the Romanian authorities had completed their task with every bit of the morbid perseverance of the German army, police, and SS units elsewhere. With the exception of people who somehow managed to hide their identity, there were only a few-dozen Jewish artisans working in a small, state-controlled workshop in the city center, and most of them were not originally from Odessa.[33] The person overseeing the deportations was decorated by the papal nuncio for his diligent management of Romania's newly acquired eastern territory.[34] He was an obscure Romanian professor who now held the weighty title of governor—*guvernator*—of Transnistria.

GHEORGHE ALEXIANU was a missionary of sorts. He was a member of the hopeful generation of 1918, the group of young men and women who witnessed the creation of "Greater Romania" at the end of the First World War. Romania had been a victor power in that conflict, and to the victor went the spoils: the territories that his generation of Romanians saw as rightly belonging to their own nation-state. He looked toward a bright future in which the newly gathered lands—territories such as Bessarabia, Dobrogea, Transylvania, Bukovina, and the Banat, absorbed into the Romanian kingdom from its defeated or defunct neighbors, Russia, Bulgaria, and Austria-Hungary—would be transformed into a Romanian-speaking paradise.

Alexianu was born in 1897 in the county of Vrancea, an ancient district of the old kingdom of Romania. Once the kingdom expanded to include lands acquired in the postwar peace settlements, he set out, like many of his generation, to the new eastern frontier. These corners of Greater Romania were Romanian in name only. Each had sizable populations of ethnic Romanians—

even majorities, depending on how and whom one counted—but there were minorities too: Ukrainians, Russians, Bulgarians, and, especially in the districts that had formerly been part of Russia's Pale of Settlement, Jews. Many men and women of Alexianu's generation saw their supreme duty as bringing Romanian culture to the benighted lands of the east. They signed up as schoolteachers, university professors, regional administrators, agronomists, journalists, and any other profession that would help to develop—and make truly Romanian—the lands that had once been captive to Romanovs and Habsburgs.

Alexianu ended up as a professor of administrative law at the university in Czernowitz, a once thriving Austrian-controlled city located in the district of Bukovina, in what is today western Ukraine. What he encountered there was different from what he expected. Far from being truly Romanian, the city seemed overwhelmingly German-speaking and Jewish. It was, in fact, one of

Gheorghe Alexianu (standing) at a formal dinner.
Romanian National Archive, I/6003.

the great centers of Jewish culture in central Europe, home of the future German-language poet Paul Celan (born 1920) and a haven for provincial intellectuals and artists.

Alexianu's task, like that of other professors, schoolteachers, and local administrators, was to "romanianize" the city and its hinterland, to make the mélange of peoples and cultures into loyal citizens of the Romanian state. School curricula were reworked to tell a Romanian version of history. Minority languages were suppressed. Jews were excluded from universities and restrictions placed on their participation in civic life. His skill and enthusiasm attracted the attention of the central authorities, and in 1938 he was named *rezident regal*—the Romanian king's personal representative and the effective governor—of all Bukovina and several surrounding counties.

When Stalin annexed Bessarabia in the summer of 1940, part of Bukovina was included in the bargain. The Soviet invasion had a galvanizing impact on local nationalists like Alexianu, who fled grumbling and vengeful back to Romania. His adopted city, Czernowitz, was now overrun by the Red Army. The Romanian-speaking peasants whom he had lauded as the repositories of an ancient national ethos were punished as imperialist stooges by the new Soviet masters. Jews in the city likely saw the Soviet arrival as a form of liberation, or at least something of a relief compared to the intense nationalism that, for some two decades, had promoted Romanians and Romanian culture at their expense. Stories circulated of locals jeering and spitting at Romanian troops as they pulled out in advance of the Soviet arrival.

Once Romanian armies joined Hitler's push to the east in the summer of 1941, Alexianu was a reasonable if not obvious choice for governing the newly "liberated" lands. He had never had more than a provincial administrative appointment, but his nationalizing zeal and direct experience as a professor in one of the kingdom's border provinces gave him a certain familiarity with the methods necessary to rebuild what the Soviets had destroyed. He knew how to get things done in a Jewish city. His major achievement as an administrator in Czernowitz seems to have been out-doing the central government in its anti-Jewish legislation. Before he had been in office a year, he had forbidden local citizens from using Yiddish in public.

In August of 1941, even before Romanian and German troops had secured effective control of Transnistria, Alexianu was named the region's *guvernator*, at the head of an array of local prefects, police units, and eventually the mayoralty of the province's new capital, Odessa. Thick-waisted and balding, with a penchant for fine suits and a tiny Hitler-style mustache, Alexianu was obsessed with hierarchy and protocol. Even his preferred form of address revealed the social anxiousness of a provincial arriviste. Right up to the end of the Romanian occupation, he always signed his letters and decrees as "Professor" Gheorghe Alexianu. He set up his office in Count Vorontsov's old palace overlooking Odessa's port. The large mural of an avuncular Stalin amid a gaggle of dancing Soviet children—left over from the days when the palace served as head-quarters of the Communist children's league, the Young Pioneers—disappeared beneath several coats of paint.[35]

In the fall of 1941, as the *represalii* were winding down and the bureaucracy for rounding up Jews was coalescing, Alexianu allowed himself a moment of reflection on the historical significance of Romania's eastern project. In a rambling and flowery letter to Antonescu, he proposed resurrecting the Preobrazhensky Cathe-dral, leveled by the Soviets in the 1930s, as an homage to Romania's eastern expansion: "As ever did our Princes of old after a victorious battle, so should we ourselves signify the most glorious moment in the life of our people, when the expansionist might of Romanian warriors has caused our country's banner to be hoisted on the walls of Odessa." He saw himself as part of a great historical pageant. It trailed back to the sword-wielding princes of the Middle Ages who had stood valiantly against Slav, Mongol, and Turk. It marched forward to a time when people would look on what the nation had achieved in Odessa as "a most magnificent icon, from age to age, of times past, of the exalted life of Romania." As the country carried on with its mission, it should therefore be conscious of how it would be judged by history—which Alexianu believed would necessarily reveal Romania's selfless and humanitarian response to the call to greatness.[36]

But then it was back to work. Alexianu, like his superiors in Bucharest and his colleagues in the military and gendarmerie, was deeply concerned with identifying Jews. Senior officials looked on the eastern province as a territory inhabited first and foremost by blood-defined groups, not by individual people. Determining the size and membership of each of these racial or ethnic groups was a basic task of administration, much like registering automobiles or issuing licenses to liquor shops. German comrades in the Wehrmacht liaison office and SS detachments in Transnistria no doubt approved of and even encouraged that process. But Alexianu had long experience with such matters from his time in Bukovina. Administrators were also convinced that finding Jews— or, by process of elimination, first identifying all non-Jews—would somehow contribute to the security of the city. If Jews were crypto-Communists, and if Communist agents had been responsible for the explosion at the military headquarters, sorting out which Odessans could be trusted became a principal task of government.

Alexianu and his team devised an entire system of checking and verifying identity, especially that of men. At its core was a registration system in which, if proper documentation could not be produced in other ways, Odessans might provide witnesses to their identity. The form provided by Alexianu's administration made the task simple:

I, the undersigned, _____, living at _____, with passport
number _____, declare that I have known Mr. _____
since the year _____, that I know he is not a Jew but is of
_____ ethnic origin, that he was not in the Communist Party,
and that he was living in Odessa [before the occupation].[37]

Alexianu was at times fulfilling orders given by Antonescu himself, but as a man who paid attention to details, he took particular care to shape the way in which orders were applied. His
personal margin notes can be found in the periodic reports on
the deportation of Jews from the city, often with stern comments evidently meant to encourage or reprimand his subordinates. Once the deportation of Jews was under way, he reminded
the gendarmes that any Jewish children left behind by deportees
were not to be taken in by Christian families; a special orphan-
age would be constructed for them in the camp at Berezovka.
When the chairman of the evacuation commission reported
that Jews were still thought to be hiding outside the ghetto in
other parts of the city, Alexianu's orders, jotted down in pencil
in his economical script, were clear: "Raids are to be conducted
and sanctions applied."[38]

Nevertheless, his own conception of identity could be as slip-
pery as that of the grotesque and quixotic province he helped
create. Sometimes Jewishness depended on blood. Sometimes it
depended on faith. Following a policy established by Antonescu,
Alexianu decreed that Jews who could verify they had been baptized as Christians would not be subject to deportation. He personally intervened in at least one instance to save a baptized,
presumably ex-Jewish woman at the request of her priest.[39] But
that was one of the many terrifying features of the government
over which he presided with officious passion. With the life and
death of individual Odessans and other Transnistrians determined
literally by the stroke of his pen, Alexianu possessed a power that

not even Antonescu—busy mapping troop movements and taking salutes—could exercise with the same pinpoint accuracy.

———————

WHAT DID THE ROMANIANS think they were doing in Transnistria? The answer would have depended on which Romanian one asked and when. Sometimes officials were simply copying the Nazi experience in the General Government or the Reich Commissariat Ukraine—killing, deporting, confining, and then killing again— even though survival rates in Transnistria were an order of magnitude higher than in some German-controlled areas. Sometimes they were creating their own micro-empire on the fly, a poorly organized and inconsistent effort to have their own colonial possession in the Slavic east, which could supply labor and raw materials for the motherland.

At still other points, they were crafting a distinctly Romanian project, preparing the groundwork for a postwar state that would be even larger and ethnically cleaner than the one created in 1918. Romania's borders had already been changed by force, and there was some expectation that at least a portion of those changes would remain in place after an Axis victory. The friendly Germans had awarded a sizable chunk of Transylvania, in Romania's north, to equally friendly Hungary around the time the enemy Soviets had grabbed Bessarabia and northern Bukovina. Surrounded by such acquisitive friends, the Romanians reckoned, securing Transnistria might be an insurance policy against the permanent loss of Transylvania—a much more valuable piece of the Romanian heartland that remained the preeminent territorial concern throughout the war.[40]

Cultural antisemitism, formalized by the institutions of the Romanian state, was fundamental to these efforts. By September of 1942, Antonescu and Alexianu finally got around to closing the circle by outlawing Jewishness itself: ordering that Judaism would henceforth be considered an illegal religion while also prohibiting cultural Jews from espousing other faiths.[41] One of the newly established newspapers, the Romanian-language *Gazeta Odesei* (Odessa Gazette), tried to capture the transformative power of Romanian rule and its relationship to the Jewish question:

> Odessa used to impress its visitors mainly through the smell of dirty yid diapers and the decomposing waste of the Privoz market.... You'd think that only yids lived there, racing through the streets, crowding into shops, and forming great herds at the entrances to buildings.... But then came the Romanian army and, after that, the Romanian administration. And the Jewish hullabaloo was put to an end. Odessa started to heal its wounds and cleanse itself of the filth that had accumulated over many years. The repulsive smell of Jewish courtyards disappeared with time. Odessa awoke to a new life, full of luminous hope.[42]

But there were other motivations beyond anti-Jewish sentiment. Romania was bound by a vague sense of manifest destiny to its east and by the desire to create a territorial buffer zone around a liberated Bessarabia and Bukovina. Once the state began the large-scale deportations, it took on a set of responsibilities that it was both unable and unwilling to meet. In the end, with Jews and Roma/Gypsies lying hungry and diseased in atrocious facilities, the Romanians got rid of the problem by turning it over to someone else—in many cases the ethnic Ukrainian and German villagers in whose laps the deportees had been dumped. Emboldened and outfitted by the Nazis, local ethnic Germans, or *Volksdeutsche*, descendants of the sedulous German farmers originally invited to the region by Catherine the Great, sometimes killed the starving people they had never really thought of as neighbors anyway. The desire to unburden the state of human encumbrances was often one of the most powerful and grotesque sources of Romanian behavior.[43]

Thousands of average Romanians well below Antonescu and Alexianu saw in the Transnistrian experiment the chance to realize a particular pet project or further their own careers. Romanian officials did not by and large suffer from what the Germans called *Ostrausch*, the intoxicating effects of working far from home, in a place seen to be inhabited by subhuman Jews and savage Slavs. But the possibilities afforded by Transnistria were not to be ignored. Academics explored the riches of the region between the Dniester and Bug rivers and prepared for the wholesale restructuring of its population. Scholars organized anthropological expeditions, measuring heads and studying the brow lines of villagers to sort out true Romanians from hybrids. (Twenty-five percent Romanian blood, it was agreed, would suffice to make someone genuinely Romanian—a far more capacious definition of national identity than that applied by the Nazis.) A new "national eugenics institute" was proposed as a way of putting the Romanian nation on a more solid genetic footing. In the summer of 1942, Romanian authorities began the process of identifying ethnic Romanians who lived to the east of the Bug River, inside the Reich Commissariat Ukraine. The plan was to relocate them to the west, into Transnistria, where they would help build a flourishing and more ethnically pure province, the Latin equivalent of Germany's "repatriation" policies toward its own *Volksdeutsche*. Some Romanian families were resettled before the tide of war began to turn against the Axis.[44]

Liberals and humanitarians spoke out about the treatment of the country's own Jews, while prominent Jewish leaders in Romania organized aid missions to assist Jews in the Transnistrian camps. The most enthusiastic nationalists welcomed policies that involved moving people, changing borders, and purifying territories thought to be contaminated by the racially or ethnically alien. But to most Romanians, the fate of Jews in the occupied region was probably of only passing concern. Even worldly intellectuals had a particular blind spot when it came to what was happening in the east. The eminent historian Gheorghe Ioan Brătianu traveled with a Romanian cavalry unit all the way to Crimea, but he was moved mainly by the long rows of soldiers' graves and the heavy toll that artillery had taken on the region's antiquities.[45] The province and its capital city were not the sole purview of a limited, secretive, and depraved cadre of officials and soldiers. Through acts of commission or omission, Transnistria was very much a participatory affair.

In Odessa all this would have seemed clear at the time. As one secret agent working for the occupying forces reported, some Odessans thought of the many Romanians now patrolling the streets and serving in government offices as representatives of a "soft nation," whereas the Germans were "strong . . . they would have quickly brought discipline" to the city—that is, they would have restored order, kept the streets clean, rounded up criminals, and stamped out official corruption.[46] That was probably the dominant view among Russians and Ukrainians: having Romanians in charge wasn't the kind of occupation one would have chosen, but nevertheless there it was. And in any case, as brown leaves floated down to empty pavements in the autumn of 1941, the basic task that the occupiers had set themselves seemed obvious: they had come to get rid of the people the Romanians called *jidani* and whom Odessans knew in everyday Russian as *zhidy*—that is, the yids.

CHAPTER 10

"I Would Like to Bring to Your Attention the Following"

A city liberated: The Soviet Union's 62nd Stalingrad Army marching down Richelieu Street, April 10, 1944. *Photo by Georgii Zel'ma, courtesy of the Prints and Photographs Division, Library of Congress.*

After the war every Odessan schoolchild could recite the dates that bracketed the occupation: the Red Army's strategic retreat on October 16, 1941, and its triumphant return on April 10, 1944. Those 907 days were treated as a brief interregnum before the restoration of Soviet power and as a time of communal suffering, when the city was held in the strangling clutch of foreigners.

Even today, along the Alley of Glory in Shevchenko Park (the former Alexandrovsky Park), a sloping walkway is flanked by memorials to the war dead. It leads to the obelisk of the unknown sailor and a sputtering eternal flame. On public holidays the memorial is patrolled by goose-stepping, uniformed children, who compete for the honor of standing to attention at "Post No. 1." From there, visitors can look out on the harbor and the high-rise apartments beyond, evidence of the city's journey from victim to victor.

Soviet historians tended to label the old enemy as "fascists" or "German-fascist occupiers," especially once Romania became a Communist state and an ally in the Warsaw Pact. The former enemy had become a socialist friend, so painful episodes from the past were quietly put aside. Few people, even in Odessa itself, know of the wartime experience in any detail—in part because of the passing of the generation that still remembers the war, in part because a half century of Soviet propaganda emphasized the city's defenders and downplayed its foreign occupiers and local collaborators.

The Soviet narrative of resistance is still powerful. Schoolteachers walk their classes through the twists and turns of the catacombs, where guerrillas plotted raids on the enemy. Commemorative plaques still mark the former homes of heroes, patriots, and partisans. Only a few Odessan writers have begun to question this version of events. For over two and a half years, were citizens really thinking only about "how to blow up the enemy headquarters, rub out an enemy soldier, or at least puncture the tires of a Romanian car?" asked one author wryly.[1] But today we know—or at least can know—a great deal more about the local response to the wartime occupation.

By the 1940s the Romanian kingdom had developed a substantial provincial bureaucracy, with more than two decades of experience in governing new and troublesome districts. Much of that bureaucratic apparatus reproduced itself in Transnistria: directorates and sections, subsections and offices, all with the dual task of real-world administration plus the diligent production of paper trails. The Soviets, who scooped up these documents when the region was retaken, were good custodians. That collection now contains more than fifty-two thousand separate files and hundreds of thousands of pages of text. Many have been microfilmed and are stored at the United States Holocaust Memorial Museum in Washington, D.C. Many more are barely kept from the ravages of mold and mice by a valiant staff at the state archives in Odessa.

The files hold detailed memos and telegrams about the establishment of the ghetto and its liquidation, the deportation of Jews to work camps and internment centers elsewhere in Transnistria, and their deaths from disease, exposure, and systematic slaughter. Yet of all the horrors in the archives, some of the most disturbing reading—especially from a city that still takes its cosmopolitanism seriously—comes in the written denunciations and secret agent reports that average Odessans filed with the Romanian authorities: hundreds of pages scrawled in ink or grease pencil on onion-skin writing paper, the backs of old posters, even the inside of candy wrappers. Along with the lists of class aliens and enemies of the people arrested and shot under Stalin, the bulging files pay bleak witness to the darker city that lurked behind the enlightened one.

ODESSANS BEGAN DENOUNCING each other almost as soon as the Romanian cavalry trotted down a deserted and sandbagged Richelieu Street. After the bombing of the military headquarters on October 22, 1941, the volume picked up. The demand to unmask hidden Bolsheviks before they could stage further terrorist attacks was greater than ever, and the supply of Odessans eager to avoid suspicion themselves probably spiked as well. After all, it was hard to have survived the 1930s without embracing to some degree the Soviet system, and in the topsy-turvy world of war and occupation, every virtue conjured from necessity was now a vice waiting to be revealed.

It really was like stepping through the looking glass. The dueling denunciations of Skopov and Labunsky are an instructive example.

In November of 1941 one Grigory Skopov wrote to the Romanian military command to denounce his neighbor, Pavel Labunsky, as a Communist and NKVD agent. He supplied a list of people who could verify this information and gave a detailed record of Labunsky's determined opposition to the Romanian state. When Labunsky heard from others in his apartment building that he had been denounced by Skopov, he quickly shot off his own handwritten note to the authorities. He affirmed that he had never been a member of the Communist Party. He noted that he had been born into a family of reasonably well-off landowners. He had been married in an Orthodox Christian ceremony. He had been "repressed" on several occasions by the Bolsheviks. His brother had fought on the side of the Whites during the civil war, for which he was sent to the gulag and had his property confiscated. In turn, Labunsky had been left with the task of caring for his brother's wife and two children. When the new war started, Labunsky was drafted into the Red Army, but he immediately deserted. Beyond all that, he wrote, the person the Romanians should really be worried about was his denouncer. He was merely trying to cover up his own Bolshevik past and well-known felonious ways by casting aspersions on someone else. "Skopov is the absolute worst enemy of the new order, which has come to liberate humanity from the hated Bolsheviks," Labunsky concluded. "Skopov should pay for his past criminal activities." He then appended a list of eleven neighbors and other witnesses who could verify his claims.[2]

A few years earlier, all the bits of biography that Labunsky offered as bona fides—his class background, his religiosity, his brother's service with the Whites—would have marked him as an enemy of the Soviet state. But in the new order, things that had been liabilities now became advantages to be valued and marketed. For plenty of Odessans, the way to demonstrate a healthy sense of civic duty was by stepping up and being of use in the maintenance of law and order, the discovery of underground Soviet agents, and especially the exposure of hidden Jews.

Alexianu's administration saw all Jewish Odessans, at least in theory, as Soviet agents. The equation between "Jew" and "Communist" had a long and gruesome history throughout eastern Europe. But given that the Romanians were not only fighting a war but also conducting a counterinsurgency campaign—against real underground fighters hiding out in the catacombs, disrupting transport, and at times targeting senior Romanian officials—the search for hidden Jews was not simply a matter of what would now be called ethnic cleansing. It was also, from the perspective of the occupier and many of the occupied, a matter of security. Latent and at times enthusiastic antisemitism, fear of a Soviet return to the city, paranoia about being denounced oneself, and the universal neighborly emotions of greed, envy, and resentment were twisted together in the motivations of Odessa's collaborators.

Unmasking pretenders was a common theme in many of the agent reports and voluntary denunciations. One Igor Brizhitsky reported that he had heard of a man named Strizhak, then living on Greek Street, who had worked as an employee of the NKVD and had participated in the Stalinist repression of ethnic Germans in the Odessa region. Strizhak's passport said that he was an ethnic Ukrainian, Brizhitsky claimed, but a next-door neighbor confirmed that "his own sister is a yid."[3] In the same report, Brizhitsky went on to detail the more complicated case of a husband, wife, and son, the Zagalsky family:

KLEIMAN and ZAGALSKY—58 Uspenskaya Street (entry via the courtyard). Director of School No. 8, Aleksey Ivanovich Zagalsky, is hiding the fact that his wife, Klavdiya Isaakovna Kleiman, is a Jew. And that her son by her first husband, by the name of Vadim Kleiman, eighteen years old, is also a Jew. And that Zagal-

sky adopted him and gave him his surname and makes out that
he is Ukrainian. Klavdiya Isaakovna Kleiman, with the help of the
yid-run Soviet *militsiia* [police], managed to get a passport in the
surname of her husband, Zagalsky, and in that passport she makes
out that she is not a Jew but a Ukrainian. A teacher at School No.
68, Adolf Poze, enabled all these machinations. This information
is given by Stasenko, a teacher at School No. 92.[4]

Odessans were naturally accustomed to hiding from the view
of the state. Smugglers, *goniffs*, and underground political groups
had perfected the art of avoidance. But in 1941 the idea of shining light on the vast underworld—now thought to be populated
by Bolsheviks and secret Jews—took on a deadly cast. Sometimes
people could be hiding in plain sight. Agent No. 61 reported that a
man who was working as a driver at a local factory by the name of
Shvidkoy was in fact the same Shvidkoy who had previously been
a well-known Communist, a member of the leadership of the factory's party organization, and "a fairly evil-doing kind of person,
always doing things on the sly." Plus, the agent continued, citing
the testimony of a Mr. Kritsky, "despite his Russian name and surname, [Shvidkoy] is a yid."[5]

Denunciations were not always directed at specific individuals,
although that is the information the Romanian authorities found
most useful. A receiving officer in the military headquarters would
sometimes make handwritten notations on denunciation reports,
requesting that the writer be more specific about who said what
and provide accurate addresses of both denouncer and denounced.
It took time to train people to do their job effectively. Still, some
Odessans continued to report any trivial fact or pet theory they
thought might be of use to the authorities. "I would like to bring
to your attention," wrote one Valery Tkachenko, "that in the basement of 13 Tiraspol Street a group of yids get together and discuss
political issues, and they say that the Romanians and the Germans

are drinking our blood by the glassful but that we will drink theirs by the bucketful. And that America is helping us."[6]

Others denounced people who were not harboring Jews but rather harboring their old clothes, safeguarding the personal effects of those who had been sent away. Still others reported that a neighbor had benefited unduly from items left behind when Jews were rounded up by the Romanians—that is, complaining that the person was not sharing the spoils with other residents in the apartment building. Amateur analysts gave their own interpretation of goings on around them, working as informal detectives rather than as simple informants. The mysterious paper found in one apartment might be the residue of an underground printing press, surmised one local woman. The portraits of Hitler, Antonescu, and Romania's King Mihai that had begun to appear in local bazaars were very poorly done and needed to be policed, said another. One neighbor reported that an acquaintance was usually hanging out with bad elements and probably up to no good. "At the same time his apartment is the meeting place of hidden terrorist-Communists. And besides that, his wife is a yid and is entirely surrounded by yids."[7] Another person gave a checklist by which authorities could smoke out Jews still hiding in the city. "Identification and inspection of the Jew may be made in the following way," wrote "An Observer":

1. the face and appearance of a Jew
2. a corrupted way of speaking
3. the official documents he possesses (and also those of his relatives)
4. the genital organs (for men)[8]

Romanian propagandists sought to market the occupation by portraying it as liberation, the final curtain on more than twenty years of Bolshevik terror. But the erstwhile liberators reinforced the basic habits and pathologies of the Soviet system. The paranoia, the self-serving indictments, and the mania for unmasking, exposing, and rooting out potential enemies of the state were ways of behaving to which the city had become accustomed already in the 1920s and 1930s. The format of the denunciation letters and the complaints they contained were often near copies of those used during the earlier Stalin period, from the standard Russian opening line—"*Dovozhu do Vashego svedeniya nizhesleduyushchee*," or "I would like to bring to your attention the following"—to rote-sounding endings that attested to the letter writer's good faith and honesty. Where the occupying power sought clear and actionable intelligence, Odessans were sometimes simply enacting a well-drilled script—one that had a great deal to do with the practiced art of surviving under an oppressive regime.

Lack of political loyalty, employment in an administrative post in the previous illegitimate regime, abuse of power by government officials, or exhibition of a sexual peccadillo or other immoral behavior could all be grounds for denunciation, under both the Soviets and the Romanians. The temptation to inform on one's neighbors and take over their living space—especially in overcrowded apartment buildings in the desirable city center—was also a direct inheritance from the Soviet system.[9] The difference now was the clear equation between being an enemy and being a Jew, a union that few Odessans seemed to have difficulty accepting. The city had been fed a steady diet of conspiracy theories and antisemitic propaganda for decades—from the supposed threat posed by Jewish self-defense organizations in the early 1900s to the more recent efforts of German and Romanian hearts-and-minds campaigns to portray the Soviets as an arm of world Jewry. Older cleavages between Jews and their neighbors now became canyons that only the most heroic Odessans were able to bridge. "They consider the Jews a very perfidious, wily, and unforgiving nation," reported an agent, "and one that is still capable of a whole range of dirty tricks."[10]

The personal testimonies of survivors corroborate the stories told in the official documents. David Senyaver was born in the town of Balta, to the north of Odessa, where his family worked as fishmongers. When their house and business were requisitioned by the Soviets in the early 1930s, the family moved into a small shed, paying the price for having been denounced as bourgeois-class enemies. During the Ukrainian famine of the early 1930s, they decamped to the city, but life was equally hard there, since the family bore an undesirable and potentially deadly class label.

Senyaver was fifteen when Romania took control of Odessa, and he remembered distinctly the crowds that gathered when Jews were told to assemble in the Privoz marketplace near the city center. "The local population, especially the Ukrainians," he recalled, "were eager to help the Germans and Romanians hunt down their victims, children and youths, hiding in cellars." When he was expelled from the city in early 1942, destined for the camp at Domanevka, gangs of locals hurled rocks and called out, "You crucified Jesus Christ." But in his testimony, Senyaver wanted to be clear on a particular point: a local villager, whose Slavic name he recalled decades later, had taken him in after his deportation. It was the Odessans, not the Ukrainian peasants in the countryside, whom he remembered shouting and throwing stones.[11] An urban population practiced in unmasking class traitors, exposing the wreckers of socialism, and rooting out enemies of the people easily transferred those techniques to uncovering secret Jews.

Jews did manage to survive in Odessa throughout the war, but they were few. Some hid in plain sight by obtaining or forging official documents that certified their status as Karaim, the ethnically distinct pre-Talmudic Jews who were generally left alone by the authorities. Others passed as Ukrainians, Armenians, or members of other ethnic groups, especially if they were able to move to a part of the city where neighbors were unlikely to know their true identity. Careful planning and raw chance mattered in equal measure. Lyudmila Kalika, a teenage girl, survived with her family through a combination of luck and neighborly piety. When the war broke out, they were living in a communal apartment—common in the early Soviet period—and shared their space with another family.

That fact turned out to be a blessing. When the Kalikas decided to go into hiding rather than report to the ghetto, the other family simply expanded into the unused space, rather than have it expropriated by the building superintendent or the occupation authorities. The Kalikas' flatmates were Jews who had managed to acquire papers that identified them, falsely, as Karaim. The apartment, located on the ground floor, had a cellar big enough to hold several people, and the small space became the Kalikas' refuge as Jews were being shot or forced out of town. Another neighbor, a Ukrainian woman, provided food and water to the hidden Jews and assisted the putative "Karaim" in keeping control of the communal apartment. She convinced any nosy residents that the Kalika family was either deported or dead. This swirl of circumstance allowed Lyudmila and four other Jews to remain hidden in the cellar for 820 days, until the city was retaken by the Red Army.[12]

There was a marked falloff in denunciations after early 1942. Most Jews had been identified and shipped out of the city. Most of the lethal, Soviet-funded partisan brigades had been scotched, their hiding places in the catacombs discovered and sealed. Agents and informants were still active, but their tasks now included delivering newspapers and posting propaganda fliers, not systematically reporting on their neighbors. People who remained in the city were learning how to get on with their daily lives.

Odessans were in no sense ignorant of what was happening in the camps and ghettos to the north. They had seen Jews hanged and shot en masse. Later, stories circulated in the bazaars about Jews being killed throughout Transnistria. Some people even worried about what would happen in the future if troops were not around to protect the city from Jewish avengers. "When you take off, the yids will be able to hurt us," women were reported yelling at Romanian soldiers. "Why haven't you made the yids kaput?"[13] Another agent wrote in the spring of 1942 that a few Jews had escaped back to Odessa and were spreading rumors about people being machine-gunned in a ravine at a place called Berezovka. We now know those rumors to have been true. The escapees were reporting one of the worst massacres to have taken place under Romania's watch, the killing of about twenty-eight thousand Odessa Jews by SS units recruited from among the *Volksdeutsche*.[14] But with Jews no longer being hanged in the streets or crowding the squares before deportation to the countryside, it was easy for Russians and Ukrainians to pretend that news of further horrors could be easily ignored.

ODESSA'S HOLOCAUST MEMORIAL lies on a busy street near the green warren of Moldavanka. An alley of newly planted trees leads to a central fountain. At the top stands a tiny but haunting work by the sculptor Zurab Tsereteli, a cluster of naked men and women huddling before a small staircase, all surrounded by a jumble of barbed wire. The fountain doesn't work, the pavement is cracked and broken, and the trees want watering. An inscription inaccurately reminds visitors of the crimes committed by the "Nazis," not by Romanians or local Odessans. The small park in which it sits is littered with plastic bottles and overflowing trash bins.

Yet the truly striking thing about the memorial is that most of it is a monument to people identified as Odessa's ninety righteous, the men and women, mainly Ukrainians, who risked their own lives to save Jews. Each tree is labeled with a name of one of the heroes. It is all a singularly manufactured way of thinking about the city's wartime experience, for the more somber truth is that an entire forest of Odessans behaved differently: cooperating with the Romanian authorities, eagerly denouncing Jews, or silently going about their lives as if unaware of where one in three of their neighbors had gone.

The heroes were there, certainly, but they are hard to spot among the betrayers and the whisperers, those whose formal letters and urgent notes peek out from archival files. One way to understand the vast number of Odessans not memorialized in the alley of the righteous is to come at the matter obliquely, through a person who spent longer in the city than Pushkin or many of the other famous figures now assumed into the pantheon of honorary Odessans: the Romanian mayor Gherman Pântea.

Whey-faced and stocky, with a thick head of hair that went from pompadour to mane in his old age, Pântea was one of the most qualified administrators the Romanian government could have placed in Transnistria. He was a product of the borderland, born in May of 1894 to a Romanian-speaking family in northern Bessarabia, a time when the region was still, as it had been for nearly a century, part of the Russian Empire. He served in the imperial army, but like many of his Bessarabian comrades he converted to the cause of Romanian nationalism during the breakdown of military discipline and the collapse of the eastern front in 1917.

He was elected as a military representative to the local parliament that formed when the Russian Empire disappeared and then worked as a minister in Bessarabia's briefly independent government. He was part of the group that opted in 1918 for union with Romania, just as the Bolsheviks were preparing to descend on Kishinev, the Bessarabian provincial seat. Once absorbed into the Romanian kingdom, Pântea served three terms as Kishinev's mayor. As the son of poor Bessarabian villagers but educated as a lawyer in the tsarist system, he was bilingual in Romanian and Russian. He even knew something of Ukraine, since he had studied briefly at Ilya Mechnikov's old institution, the university in Odessa. When the Soviet army invaded Bessarabia in the summer of 1940, Pântea joined the masses of Romanian soldiers and officials retreating westward.[15]

Although he did not know Ion Antonescu personally, the Romanian leader called him to a meeting at the train station in Kishinev in August of 1941. He was informed of Antonescu's intention to name him mayor of Odessa once the city was captured by German and Romanian troops. His considerable experience in Bessarabia would have made him a reasonable choice; perhaps liberal politicians in Bucharest—those already concerned about Antonescu's harsh policies at home—pushed him forward in hopes of softening the regime's behavior in the occupied territories. In any case, when the city finally fell, Pântea was duly named to the mayoral post, arriving in Odessa on October 18, less than a week before the fateful bombing at the military headquarters.

Pântea was a direct witness to the "reprisals" carried out against Jews in the days following the attack. He wrote a personal letter to Antonescu—avoiding Alexianu and jumping up the chain of command—in which he recalled coming back from the recovery effort at the ruined building near Alexandrovsky Park to find people hanged along the major streets and intersections. He learned that the military command had ordered Jews to assemble for deportation to Dalnik, the place where many were eventually shot or burned alive. "If you were informed precisely about the situation, in particular that the population had no involvement in the act of October 22, . . . you would revoke the order for reprisals, and innocent people would not be punished," he wrote. Pântea even requested that Antonescu name someone else as mayor since his power was dwarfed by that of the local military authorities. He stopped short of resigning, however.[16]

For all his objections, Pântea nevertheless attended the crucial meeting that determined the fate of Odessa's remaining Jewish population. Through Ordinance No. 34 in January of 1942, Alexianu had ordered the creation of a special "commission for selection and evacuation" to supervise the cleansing of the capital city. On January 6 the first session of the commission met, chaired by Colonel Matei Velcescu, the police prefect for the Odessa region. At that session the members decided the manner in which

Alexianu's order would be effected, including the systematic emptying of the ghetto in Slobodka. Although the people charged with
doing the work on the ground were local police and gendarme
units, Pântea had been present at the creation of what amounted
to the final solution of the city's Jewish problem. He attended no
more sessions of the "selection and evacuation" committee and
named one of his deputy mayors as a stand-in. He remained in post
as mayor until briefly handing control of the city to German forces
in the spring of 1944.[17]

Pântea's authority was severely circumscribed by the overweening power of Alexianu as well as by that of the Romanian military
command, which had final say over local affairs. But within the areas
under his control and within the bounds of a wartime economy,
the city seemed to be on its way back. Public works were restarted,
including the provision of water and electricity. Restaurants and
markets reopened. For the first time in two decades, individual vendors were allowed to sell produce and manufactured goods in private
shops and stalls. Cinemas offered films prohibited under the Soviets, and their upkeep became a particular concern to the occupation
authorities.[18] Movies had the huge potential for keeping the local
population happy and entertained, and Romanian propaganda films
regularly highlighted the progress of the war and the depravities of
Stalin—the latter, at least, a point about which many citizens did not
need to be convinced.

Corruption was rampant in the newly energized economy, but
then the city had hardly been a paragon of economic virtue under
the Soviets. Citizens learned to respond with the dark and corny
humor for which Odessa was already famous. In the open-air markets, sellers taunted strolling Romanian soldiers and bureaucrats
with creative wordplay. The standard Romanian greeting "*Bună
dimineața*"—"Good morning"—became the Russian "*Budem'te
meniat'sia*"—"Let's make a deal!"[19]

Even if the final status of Transnistria after an Axis victory was still uncertain, the Romanians were committed to managing affairs in ways that would appeal to local Russians, Ukrainians, and Germans. The major city streets were rechristened in forms consonant with the new order. Karl Marx Street became, a bit too obviously, Hitler Avenue. Jewish Street was renamed for Mussolini. One of the city's great landmarks since the 1870s, the Opera, had been severely damaged during the siege. The roof was caved in, every window smashed, and heating and water systems broken. Already by the end of 1941, the city government had arranged for the windows to be replaced. Soon the theater's magnificent organ, long dysfunctional under the Soviets, was in working order (a project overseen by the same deputy mayor who spent the rest of his time attending meetings on the liquidation of the ghetto). During the 1942–43 season, Odessans walked into a fully reoutfitted building, freshly plastered and painted, with the chance to buy tickets for one of fifty-eight separate productions, from *La Bohème* to *Eugene Onegin*. The city administration made no effort to "romanianize" the musical repertoire. Three-quarters of the productions were the standard European classics, while a quarter were Russian works.[20]

"Pântea was a popular man in Odessa," recalled one local actress in the late 1950s, "and even today the population remembers him fondly."[21] A constant stream of Romanians journeyed from the kingdom to see for themselves the new experiment in neighborly imperialism. Students and professors from Bucharest University, representatives from the Romanian Association of Teachers, delegations from Romanian villages, and choirs, dance groups, and journalists all visited the city at the expense of the government. The Lawn Tennis Section of the Sports Association of Romanian Railways organized a two-day match with guest invitees. Even a prize-winning group of Bucharest schoolchildren, selected as the Romanian capital's most promising pupils, were rewarded with a tour around the province they would presumably one day rule.

Ion Antonescu visited on three occasions—once in 1942 and twice in 1943—to see the wonders being wrought on the eastern frontier.[22] The flow of visitors became so great that lower-level functionaries called for the creation of special *cantine turistice*—tourist hostels—to accommodate the missions of artists, musicians, educators, students, and dignitaries coming weekly from the motherland.[23] Overall the city exuded freshness and vitality, a place "full of young people," as one visitor recalled, a marked contrast to the empty streets and squares in other parts of occupied eastern Europe.[24]

Pântea had nevertheless been perfectly aware of, and deeply troubled by, the events of the first year of the occupation. When the systematic removal of Jews from Odessa began, he wrote to Alexianu protesting the move. "I have reported to you verbally and in writing," he said, "that this evacuation is wrong and inhuman, and since it is taking place in the depths of winter, it has become truly barbaric." Repeating the argument he had made earlier to Antonescu, he complained that the governor's advisors had mistakenly convinced him that Jews represented a security threat in the city. Pântea insisted that they were in fact working hard to rebuild it. But with the transport trains and columns of marching Jewish Odessans already on the way, Pântea wrote that he now wished to make "the last attempt to save as much as may be saved." He asked specifically for Jewish craftsmen and teachers to be exempted from deportation, along with the roughly one thousand Karaim still living in the city. No sizable effort was made to sort out the first two categories, although the Karaim, as in the past, were generally passed over as not "racially" Jewish (a view developed by Nazi race theorists and adopted by the Romanians).[25]

But because of his protests against Romania's Jewish policy, the mayor remained deeply suspect in the eyes of Alexianu and his other superiors, all the way to Bucharest. He was surrounded by Bessarabian Romanians, who—as people of the frontier and bilingual in Romanian and Russian—had always been considered by officials from the old kingdom as being of dubious loyalty and imperfectly versed in the ideals of Romanian nationalism. (As early as 1939, the

Romanian ministry of defense was gathering intelligence reports assessing whether Bessarabians were likely to fraternize with Soviets rather than fight them.)[26] Pântea used Russian as the working language of the mayor's office and communicated decrees and other bureaucratic acts to Odessa's population primarily in that language. This, again, raised suspicions about his nationalist credentials, even while certainly easing the task of city administration.

Yes, most of the functionaries in the mayor's office were former Communists, he wrote to Alexianu, but that was to be expected in a city that had been under Soviet control for two decades. Moreover, the entire idea of Communist agents sneaking around in the city was largely a fiction. "It is not true that the local population is agitating [against Romania]," he wrote. "On the contrary locals have gotten down to business, going to work in all senses, and participating effectively in the rebuilding of Odessa. Fabrications about the 'agitation' of the population are circulated by various secret organs of the State, which have full interest in stirring up things in order to justify their existence and their expenditures. That is why these organs speak of the Communist threat to Odessa, of plots, of the catacombs' being full of Communists, Jews, and so on."[27] Both the eager denunciations by locals and the equally eager receptivity on the part of Romanian security services, he suggested, were more a matter of self-interest than real threat. The former sought to ingratiate themselves with the new power. The latter hoped to convince their higher-ups that they were doing their job. As even the city's mayor knew, Odessans and their occupiers were locked in a mutual, and at times mutually beneficial, embrace.

———————

WE KNOW THE DETAILS of the careers of Alexianu and Pântea because both were put on trial after the war. Shortly after Romanian forces pulled out of Odessa, leaving the city and the wider Transnistria region notionally in the hands of the Germans, Romania itself switched sides. With the Soviets pushing ever westward and the Axis war effort crumbling, in August of 1944 the Romanian king, Mihai, overthrew Ion Antonescu and declared Romania's accession to the Allies—just in time to stave off an all-out fight against the Red Army, now pursuing its own version of blitzkrieg. At the end of the war, the Soviets gradually installed a Communist government in Romania, which cemented its position by forcing Mihai to surrender the throne and leave the country at the end of 1947. One of the new government's first tasks was to prosecute—or in many cases re-prosecute—the leaders of the old regime.

Alexianu was one of four defendants found guilty of war crimes, sentenced to death, and executed by the Communists. The others—the powerful vice chairman of the Council of Ministers, Mihai Antonescu; the brutal deputy interior minister, Constantin Vasiliu; and the *conducător* himself, Ion Antonescu—had been visible public figures, working in the central government in Bucharest and tacking back and forth between their own profound antisemitism, the exigencies of war, and the demands of their patron, Nazi Germany. Their hatred of Jews tended to be of the conservative kind found among traditional right-wing parties throughout central Europe, not necessarily the rabid, revolutionary variety preached by Nazi propagandists. It was activated into a political program by the experience of being an occupying power and by the infectious zeal of the SS, German liaison officers, and Hitler himself. However, what emerged in the trials was that of all the senior officials, the relatively obscure Alexianu, diligently issuing decrees from halls that had once hosted Lise Vorontsova's famous soirees, was perhaps the truest of the true believers.

Alexianu denied having any role in the massacres of late 1941, attributing those to excesses by the secret police and the gendarmerie. But he stood by his efforts to administer Transnistria in ways beneficial to the Romanian state, especially by shipping as much of its wealth as possible to the motherland and, where necessary, removing Jewish populations he believed presented a threat to public order.[28] Unlike many at the top of the administrative hierarchy, he seems not to have benefited personally from his role in the war. Investigators found him living in a modest apartment in Bucharest, with no major property holdings elsewhere in the country, no transfers of funds to foreign banks, and no hidden accounts in which he could have stashed the loot taken from the Jews who were deported and killed during his nearly three-year reign.

Most of his remorseless testimony was taken up with defending his husbandry of the provincial economy—the very issue that had meant the end of his career: Antonescu had sacked him from the governorship in January of 1944, shortly before the entire Transnistrian adventure came to an end, for being a bad manager.[29] Even as he faced death, he was still defending the nobility of the national cause, a scene captured by a newsreel camera at the time. Standing before their joint firing squad, Vasiliu and Mihai Antonescu fidgeted, while Ion Antonescu raised his homburg in a theatrical salute to his fellow soldiers and executioners. Alexianu, thin and clean shaven, stood glum and ramrod straight.

Pântea's fate was different. Already in 1945, he was discovered hiding under an assumed name in Romania and was put on trial for allegedly selling gravestones from one of Odessa's Jewish cemeteries. He was acquitted and freed the next year, but went into hiding again with the advent of the new Communist government. He passed from one friend to another, carrying false identity papers and a signed copy of his letter to Antonescu protesting the "reprisals," a talisman of sorts against the gathering storm.

Most nights he slept at the Gara de Nord train station in Bucharest to avoid detection. He was arrested again in 1949, retried, found guilty of war crimes and crimes against humanity, and sentenced to ten years' hard labor. It was a sign of the times that his chief transgression was now classed as "causing the deaths of thousands of workers," not killing Jews or looting graves.[30] Even though he was eventually released from prison, as late as the 1960s he was still being tailed by the Securitate, the Communist-era secret police, for hanging out with "anti-socialist" elements.[31]

Pântea might have resigned his post as mayor. He might have done more than send his deputy to those unpleasant meetings on the deportations. He could have prevented Jews from being killed by simply notarizing their certificates of baptism as Christians, a last-ditch escape route that many attempted as the ghetto was being emptied.[32] He might have done much more than send a few letters of protest. "I am no defender of Jews," he declared flatly to Antonescu as bodies were still hanging from makeshift gallows.[33] But for all these reasons, Pântea was uniquely representative of the city that he oversaw as mayor. Beyond the actions of the most abhorrent architects of the Holocaust, Pântea's behavior was, in the end, close to that of many Odessans through war, occupation, and atrocity—born of a steely willingness to disregard what was happening right before his eyes.

Other parts of Ukraine suffered more in sheer numerical terms. In some regions, more than 90 percent of prewar Jewish populations were wiped out. An estimated 40 percent of Jewish citizens perished during the war years in the Odessa region, with the figure surely higher for those killed inside the city itself.[34] In Transnistria as a whole, perhaps 50,000 of the 300,000 local Jews remained alive once the region came again under Soviet control.[35] Individuals survived by falsifying their identity, relying on the kindness and propriety of a villager or neighbor, or living silently and fearfully inside cellars and attics. In time, some even returned to their old homes, where they were joined by evacuees returning from refuge in Central Asia or other parts of the Soviet Union. But communities were now gone. In November of 1944, after the Red Army had been in charge of Odessa for several months, Soviet officials counted forty-eight Jews living there.[36]

PART III

Nostalgia and Remembrance

CHAPTER 11

Hero City

Memory and myth: Movie poster advertising the 1943 film *Two Warriors* starring Mark Bernes (left). *Russian State Library/Abamedia.*

A Romanian secret agent reported in the winter of 1941–42 that Odessans in the Privoz marketplace regularly speculated about their city's return to greatness. With the Soviets out of power, one man allegedly proclaimed, "Odessa will once again be a free port and will return to the golden age of Count Vorontsov and the duc de Richelieu under the patronage of His Highness King Mihai of Romania and His Excellency the Supreme Leader of the German Empire Adolf Hitler."[1]

Few people at the time were that mawkish or self-servingly deferential to the occupiers, but the general sentiment was not uncommon. With enough optimism and bravado, Odessans could imagine a future in which their city might be put back on the track it had left at some point in the nineteenth century. Nostalgia was not just a way of longing for the past. It was also a method of conjuring a distant but radiant future. Anyone who was paying attention knew that these were temporary fantasies, however. One cooperated with the occupiers when it made sense and found ways to avoid them when it didn't. Ducking and weaving were Odessan habits, and the war years only sharpened old skills: skirting customs agents, buying off the police, studiously ignoring the entreaties of government officials, and generally bending to avoid breaking. Survival was a special kind of flourishing.

Odessa was not quite a blank slate at the end of the Second World War, but it was something close: a city denuded of a major ethnic and religious community and with much of the rest of its population hunkering in cellars or dispersed to outlying towns and villages. The city was still reeling from artillery hits, aerial bombing, partisan raids, and the ravaging of its Jewish core. Odessan evacuees could be found throughout the Soviet Union, some as far away as Uzbekistan. Barely 200,000 people remained in the city, perhaps a third of its prewar population. The buildings and infrastructure had been looted by the retreating Axis armies. The costumes and seats from the opera house were gone. The docklands and grain elevators were smoldering ruins. Even the trolley cars were now doing service in Romania.[2]

Crime, which the Romanians had sought to control but never rooted out, returned in force. Former partisans became bandits, visiting on the restored Soviet authorities the same kind of raids they had inflicted on the Romanians. Theft and robbery were common, and the boldest of the criminals left messages to the Communist authorities scrawled on city walls. "The day is yours before seven o'clock," declared one graffito, "but we own the night."[3] Petty violence ran parallel to the state's reckoning with those who had aided and benefitted from the occupation. Alleged collaborators were identified by Soviet archivists and apparatchiks who pored over the careful records kept by the Romanian authorities. Those without the good sense to have left with the fleeing Romanians were arrested, imprisoned, or shot. Even having lived in Odessa during the war was cause for suspicion, on the assumption that survival entailed some sort of compromise with the fascists. A new but short-lived wave of denunciations swept over the city, with neighbors fingering people who had supposedly worked for or sympathized with the "Romano-German barbarians," as the language of the time cast the ousted occupiers.

At the same time, Soviet officials worked to uncover the fate of those who had fallen victim during the war. In a massive effort at documenting human and material losses, an "extraordinary state commission," working throughout much of the formerly occupied territory of the Soviet Union, assembled data on victims. Based on sworn oral affidavits, the commission's reports were often rendered in striking detail. The lists of killed and deported still provide some of the most fine-grained assessments of the war's toll, particularly on Odessa's Jews. From these postwar assessments, for example, we know that sixteen people were removed from 74–76 Pushkin Street at some point during the war, including members of families identified as the Leidermans, Likermans, Kotliars, Shvartsmans, Kogans, Figelmans, Ashkenazis, and Katzes, among others. At 9 Shchepnoy Lane, twenty-three people—from sixty-five-year-old Chaim Tsyperman to nine-year-old Lusya Kravets—were "sent away by the fascists," in the language of the affidavits.[4]

No doubt some of the people who gave testimony to the commission were those who had enabled the deportation of the Jews in the first place. The same mix of motives that underlay the wartime denunciations were probably at work in the postwar accounting of victimhood. Goodness, neighborliness, and regret were present, but so too was rational self-interest. An official document certifying the displacement of residents from a precise address could also serve as a certification of abandonment, a key bureaucratic tool for neighbors seeking additional living space. There was a surfeit of housing in Odessa immediately after the war, given the relatively small population during the occupation period. But in the rush for housing after 1945—as both Jewish and non-Jewish evacuees returned home—empty properties were at a premium.

Sura Sturmak had been deported to the camp at Domanevka during the war. She ended up confined to an old farm where Jews were made to live in a repurposed pig shed. Her sisters, brother, and mother were killed; her husband, a Red Army soldier, was missing in action. When she returned to Odessa after the war, she found the family apartment occupied by ethnic Russians. But by assembling affidavits and other legal documents, she secured a court order that pitched out the squatters and restored the space to its former inhabitant.[5] For Jewish survivors, being on the lists of those "sent away" was a critical official validation of their claim to former property, now occupied by acquisitive neighbors. The commission affidavits, drawn up on old scraps of paper and pages torn from printed books, are a telling archival bookend to the denunciation reports of a few years earlier. In 1941 to be listed as a Jew, with a precise address and with all one's family members named and accounted for, was the first step toward deportation and perhaps death. For the survivors after 1945, not being on a similar list meant effectively losing one's apartment and residency status. In both cases, a bureaucrat's scrawl meant the difference between being a real Odessan and an illegitimate one.

Jews would never again be a sizable ethnic group in the city. By the time of the 1959 Soviet census, they accounted for only 12 percent of the population in the Odessa region, which included the city itself and several small towns—an increase from the wartime era, to be sure, but only a fraction of the prewar figure. That percentage declined steadily as Jews migrated to other parts of the Soviet Union or left to build new lives abroad, and as ethnic Ukrainians and Russians took their place in the city center and the industrial suburbs. But just as local Odessans had worried about what would happen if the Romanian occupiers left and Jews were allowed to exact "revenge," Soviet officials sought to limit the effects of Jewish return on the postwar city.

Official antisemitism, in both subtle and overt varieties, was a common feature of postwar life, in the Soviet Union and other newly Communist states in eastern Europe. A group that had been viewed as crypto-Communists by the Romanians was now seen as unreliable, rootlessly cosmopolitan, and—especially after the establishment of the State of Israel in 1948—crypto-nationalists. Jewish religiosity was a particular target. Immediately after the war, the Soviets launched a campaign to "liquidate the minyans"—the groups of ten men required for ritual prayer—that had emerged spontaneously after the withdrawal of Romanian and German troops. By the early 1950s, even synagogues that had been allowed to reopen after the war were once again closed, part of a spiraling frenzy of antisemitism throughout the Soviet Union shortly before Stalin's death. In an attempt to separate Jewish religious practice from Jewish national aspirations, the ritual phrase "Next year in Jerusalem" was ordered removed from prayers recited on Yom Kippur and Passover.[6]

Antisemitism in Odessa long predated the arrival of the Axis powers, and it was still there when the city came back into the Soviet fold. "The vermin have returned," Saul Borovoi heard Odessans saying about the arrival of evacuated Jews after the war.[7] The writer Emil Draitser came back to the city with his parents after the war and lived there throughout the postwar reconstruction. "All Jews are cowards," he recalled his schoolmates jeering. "During the war, they hid in Tashkent."[8] For some Jews, part of the cruel taunt was true, and providentially so. The ships that left the packed quayside in the autumn of 1941 carried tens of thousands of Jewish Odessans toward safety in other parts of the Soviet Union, the beginning of what would become, throughout the rest of the twentieth century, a mass exodus of Jews to other Russian and Ukrainian cities as well as to Israel, the United States, and other foreign countries. Between 1968 and 1980 alone, more than twenty-four thousand Odessan Jews—a little under a quarter of the Jewish population—left the Soviet Union for good. More followed during the Gorbachev era and after.[9]

The end of Jewish Odessa produced an Odessan diaspora that gave the city a new kind of life well beyond the harbor and Deribasovskaya. In time, Odessa became revered as the Soviet Union's imaginary Mississippi Delta, a remarkable incubator for music and dreamy nostalgia, yet also a place whose creative power really became evident once people managed to escape it. The city already had its Mark Twain in Isaac Babel, a writer who grasped the distinctive speech, social mores, and colorful characters of an age whose passing few people actually regretted. What it lacked was its Robert Johnson or Muddy Waters—the musicians who provided the soundtrack for a lost world. After the Second World War, Soviet officialdom and popular culture managed to do something that Babel, shot by his Stalinist captors nearly two years before the Romanians had marched into his hometown, could not have foreseen: to transform the old city into an object of schmaltzy and melodic longing.

———

WHEN SERGEI EISENSTEIN sat down to compile his fragmentary and poetic memoirs, he wondered somberly about the fate of the hundreds of extras in *Battleship Potemkin*, the men and women he had sent racing up and down the Odessa steps with a few shouts through his megaphone. He could remember many of them, since he had always made a point of learning the names of as many people on set as possible. But the identity of the film's most famous actor—the baby in the carriage that bounces down the bloody staircase—remained a mystery. "He would be twenty now," Eisenstein wrote in 1946.

> Where is he—or she? I do not know whether it was a boy or a girl.
> What is he doing?
> Did he defend Odessa, as a young man?
> Or was she driven abroad into slavery?
> Does he now rejoice that Odessa is a liberated and resurrected town?
> Or is he lying in a mass grave, somewhere far away?[10]

Any of those fates would have been possible, but the city had had enough of villains and victims. By the time the Red Army goose-stepped down Richelieu Street, with smiling faces and submachine guns strapped across worn tunics, a pantheon of heroes was already emerging in popular lore and Communist Party history-writing. There were NKVD agents such as the famed Molodtsov-Badayev gang who launched daring strikes from their hideouts in the catacombs during the defense of Odessa. The almond-eyed sniper Lyudmila Pavlichenko chalked up more recorded kills than any other Soviet soldier. The boy-patriot Yakov Gordiyenko, a graduate of the school the Bolsheviks had built out of marble quarried from the defunct Preobrazhensky Cathedral, ferried secret messages to the Communist underground before being shot by the fascists in 1942.

None of these stories was exactly untrue. Partisan units, outfitted and directed by Moscow, had disrupted the early months of the Romanian occupation. But the postwar tales of sacrifice and derring-do often exalted minor figures in Odessa's wartime experience, marshaling bit players as evidence of the city's valiant, if only belatedly successful, stand against fascism and foreign domination. In the rebuilt city, commemorative plaques and statues served as public surrogates for private and more complex memories. An apartment where partisans hatched their plans and a building from which Soviet commanders directed the countersiege became everyday monuments to Odessa's misremembered heroism. These tales of sacrifice and achievement were put on display in a new Museum of the Defense of Odessa, which registered tens of thousands of visitors annually.[11]

Odessa was one of the first four Soviet cities—along with Leningrad, Sevastopol, and Stalingrad—to be awarded the title *Gorod-Geroi*, or "hero city." Leningrad held out against a withering German siege for nearly two and a half years. Sevastopol withstood nine months of heavy artillery barrages. Stalingrad was the anvil on which Germany's war on the eastern front was eventually crushed. Odessa was an oddity in that illustrious group. Most of the population spent the war safely evacuated to the east. Much of the rest found ways of cooperating, either actively or grudgingly, with the Romanians. But Odessa was the only major Soviet center held captive by an invader other than Nazi Germany, and being a martyr, however ambiguous, conferred a special kind of status.

In time the hero city came to outshine the real one. The Soviet narrative of resistance and valor signaled Odessa's passing fully into the realm of nostalgia. The myth of its experience in the Second World War was now woven into a new set of characteristics that were thought to define it: amicable multiethnicity, good beaches, faux-Mediterranean jocularity, and a zest for life that was only vaguely Jewish. As a favorite and sun-drenched locale for workers' holidays, Odessa was becoming famous again as precisely the frontier destination that Catherine had intended, an important attraction on the Soviet Union's southern coast.

The whole process of remaking Odessa had begun even before its liberation. Just as Gherman Pântea was overseeing the reconstruction of the Odessa opera house and Gheorghe Alexianu was

finding the most efficient way of squeezing a profit out of Transnistria, the Soviets were making another Odessa movie. *Two Warriors* is a forgettable piece of wartime propaganda produced by the
Tashkent Film Studios, home to filmmakers and actors evacuated
from occupied parts of the Soviet Union. The picture is the Soviet
equivalent of minor Hollywood films that were eventually eclipsed
by those with some claim to greatness, the handful of Errol Flynn
and John Wayne vehicles that added complex characters to the
standard model-navy battle sequences and patriotic sermonizing.

The film tells the story of Arkady Dzyubin and Sasha Svintsov,
the two soldiers of the title, and their adventures during the siege of
Leningrad. The comrades share the deep bond of frontline friend-
ship, the kind that allows Dzyubin to rib Svintsov to the point of
anger, but also the kind that pushes Svintsov to rush into danger—
twice—to save his friend from certain death. Dzyubin is a wingman
par excellence. When the tongue-tied Svintsov gives up on getting the girl, a charming blonde Leningrader with a winning smile,
Dzyubin steps in to ghost-write the love letters that win her heart.

Critics didn't think much of the movie when it was released in
1943. The plot is shaky at best, and the musical numbers are pasted
awkwardly into the script. But behind the front lines, Soviet movie-
goers were soon humming the signature tunes and laughing at the
antics of Dzyubin and Svintsov. It was exactly the kind of feel-good
flick that the Soviet Union required at the time, even as its western
reaches were under foreign control. According to the poet Yevgeny
Yevtushenko, these weren't just actors "but real, authentic people"
going through the same traumas and everyday triumphs of their
Soviet comrades.[12]

No one who saw the film could have missed the basic message. Svintsov is from the Ural Mountains, the end point of European Russia and the place beyond which, in the middle of the war,
millions of Soviet citizens had found refuge. Dzyubin was from
Odessa, the Soviet Union's southern paradise, which now lay

beneath the fascist boot. The two men were from different places, but they were fighting for essentially the same thing: Svintsov to hold on to what the Soviet Union had managed to retain, Dzyubin to take back what the foreign invader had wrenched away. Beyond the patriotism, at the film's core is the wish that many of the film's viewers would have shared—the simple desire to be done with war and go home. For the next half century, if Soviet citizens were asked to name someone who represented the city of Odessa, they would probably have named Arkady Dzyubin. Plenty of Russians today, nostalgic for the films their parents and grandparents knew, would do the same. And in thinking of Dzyubin, they automatically thought of the actor who created him.

Mark Bernes was perfect for the part. He had a wide and open face, with the first hints of the furrows of wisdom and middle age, a Soviet version of William Holden or Humphrey Bogart, yet with the smiling eyes and subdued humor of Spencer Tracy. But Bernes was not, nor ever claimed to be, an Odessan—at least until he played one in a film. He was born in September of 1911 in a small town near Chernigov, in north-central Ukraine, and grew up in the regional center of Kharkov. His family was probably of Jewish heritage—Bernes's fans certainly assumed it—although Bernes himself preferred to speak of his roots as being in Ukraine rather than in any particular ethnic group. His father was a junk dealer and odd-jobs man. His mother was the real power in the household and managed to keep things together in tough times. Her ambition for her son was that he should become either an accountant or a violinist, but he disappointed on both fronts. He displayed an early attraction to the limelight, and even though he had no formal theatrical training, he seemed to relish the songs and folk poems that swirled around his native region. At age fifteen he saw his first theatrical production and fell in love with the stage. He took a job plastering theater notices around town and managed to secure a place as an extra in several productions. That experience took him to Moscow, and by 1930 he had landed a position in the famed Korsh Theater.

Bernes was still relatively unknown more than a decade later when he was cast in the film role of Dzyubin. He answered an open call for auditions, and after two weeks he was called back and given news that he had earned the part. Then began what he later called a real soldier's life. To prepare for the role, he donned a regular uniform and lived on a soldier's rations. He visited hospitals to listen to the dialect of Odessans and pick up its pronunciations and tones—the "g" that sounds like an "h" or the upward glide at the ends of sentences, usually accompanied by shrugged shoulders and pursed lips. But it was only when he got a bad haircut from an inexperienced barber—"teased-up in a characteristically Odessan way," as he called it—that he felt he was finally prepared to inhabit the character.[13]

Bernes had the ability to portray youthful Soviets in exactly the way they remembered themselves: struggling to build a young country and fight off an invader, but doing so with the good humor and comradeship they embraced as part of their national character. Bernes's Odessan became a Soviet Everyman. Russians and Ukrainians found in him a jocular but courageous hero, motivated by love of country but eager for the war to end. For others, Dzyubin's Jewish identity was unspoken but evident. "We know your kind, the Odessans," an artilleryman in *Two Warriors* sneers at Dzyubin. What he really meant would have been clear to both Jewish and non-Jewish viewers. "What kind of Odessans do you mean?" Dzyubin replies, agitated and defensive. "The women and children bombed by the Germans? . . . Don't mess with Odessa. There's sorrow and blood there." More than ever before, the qualities Odessans claimed as their own—cosmopolitanism, freedom, and resilience—were appropriated by the larger country of which they were a part. The city had once been a place of escape, exile, and adventure. Now, through the alchemy of cinema and wartime displacement, every Soviet citizen could imagine himself to be just a little bit Odessan.

One of the film's musical numbers, "Dark Is the Night," is sappy and sentimental, but it struck a chord with a Soviet populace reeling from the Axis invasion, the separation of families across front lines, and the years of privation and hardship that seemed to have no clear end. The film's other hit, "Shalandy," cemented Bernes's place as a professional Odessan. The name refers to the Russian word for scows, the flat-bottomed boats used by Black Sea fishermen to haul their catch ashore. It was a lively nonsense ditty about a goodtime sailor, Kostya, and his pursuit of the fisherwoman Sonya. The song surely had the most unappealing first line in all of pop music: "The scows were full of grey mullet." But you could really swing a glass of beer to the chorus: "I can't say much about all of Odessa, / 'Cause Odessa is very great, / But in Moldavanka and Peresyp, / They adore Kostya the sailor." This was all supreme silliness, of course, but it was Odessa's silliness, and in a time of awfulness and privation, it could make a person smile or even cry—Odessa's own version of "Yankee Doodle" or "Waltzing Matilda." It is still the closest thing the city has to a national anthem.

Almost immediately upon its release, *Two Warriors* was a smash with audiences across the Soviet Union—in marked contrast to the way *Battleship Potemkin* had sunk when it opened in theaters twenty years earlier. Dzyubin became the archetypical Soviet soldier, the kind who fought unsparingly for the homeland but also pined sweetly for his beloved. The role won Bernes the Order of the Red Star from the Soviet government. Fan letters told of the film's impact on individual lives. "Thank you from a happy viewer," wrote one of his female admirers nearly two decades after the film's premiere. "When I saw *Two Warriors*, I decided that Arkady Dzyubin was the only kind of husband for me. I found my future husband when he was demobilized, some eighteen years ago. We went out for a while, then got married. Life is great, and we have two children. Overall I'm the happiest woman in the world. Way to go, Mark Bernes!"[14]

One evening after the film's initial release, Bernes appeared on stage at a cultural club in the city of Kuibyshev, on the Volga River, to talk about the role of Arkady. He reminisced about his early childhood in Ukraine but mentioned in passing that he had never set foot in Odessa.

"You're wrong!" shouted someone from the back of the hall.

"It seems someone disagrees with me," said Bernes. "But it's strange that someone should think he knows more than I do about this, since I was the one who created the role. Maybe he would like to explain what exactly he means?"

A young army officer stepped forward, trussed up in a new full-dress uniform.

"It's me!" he said imploringly. "But I'll explain a bit later."

After the evening's program had finished, the officer appeared backstage and said that he was a native Odessan. He was so excited after seeing *Two Warriors* that he had told his young wife and in-laws that he and Bernes had been childhood friends, lolling on the beach and chasing stray cats in Moldavanka. He had been able to keep up the ruse until Bernes made his unfortunate admission onstage.[15]

Bernes went on to become one of the great purveyors of music known in Russian as *shanson*—a mix of torch-song longing, the false romanticism of criminality, and minor-key Slavic melancholy. When he died in 1969, it was as if a bit of the city had passed as well. As one of his biographers claimed, he had captured the essence of Odessa itself: "a light humor; irony combined with a tender, almost sentimental soulfulness; and an openness and simplicity that were reflected in an outward sharpness of judgment."[16]

Bernes was one of several Soviet pop stars who made being Odessan into a profitable profession. Some of them were actually from the city. The Falstaffian and expansive Leonid Utesov—Jewish and Odessan by birth, and one of the fathers of Soviet jazz in the

1930s—managed to survive both Stalinism and the war. He gave concerts on the eastern front and bucked up war-weary audiences with his own versions of "Shalandy" and other hits. He went on to become a central figure in the postwar expansion of the myth of "Old Odessa" across the Soviet Union, including the legend that jazz had been originally fashioned in the crucible of Odessa's gangster haunts, klezmer bands, and sailor pubs. "Odessa has a lot to it," he wrote in his conversational and saccharine autobiography.

> But more than anything there's music.
>
> They sing from morning to night.
>
> Take the courtyard of our building, for instance.
>
> A summer morning. The gentle Odessa sun. The wind is a tonic. If you drink it, you're tasting the gifts of the earth, and they go down pretty smooth. Those gifts work their magic on you, too. Of a morning, each courtyard is a bazaar. A musical bazaar.
>
> "Meeee-loooons, meeee-loooons by the slice!" intones the heart-rending bass. . . .
>
> A hysterical tenor joins the aria. Then the baritones weave themselves into the duet.
>
> "Froooo-zeeeen iiiic-eeees!"
>
> "Knife sharpening! I fix razors!" . . .
>
> So it's no wonder that I've loved music since childhood.[17]

Utesov's orchestra—like his prose—had the power to transport audiences to a warmer, cheerier place, but one where reveling in being rough around the edges and thumbing your nose at authority were the standard. His contemporary, the writer Konstantin Paustovsky, waxed lyrical about his own childhood in the city and, through his short stories and autobiographical tales, introduced a new generation of postwar Soviets to the universe of multiethnic cheats and witty men on the make. It was if nothing at all had happened between Babel's day and the postwar era. The First World

War, Stalinism, bombardment and occupation, and the draining of Odessa's Jewishness all disappeared behind the veil of romanticized memory and selective forgetting. The hero city again became the home of likable and rebellious antiheroes.

Utesov's music and his cheeky memoirs, published in the 1960s and 1970s, were wildly popular with Soviet listeners and readers. Like those of Paustovsky, they re-created a world that no one could actually remember, but they were all the more powerful because of it. Whatever had been lost in the first half of the century could now be recalled in new, more interesting, and golden-hued forms in the second half. From the mid-1960s until the mid-1980s, at least a dozen major-release Soviet films were either set in "Old Odessa"—the era of the First World War through the 1920s—or featured a character with Odessa origins. Isaac Babel's *Odessa Tales* were republished in this period for the first time since the 1930s, as were Ilf and Petrov's novels featuring the exploits of the scheming Ostap Bender, some of which had five million copies in print by the end of the 1970s.[18]

Like the myth of the hero city itself, none of what Paustovsky wrote or Bernes and Utesov performed was completely untrue. But from the 1950s onward, it became part of a growing industry in literature, film, the popular press, and tourism: the substitution of memory and nostalgia for history and remembrance. In the age of Khrushchev and Brezhnev, you might arrive by train, bus, or ship on a subsidized holiday from your office or factory job, with accommodation in any of the resort hotels located along the Black Sea coast. You could take in the Odessa steps and the Pushkin monument at the end of Primorsky Boulevard (the renamed promenade known as Nikolaevsky Boulevard in the tsarist era), and if you were part of an official delegation, you could lay a wreath at the monument to the unknown sailor in Shevchenko Park. A bus ride could take you to an entrance to the catacombs, located in a nearby village and marked by a socialist-realist statue of underground fighters in sweaters and flat caps, submachine guns at the ready.

During the concert season, the Opera and the Philharmonic, which had taken up residence in the grand and Moorish commercial exchange, were packed with Soviet citizens being reminded that here, in the Soviet south, high culture and the beach could come together in ways that the capitalist West could never imagine. "Tourism is one of the best forms of relaxation," noted a typical Soviet brochure on the city. "Travel along tourist routes always enriches man's mind, helps him to become more deeply acquainted with the Motherland of yesterday and today, and provides a major aesthetic delight. . . . That is why from year to year in our country an army of tourists continues to expand."[19] The army could be seen each evening at sunset, ambling disheveled and sunburned up and down the slight incline of Deribasovskaya Street.

Fresh fruits and vegetables could be purchased a short distance away in the Privoz market all year long, something unheard of in other Soviet cities. Giant flea markets flourished in Moldavanka, even at times when such unofficial commerce was frowned upon by the Soviet state. But the visitor's experience in the city was a carefully managed one. Crime remained a problem. If you were a Soviet tourist, you knew that you could be mugged or stabbed even in the city center, a relative rarity in other urban areas. If you happened to stop by a local library, you would not find many books on the city's Jewish heritage, since zealous librarians would have removed most of them for fear that they were actually Zionist tracts at odds with the message of Soviet universalism.[20] The city's wavering relationship to its Jewish identity remained even after few Jews were left to argue the case.

The roots of Odessa's brand of nostalgia lay in the nineteenth century; the sense that the best of times had already passed was a feature of its artistic and cultural life already in Count Vorontsov's day. But "Odessa-Mama"—the appealing and warm mother-city that Soviet crooners and writers extolled—now became a surrogate for the knotty realities that had defined the city in the first half of the twentieth century. The Soviet version of Odessan patriotism covered a darker and more recent past: the inescapable fact that the Jewish heritage celebrated mainly in code—in countless stories, novels, plays, films, joke books, concerts, musicals, and other ribaldries—had been actively erased in the living memory of those who now sought to re-create it.

TODAY THE EPICENTER of tourist Odessa is still Deribasovskaya Street. Its hipster cafés, Ukrainian restaurants, ice cream vendors, and street artists share space with the shock troops of globalization: an Irish pub, a McDonald's, and—that universal marker of twenty-first-century cosmopolitanism—a band of Andeans with panpipes. It has been transformed from its cleaner and more restrained Soviet-era version, but even then Deribasovskaya was a destination, the place to which you repaired when you had had enough of the beach and the obligatory stops at the sites of sacred patriotic memory.

Some of the excitement and tumult of postwar tourism can still be felt just off Deribasovskaya in the City Park, a small and manicured green space shaded by some of the most beautiful and stately trees in town. The park was laid out not long after the city's founding. It anchors the vibrant street life in the old center as it has done for more than two centuries. In the warmer months, wedding parties promenade there. A brass band gives concerts in the gazebo. Young people ogle and flirt on the benches. But there are two attractions that are post-Soviet in vintage.

One is an empty chair, the other a statue of a round man seated on a small bench. Both, in their way, are monuments to the power of dreams and invention. The former recalls Ostap Bender, the fictional swindler of Ilf and Petrov's novels *The Twelve Chairs* and *The Golden Calf*, a literary character immortalized as typically Odessan: a person of Oriental cunning and larger-than-life ambitions, whose picaresque exploits involved the search for a set of dining chairs thought to contain a magnificent treasure. The latter is the jazzman Leonid Utesov, his arms outstretched toward any visitor who wants to sit down for a rest or a snapshot.

· Although both monuments were erected only after the Soviet Union collapsed, they shine from the people who have clambered over them or patted their bronze surfaces for good luck. The Bender and Utesov monuments are among the few places in Odessa—perhaps in all of Ukraine—where visitors habitually stand in polite and orderly queues, lining up to capture a picture that will link them with two of the city's most famous native sons. But in the short space between the two, between a wholly invented life and an energetically embellished one, lies the past of the real Odessa— a city that, like Utesov's klezmer-infused music, remains largely improvisational, shifting wildly between the solo and the communal and always threatening to slip out of control.

CHAPTER 12

Twilight

Odessa in Brooklyn: Russian veterans of the Second World War, many
wearing their medals, march along Coney Island Avenue in Brighton Beach,
Brooklyn, in commemoration of Soviet victory day, May 2009.
Photo by Todd Maisel/NY Daily News Archive via Getty Images.

On the Brighton Express from the Atlantic Avenue station, I
sat down beside an elderly man with a veined and bulbous
nose, a small Pekingese dog standing primly on his lap.

"Is this the train to Sheepshead Bay?" he asked in Russian—
"Shipskhit Bey"—as the brick mid-rises and small frame houses of

outer Brooklyn sped by. I told him it was and that I would let him know when we were getting close to his station.

"Ah, you speak Russian," he said. "I could see that you were a Russian." He waved his open hand in circles in front of his face. "Not like them." He crinkled his nose and flicked his wrist toward three lanky Caribbean men, in sunglasses and dreadlocks, who had been talking loudly in the seats opposite.

The man said he had emigrated from Odessa ten years ago but never really needed to learn English in his new home. He had started out just down the subway line in Brighton Beach, where it was easy to thrive in a Russian-only environment, but had moved some time ago.

When we reached his stop, he waddled slowly, dog in tow, toward the opening subway doors. He said people were more "aristocratic" in his new neighborhood. The old one now had too many people like them, he whispered, still in Russian, tilting his head toward the Caribbean men across the aisle.

One stop down the tracks, though, and Brighton Beach seemed to be full of people like him.

On the boardwalk, elderly neighbors, pink-skinned already on a hot day in spring, sat in silence on wooden benches, the men with their shirts open and legs splayed, the women with their eyes closed and faces turned to the sky. Floppy beach hats and plastic nose shades discouraged the April sun. A cool breeze swept occasionally across the flat, damp sands, blowing eastward from the towers and roller coaster humps of Coney Island. A Russian shop sign advertised "*Morozhennoye na lyuboi vkus*," rendered below in liberal and pregnant translation as "The Tasteful Ice Cream in Town."

"In Odessa you can smell Europe," Pushkin once wrote. In Brighton Beach, you can smell Odessa. It hits you as soon as you step down from the elevated train platform onto the avenue: the fishy sea air, a whiff of old cooking oil, the sweetness of overripe fruit, dark traces of motor oil and axle grease, the tang of dill and parsley, the alcoholic sting of cheap perfume, and the assertive revival of vintage sweat, all braided like a garland of garlic, silent as to source or cause. Odessa's oddities and incongruities are there too. A Starbucks sits uneasily between the Detsky Mir toy store and the Tel Aviv Fish Market. A parade of granny carts trundles beneath the overhead trains.

Tourist T-shirts now market Brighton Beach as "Little Odessa by the Sea," but that would have seemed bizarre to the neighborhood's founder. William A. Engeman knew a good deal when he saw it. A wealthy railway man and arms dealer who had profited by selling weapons to both sides during the American Civil War, Engeman arranged in 1868 for the purchase of several hundred acres of oceanfront property near the village of Gravesend in Brooklyn. The area had already begun to develop shortly after the war, when New Yorkers, seeking a respite from the grime and gloom of Manhattan, were drawn to the unspoiled beaches lying at Brooklyn's southern tip.

Engeman was slow off the mark, however. Coney Island and Manhattan Beach were already developing as major destinations. Sandwiched between the two, Engeman's project had little hope of overtaking the more established resorts. He needed a gimmick, and he ended up with several. In addition to a pier, hotels, and eventually a boardwalk, Engeman built entertainment venues: a music hall, a pavilion, a theater billed as "the handsomest seaside theatre in the world" located at the end of the quarter-mile pier, and, through his connections to Tammany Hall, a racetrack. Engeman's genius was not to compete directly with his neighboring developments, which always offered bigger headliners. His strategy was to provide affordable entertainers just glitzy enough to draw a crowd. As the destination became more and more popular, Engeman staged a public contest to name the development. The winning entry was "Brighton Beach," after the famous resort town on the southern coast of England.

By the time of Engeman's death in 1897, people were arriving in droves—but not exactly from the source that the old developer would have expected. Engeman had intended Brighton Beach to be a more family-friendly environment than its rival Coney Island: an entertainment venue open to middle-class New Yorkers but free of the riffraff that had caused other parts of coastal Brooklyn to acquire seedy reputations. For Engeman, this meant informally excluding Jews, among other undesirables. But over the next century, whenever the neighborhood looked in peril of decline, with dropping house values and a sliding population, a new wave of Jewish migrants always rescued it just in time.

Jews from the Lower East Side had already begun to make their way to Brighton Beach at the turn of the century, seeking an alternative to the cramped quarters of Delancey Street. Boarding houses and bungalows sprouted along the neighborhood's three major avenues, butting up against each other in the small but airy fifteen blocks that defined its boundaries. A greater influx of Jewish immigrants arrived following the 1903–1905 pogroms in the Russian Empire, especially those fleeing Odessa and the borderlands of Ukraine. By 1918 the old Brighton Beach Music Hall, which had featured some of the greatest performers in vaudeville, had become a theater specializing in Yiddish-language plays, the first summer Yiddish theater in the United States. The renowned Odessan actor Jacob Adler performed there, as did the tragedienne Jennie Goldstein, the leading man David Kessler, and scores of other performers, such as the twenty Jewish chorus girls who shared the stage of the old music hall, and the composer and pit conductor Joseph Rumshinsky, billed as the "Irving Berlin of the Yiddish stage."[1]

Further waves of Jewish immigration followed: one after the Holocaust, when survivors found Brighton Beach both a haven and a melting pot for Jews from across Europe, and another after the end of the Soviet Union, when Jewish and non-Jewish immigrants from Russia, Ukraine, Georgia, and other former Soviet states were able to re-create, on a smaller scale, something of the societies they had left behind. Russian replaced Yiddish on the avenues and connecting streets. New York cops were soon sitting in voluntary Russian-language classes at the local YMCA.[2]

By one estimate, about three-quarters of Brighton Beach's new immigrants came from Ukraine, mainly from Odessa and other Black Sea cities.[3] Already in the late 1970s, journalists were calling the place "Little Odessa," and like its namesake it became a font of intellectuals who looked back with mixed emotions on their hometown. Neil Simon's play *Brighton Beach Memoirs* is the most famous of the products of Engeman's old neighborhood, but the local Abraham Lincoln High School educated other makers of culture, both high and low, from Arthur Miller and Joseph Heller to Mel Brooks and Neil Diamond. "They send us their Jews from Odessa," the violinist Isaac Stern reportedly remarked about immigration and cultural exchange with the Soviets, "and we send them our Jews from Odessa"—in the form of American-trained musicians, writers, and artists with distant (even imagined) Odessan roots.[4]

Achievement and weirdness were as much a part of Brighton Beach's identity as they were of the original Odessa's. In the early twentieth century, the summer crowds that followed the newly extended train tracks to the coast found a place of mud and dust, with unpaved streets but plenty of people still pouring through Brooklyn to take in the sea air and a show. Seaside evangelists set up shop to rescue the beachgoers from themselves. The *Brooklyn Eagle* reported solemnly in the late summer of 1916 that a total of 379 people had accepted Christ and another 762,352 had heard the gospel in the last four years as a result of open-air proselytizing by a team featuring "Miss Marion Bushnell, cornetist."[5] (The low rate of return did not seem to discourage Miss Bushnell and her associates.) Even through the peaks and troughs of the neighborhood's development—the flourishing Yiddish culture of the

Pedestrians walk along a street beneath the elevated train tracks in "Little Odessa," the Brighton Beach neighborhood of Brooklyn, New York, 1994. *Stephen Ferry/Liaison/Getty Images.*

1920s, the population growth at mid-century, the urban blight and out-migration of the 1960s and 1970s, and the Russian invasion of the perestroika years and after—the mixed and colorful street life remained. Even the crack-addled eccentrics and performers who roamed Brighton Beach Avenue in the 1980s—known to some locals as the *mishe goyim*, or the "crazy gentiles"—were said to speak at least a little Yiddish.

Today Brighton Beach resembles Odessa even more than its marketers might realize. It is still a place of loud voices and too much food, where the freezing mist of a January stroll along the empty boardwalk is as much a part of city life as the crowds of beachgoers on a July afternoon. The smells of knishes, khinkali, and a dozen other combinations of meat, dough, and root vegetables waft down the avenue, just as on Deribasovskaya. But it is also a place perched between reality and memory. It is mainly a retirement neighborhood, at least in the off-season, with perhaps the largest collection of walkers and scooter chairs outside Florida. All old seaside towns live partly in twilight, always on the far side of some golden age, but on the crowded or empty boardwalk, with the lights of Coney Island flickering through the sea breeze, the shadows of Little Odessa's forebear appear in stark relief.

ODESSA, TOO, is now in many ways a twilight town, sitting uneasily inside a new country and more comfortable marketing its distant past than presenting itself as a city of the future. But over the last two centuries, Odessa managed to produce a local culture woven from uneasiness, a way of living that may hold lessons about the creative and destructive power of being in-between. Richelieu and Vorontsov saw in Odessa a plain palette on which they could realize their enlightened visions of modernity and culture. Pushkin found the scent of the exotic. Jabotinsky and Babel sought both to escape their origins and to reshape them. The likes of Alexianu worked to erase the landscape altogether, to possess a desirable city while conveniently ridding it of many of the people who happened to live there. Mark Bernes, Leonid Utesov, and countless lesser comics and musicians raised nostalgia to an art form. Frontiers are places that get reshaped, again and again, according to the ideals, both laudable and terrible, of those who seek to control them. But there is something about such places that remains steadfastly resistant to the best-laid plans for their reengineering.

Odessa is now undergoing yet another transformation. It is the most important passenger port of a relatively new country, Ukraine, which emerged from the rubble of the Soviet Union in 1991. The city's administrators are far more benign than those of earlier ages. In many ways, they embrace the city's multifarious past rather than seek to cleanse it. They have discovered, like their Soviet predecessors, that nostalgia sells. But the old impulses are still there. School textbooks, even in this quintessentially mixed city, tell a story of straight lines and definite end points, of the emergence of a distinct Ukrainian people since antiquity, its oppression by Russians and Soviets, and its glorious reemergence with its own independent country at the end of the twentieth century.

Odessa, true to form, has resisted. Russian-speakers prefer to use their own language rather than learn the official language of state, Ukrainian. Museums still portray a decidedly local vision of the past that is at odds with the more triumphal, more national, versions found in the capital. When the people of Kiev rose up against corrupt politicians and rigged elections in 2004—a peaceful change of government now termed the "Orange Revolution" (after the colored scarves and T-shirts worn by the protestors)—Odessans remained noticeably quiet. It wasn't that they didn't support the protestors—although plenty of Odessans were skeptical. It was just that they had never paid much attention to what was going on in Kiev anyway.

Yet Odessans have just as frequently chosen to trade the challenges of cosmopolitanism for the easier charms of nostalgia. They still apply as much energy to re-creating their past as they once gave to pulling their city out of the nothingness of the coastal prairie. Citizens have a natural affinity for, even an obsession with, what in Russian is called *kraevedeniye*, a combination of local history, just-so stories, and assiduous antiquarianism.

No city can best the volume of small-print-run historical guides, joke books, and memoirs on particular streets, buildings, neighborhoods, families, businesses, famous visitors, and obscure historical figures. On summer weekends along Deribasovskaya and in the dusty park that surrounds the rebuilt and renamed Spaso-Preobrazhensky Cathedral you can find local poets selling their self-published odes to the city, *kraeveds* flogging their latest collection of essays on nineteenth-century grain production or the city's first water collection system, and booksellers offering several different dictionaries of a notional "Odessan language"—Russian with a smattering of Ukrainian words, Yiddish intonation, and gangster argot. One publishing house, Optimum, has made its reputation by reprinting scores of out-of-print works such as the memoirs of de Ribas's associate, the architect Franz de Voland, and an almanac from 1894, alongside breezy reference books like *100 Great Odessans*, which includes everyone from Wassily Kandinsky and the violinist David Oistrakh (both of whom spent their childhoods there) to Pushkin, Catherine the Great, and the British spy Sidney Reilly.

Odessa gobbles up famous personages like an enthusiastic camp counselor rattling off lists of Jewish movie stars or notable athletes from Cleveland. With enough research and imagination, lots of geniuses can be discovered to have had Odessa connections of some sort. In the past twenty years, however, the state has gotten into this memory game as well, with results that are by turns ridiculous and disturbing.

Dig down deep enough into the city's past, the logic goes, and Odessa's true origins will reveal themselves. In 2005 the remains of the Vorontsov family were dug up from their suburban cemetery— where the count and countess had been relegated by the Soviets— and, after a solemn procession through the city, were reinterred in the Spaso-Preobrazhensky Cathedral. Three years later local archaeologists opened a permanent exhibit on Primorsky Boulevard above the harbor. A glass canopy covers the remains of a stone wall, a ship's anchor, the jawbone of a cow, some scattered pottery sherds and broken amphorae, and the skull of a dog. According to the accompanying sign in Ukrainian and English, these are remnants of the ancient culture that flourished there from the fifth to third centuries BCE—Greek or Roman perhaps, or Greco-Scythian, or perhaps proto-Cossack. The viewer is left to decide. But it is a whole-cloth invention: not an actual open-air dig but a mock-up of an archaeological site, an imagined and frozen scene meant to connect the present-day city with a real and non-Russian past. Being rooted, however imaginatively, still competes with the rootless cosmopolitanism that both built Odessa and helped to unmake it.

Odessa has been mainly Ukrainian in demographic terms since the late 1970s. At the time of the 1979 census, Ukrainians were on the cusp of becoming an absolute majority, at 49.97 percent of the population in the Odessa region as a whole. But until very recently, that fact said little about the feel of the city in cultural terms. Even after the Second World War, the city remained a confusing space to Soviet demographers and social engineers. By 1959 it was the most linguistically mixed place in all of Ukraine. More people considered their native language to be different from the language of their self-reported ethnic group than anywhere else in the republic. Most Jews and more than half the ethnic Ukrainians in the city spoke Russian as their everyday language. Nearly a third of ethnic Moldovans spoke Ukrainian. The smaller communities of Bulgarians, Belorussians, and others got along by using Russian, Ukrainian, or another language entirely.[6] The Soviet system was based on the faith that modernity would cause the dividing lines among peoples to fade into insignificance. But in Odessa those lines became indecipherable squiggles as the main markers of ethnicity, language, and even religion combined and overlapped in unpredictable ways.

The Jewish population has remained tiny. There were just under 70,000 Jews in the entire Odessa district in 1989, the time of the last Soviet census; most were living in the city of Odessa proper. Their share of the population—under 4 percent at the time— declined even further once Jews, as well as their neighbors, were free to emigrate after the fall of Communism. Today, no one knows exactly how many Jews make up the small community in a city of 1.2 million people; some estimates put the figure at 36,000, although that is probably too high since the last Ukranian census, in 2001, recorded only around 13,000 Jews in the entire Odessa district.[7] Still, the main synagogue, the Glavnaya, has been restored to some of its old magnificence, with a kosher restaurant in the expansive basement. There is enough of a Jewish presence—or popular memory—for travel agencies to offer tours of "Jewish Odessa," including a stop at the hypermodern Jewish community center.

Ukrainians—at least those who claim that ethnic label in censuses—are now an absolute majority, forming close to two-thirds of the total population. But with a sizable ethnic Russian minority and nearly complete agreement on Russian as the city's lingua franca, political factions have spent the past two decades waging a struggle over public memory on literally a monumental scale. A block away from the Odessa steps, the city administration removed a Soviet-era statue that commemorated the *Potemkin* mutiny. In its place went a restored statue of the city's founder, Catherine the Great, which had itself been removed by the Bolsheviks (who had substituted a huge bust of Karl Marx). Catherine's left hand now points not only toward the port but also toward the north, to Russia, which many Odessans, regardless of their ethnic provenance, still see as their cultural and spiritual home. Predictably, demonstrations—both pro and contra—accompanied the unveiling.

Elsewhere, Ukrainians were fighting a rear-guard action. Up went a statue to the poet Ivan Franko, a Ukrainian nationalist icon with tenuous connections to the city, and a memorial to Anton Holovaty, an eighteenth-century Cossack leader and, as such, a proto-Ukrainian hero. A faux-antique street sign was placed at the top of Deribasovskaya, announcing that its name would now become, officially at least, Derybasivs'ka—a ukrainianized version that few Odessans have ever been heard to utter. Since the end of the Soviet Union, the city government has reportedly removed 148 public monuments (104 of them to Lenin) and rechristened 179 streets with either their old Russian imperial names—usually spelled the Ukrainian way—or newly created ones.[8] "My nationality is Odessan!" goes a slogan often repeated in tourist brochures and local guidebooks. But in the midst of Odessa's internal struggles over community, identity, and memory, the city is still grasping awkwardly for a foundational myth that will make it something more legitimate than itself.

In the end, Odessa's past—honestly viewed and properly understood—could be an asset to both its new ruler and its older one, Ukraine and Russia. For Ukraine, Odessa could turn out to be an advantage as the young country seeks membership, down the road, in the European Union and full recognition as a geographically, culturally, and politically European state. Europe was, for a good part of the last century, the world's central battleground in serial conflicts over land, power, and identity. Today, the ideal of religious and ethnic communities managing to live together through the shock of war, scarcity, nationalism, and failed imperial ambitions, despite the siren calls of mutual loathing and convenient blame, is the European response to the reality of the recent past. Europeans now imagine themselves as humane, tolerant, and cosmopolitan precisely because their grandparents spent so much of the last century perfecting exactly the opposite values. If Ukrainians can will themselves to engage with the past in the same way—resurrecting older talents for living together while staring bravely at the horrors of the Second World War—the old vision of Odessa as an entryway to Europe may still have some life in it.

For Russia, Odessa offers a model of development that prizes the odd and the unusual, an ability to laugh at oneself, and a skepticism about grand narratives of national greatness—values that Russia, like its Soviet precursor, seems to have forsaken. During the Communist era, Odessa lost its previous position as Russia's antechamber. It became a quaint regional city, no longer the global port that it had been earlier in its imperial history. But Russia also lost one of its best hopes for defining itself as multinational, modest, and secure in its own sense of self. For a country now rediscovering its regional and even global influence—flexing its muscle as an oil and gas producer, naval power, and alternative pole to the West— Odessa stands as a reminder that the decline of the old port meant the decline of a certain way of being Russian.

Many cities balance on a thin boundary between the everyday collisions that spark real genius and the periodic explosions that leave windows smashed and communities divided. Many others, especially in eastern Europe, actively rewrite their pasts, seeking to cover up the times when the basic covenant of urban civility fell victim to the stresses of cultural difference. That Athens once had a substantial Muslim presence, Thessaloniki a Jewish plurality, and Tbilisi an Armenian core are now historical footnotes at best, understated in museums and left out of popular memory. The same purifying impulses are there in Odessa, despite its rebellious and multicultural reputation. After the Second World War, a city that had represented a hundred different ways of being Jewish or Christian or neither traded the burden of multiple lifeways for the easier virtues of memory and nostalgia.

It takes a special effort to memorialize, not just look past, the times when the urge to self-destruction won out over human achievement. Visiting Odessa today, you can feel and smell a place that, in the middle of the twentieth century, became practiced in the art of devouring itself—consumed by some aspects of its own past but painfully ignorant of others. Yet an identity that embraces people who speak with an accent, talk too loudly, and are somehow your neighbors is still there in Odessa's streets, even amid post-Soviet kitsch, Ukraine's preoccupation with national mythology, and Russia's new fascination with its old imperial vocation. With attention to the dark times as well as the golden ages, Odessans might again figure out how to make a grounded kind of patriotism out of the leftovers of empire. After all, the children and grandchildren of Ukrainians, Russians, and others who settled in the city after the Second World War—along with new migrants from Turkey, the Caucasus, the Middle East, and East Asia—now have the chance to construct their own visions of "Odessa-Mama," different from but no less complex than those of the past two centuries. Like Parisians, Berliners, Viennese, and New Yorkers, they might even be able to convince themselves of something that vanished generations of Odessans knew instinctively: that with the right combination of neighborliness and mayhem, cities really can be the highest species of *patria*.

CHRONOLOGY

5th century BCE	Herodotus describes Greeks and Scythians along Black Sea coast
ca. 1250–1350	Italian trading colonies flourish around Black Sea
1415	Village of Khadjibey first mentioned in written sources
1453	Fall of Constantinople to the Ottomans
ca. 1550–1650	Cossack sea raids against Ottomans
1762–96	Reign of Catherine the Great
1768–74	Russo-Turkish war
1787	Catherine's elaborate procession to Crimea, managed by Grigory Potemkin
1787–92	Russo-Turkish war
Sept. 1789	Khadjibey captured by Russian troops under José de Ribas
1794	Khadjibey becomes "Odessa"
1803	Richelieu appointed Odessa city administrator
1812–13	Major plague outbreak
1823	Vorontsov becomes governor-general of New Russia
1823–24	Pushkin in Odessa
1828–29	Russo-Turkish War
1830s	Beginning of large-scale Jewish immigration to Odessa
1841	Completion of famous outdoor staircase, now called the "Potemkin steps"

1853–56	Crimean War
1861	Serfdom abolished in Russia
1871	Anti-Jewish pogrom
1881	Anti-Jewish pogrom
1887	Opening of new Opera theater
1897	Jews are 34 percent of Odessa's population (Russian imperial census)
1905	Riots and anti-Jewish pogrom; *Potemkin* mutiny
1914–18	First World War
Feb. 1917	February Revolution in Russia
Oct. 1917	Bolshevik Revolution
1918–20	Russian civil war; Odessa nominally controlled in turn by French, Ukrainian, White, and Bolshevik troops
1921	Publication of the first short story in Isaac Babel's *Odessa Tales*
1922	Soviet Union established
1925	Filming of Eisenstein's *Battleship Potemkin*
1926	Jews are 36 percent of Odessa's population (Soviet census)
1935	Vladimir Jabotinsky writes *The Five*
1939–45	Second World War
1940	Execution of Babel; death of Jabotinsky
Oct. 1941– Apr. 1944	Odessa occupied by Axis powers
Jan. 1942	Romanian forces empty the Jewish ghetto
1943	Mark Bernes stars in *Two Warriors*
1953	Death of Joseph Stalin
1989	Jews account for less than 4 percent of Odessa's population; Ukrainians, 51 percent; and Russians, 36 percent (Soviet census)
1991	Ukraine declares independence from Soviet Union

ACKNOWLEDGMENTS

I have been to Odessa by car, plane, train, and ship, and on each journey I have encountered the verve and hospitality for which the city is rightly famous. I thank the State Archive of the Odessa Region (especially its deputy director, Liliya Belousova) and the Gorky State Scientific Library (especially the "Odesika" Department) for their willingness to share their treasures. Volodymyr Dubovyk spent plenty of shoe leather walking me around his hometown. A conference dinner with Richard von Weizsäcker in the charming garden of Count Mikhail Tolstoy's former mansion, laid on by the Körber Foundation, first stirred my thinking about the attractions and terror of "Old Odessa."

The staff of several other archives and libraries made my work efficient and enjoyable. These include the Library of Congress, the United States Holocaust Memorial Museum Archives and Library, the U.S. National Archives and Records Administration, Georgetown University's Lauinger Library (especially the interlibrary loan and consortium library services), the Columbia University Rare Book and Manuscript Library, the Brooklyn Public Library, the Center for Jewish History (especially the YIVO Archives) in New York, the National Archives of the United Kingdom, the National Archives of Romania, the Yad Vashem Archives in Jerusalem, and the Jabotinsky Institute in Tel Aviv.

In Odessa, Marina Vorotnyuk provided expert assistance in researching images and filling in archival holes. Andrew Robarts and Quint Simon, my U.S.-based research assistants, were intrepid and informed, an ideal combination of traits. Andrew made his own trip to the city to work on his dissertation and to pave the way for my last visit. Quint's fine paper on the history of Brighton Beach helped my thinking about the reproduction of nostalgia.

Any historian of Odessa is indebted to Patricia Herlihy. She has read nearly everything ever written on the city—including the entire manuscript of this book—and her *Odessa: A History, 1794–1914* is a foundational text. To an interloper in her field, Pat was a warm source of wisdom. I also thank the other members of America's small band of "Odessologists"—especially Tanya Richardson, Roshanna Sylvester, Jarrod Tanny, and Steven J. Zipperstein—whose research contributed to my own thinking and is recognized in the notes.

Other friends and colleagues read all or part of this book in draft form and provided generous and invaluable criticism. They include Harley Balzer, Holly Case, Peter Dunkley, John Gledhill, Thane Gustafson, John McNeill, Vladimir Solonari, and the late Richard Stites. (A package containing a copy of the entire manuscript, marked up with Richard's insightful and playful comments, arrived in my mailbox a week after his death in Helsinki. I am unspeakably grateful to Natalia Baschmakoff for sending it to me.) Participants in the Washington, D.C., Russian History Workshop, organized by Eric Lohr and Catherine Evtuhov, provided important comments on two draft chapters. Those chapters were also presented at the 2010 World Convention of the Association for the Study of Nationalities, convened by Dominique Arel. I thank the following people for helpful conversations and advice: Tommaso Astarita, Jacques Berlinerblau, Binio Binev, Jeffrey Burds, Daniel Byman, Adrian Cioflanca, Dorin Dobrincu, Anton Fedyashin, Eugene Fishel, Steve Harris, Bruce Hoffman, Radu Ioanid, Anita

Kondoyanidi, Jared McBride, Michael Oren, Blair Ruble, Hannah Shelest, Douglas Smith, Eric Steinhart, Tom de Waal, Larry Wolff, and Sufian Zhemukhov.

Lawrence and Amy Tal, Michael Thumann and Susanne Landwehr, and the American Research Institute in Turkey (directed by Tony Greenwood) were gracious hosts on my trips to and from Odessa. Georgetown's School of Foreign Service, the Center for Eurasian, Russian, and East European Studies (CERES), and the Department of Government have been wonderful homes for the last fifteen years. I thank my four bosses—Robert Gallucci, Carol Lancaster, Angela Stent, and George Shambaugh—for their support. Jennifer Long deserves special thanks for miraculously keeping the CERES trains on their proper tracks. My beloved Maggie Paxson, among many other contributions to this project, discovered that Vladimir Jabotinsky and Bahá'u'lláh nearly shared the same cell in Acre, although a half century apart.

My agent, William Lippincott of Lippincott Massie McQuilkin, was a brilliant and encouraging tutor. My editor at W. W. Norton, Alane Salierno Mason, was excited about the project from the beginning and a supportive critic as chapters came across her desk. Her pencil made the stories better and the prose sharper. Denise Scarfi helped shepherd the book through the publishing process. The sharp eye of Mary N. Babcock was of enormous benefit at the copyediting stage. Chris Robinson, with whom I have worked happily on several projects, drew the fine maps.

This book is dedicated to my mother's side of the family, especially my warm-hearted uncles, whose Mennonite great-grandparents surely knew something of Odessa's wicked charms.

NOTES

Abbreviations Used in Notes

CUR   Columbia University Rare Book and Manuscript Library, New York

DCFRJ   Ancel, ed., *Documents concerning the Fate of Romanian Jewry during the Holocaust*

GAOO   State Archive of the Odessa Region, Odessa

JIA   Jabotinsky Institute Archives, Tel Aviv

JPJ   John Paul Jones Papers, Library of Congress, Washington, DC

NARA   National Archives and Records Administration, College Park, MD

NAUK   National Archives of the United Kingdom, Kew, London

PPSS   Pushkin, *Polnoe sobranie sochinenii*

SIRIO   *Sbornik Imperatorskago russkago istoricheskago obshchestva*

TGE   Theodore Gordon Ellyson Papers, Naval Historical Foundation Collection, Library of Congress, Washington, DC

USHMM   United States Holocaust Memorial Museum Archives, Washington, DC

YVA   Yad Vashem Archives, Jerusalem

References to archival documents held in GAOO use the standard Russian-language archival designations: f. (*fond*), op. (*opis'*), d. (*delo*), l/ll. (*list/listy*).

INTRODUCTION

1. Twain, *Innocents Abroad* in *Complete Travel Books of Mark Twain*, 1: 256.
2. Jabotinsky, "Memoirs by My Typewriter," in Dawidowicz, ed., *Golden Tradition*, 399.

Chapter 1: THE SINISTER SHORE

1. Kohl, *Russia*, 417. See also Koch, *Crimea and Odessa*, 259.
2. Hommaire de Hell, *Travels in the Steppes of the Caspian Sea*, 2.
3. See Baschmakoff, *La synthèse des périples pontiques*; Boardman, *Greeks Overseas*; Nawotka, *Western Pontic Cities*; Tsetskhladze, ed., *North Pontic Archaeology*.
4. Herodotus, *Histories*, 232–33.
5. Pliny the Elder, *Natural History*, 10: 18.47–48.
6. Strabo, *Geography*, 7.3.7–9.
7. Ovid, "Tristia," in *Poems of Exile*, 3.13.28.
8. Pachymeres, *Relations historiques*, 5.30.
9. Polo, *Travels of Marco Polo*, 344.
10. Pegolotti, *La pratica della mercatura*, 24.
11. "The Journey of Friar John of Pian de Carpini to the Court of Kuyuk Khan, 1245–1247, as Narrated by Himself," in Komroff, ed., *Contemporaries of Marco Polo*, 8, 47–48.
12. Honcharuk, ed., *Istoriia Khadzhibeiia*, 5–8.
13. Beauplan, *Description of Ukraine*, 10–11.
14. Coxe, *Travels in Russia*, in Pinkerton, ed., *General Collection of the Best and Most Interesting Voyages*, 6: 889.

Chapter 2: POTEMKIN AND THE MERCENARIES

1. Ligne, *Letters and Reflections*, 1: 46.
2. Montefiore, *Prince of Princes*, 65.
3. Ligne, *Letters and Reflections*, 1: 55.
4. Ségur, *Memoirs and Recollections*, 3: 8, 91–2; Ligne, *Letters and Reflections*, 1: 39; Coxe, *Travels in Russia*, in Pinkerton, ed., *General Collection of the Best and Most Interesting Voyages*, 6: 764.
5. Ligne, *Letters and Reflections*, 1: 66.
6. Ligne, *Letters and Reflections*, 1: 41. See also Dearborn, *Memoir of the Commerce*, 1: 117.
7. Ligne, *Letters and Reflections*, 1: 74.

8. Smith, ed. and trans., *Love and Conquest*, 262–63.

9. Aragon, *Le prince Charles de Nassau-Siegen*, 237.

10. Jones to de Ribas, Aug. 1, 1788, JPJ.

11. Astarita, *Between Salt Water and Holy Water*, 7, 319.

12. Sade, *Voyage d'Italie*, 1: 177.

13. Ségur, *Memoirs and Recollections*, 3: 19–20.

14. Jones to de Ribas, Aug. 1, 1788, JPJ.

15. Jones to de Rileef, Apr. 2, 1789, JPJ.

16. Smith, ed. and trans., *Love and Conquest*, 297.

17. Honcharuk, ed., *Istoriia Khadzhibeiia*, 233–36. See also Skal'kovskii, *Pervoe tridtsatiletie*, 14–17. Some sources state that Russian losses ran to five killed and thirty-two wounded, while more than two hundred Turks were killed, but those figures seem doubtful. See Skinner, "City Planning in Russia," 34.

18. Castelnau, *Essai sur l'histoire ancienne*, 3: 5–8.

19. Smith, ed. and trans., *Love and Conquest*, 360.

20. Byron, *Don Juan*, 8.120.

21. Honcharuk, ed., *Istoriia Khadzhibeiia*, 328–30.

22. Honcharuk, ed., *Istoriia Khadzhibeiia*, 339–40.

23. Honcharuk, ed., *Istoriia Khadzhibeiia*, 350; Herlihy, *Odessa*, 7. There is sadly no documentary evidence that Catherine personally chose the new city's name, but the story of her intervention was taken as fact by the earliest writers. See for example Stevens, *Account of Odessa*, 5; Vsevolozhskii, *Dictionnaire géographique-historique*, 2: 35; and Lyall, *Travels in Russia*, 1: 161.

Chapter 3: BEACON

1. Clarke, *Travels to Russia*, 502.

2. Stevens, *Account of Odessa*, 5.

3. Anthoine de Saint-Joseph, *Essai historique*, 62.

4. Sicard, *Pis'ma ob Odesse*, 47.

5. Bremner, *Excursions in the Interior of Russia*, 2: 507.

6. Richelieu, "Mémoire sur la Russie," *SIRIO* 54 (1886): 387.

7. Herlihy, *Odessa*, 20.

8. Castelnau, *Essai sur l'histoire ancienne*, 3: 26.

9. Lagarde, *Voyage de Moscou à Vienne*, 152.

10. Herlihy, *Odessa*, 36.

11. Stevens, *Account of Odessa*, 8–9.

12. Castelnau, *Essai sur l'histoire ancienne*, 3: 43.

13. My account of the plague of 1812–13 and its victims is based on Lagarde, *Voyage de Moscou à Vienne*, 167–99; Sicard, "Notice sur onze années de la vie du duc de Richelieu à Odessa pour servir à l'histoire de sa vie," *SIRIO* 54 (1886): 53–60; "Le duc de Richelieu à l'Empereur Alexandre," *SIRIO* 54 (1886): 367–68; and Morton, *Travels in Russia*, 312–30, who in turn based his work on that of a well-informed eyewitness, Gabriel de Castelnau.

14. *SIRIO* 54 (1886): vii.

15. Lagarde, *Voyage de Moscou à Vienne*, 167.

16. Morton, *Travels in Russia*, 319.

17. Morton, *Travels in Russia*, 326–28. Skal'kovskii, *Pervoe tridtsatiletie*, gives the different figures of 4,038 infected and 2,632 dead, but agrees on the mortality rate of around 10 percent (p. 206).

18. Morton, *Travels in Russia*, 326.

19. Stevens, *Account of Odessa*, 5.

20. Lagarde, *Voyage de Moscou à Vienne*, 155.

21. Kohl, *Russia*, 419.

22. Lagarde, *Voyage de Moscou à Vienne*, 153.

23. Herlihy, *Odessa*, 141; Skal'kovskii, *Pervoe tridtsatiletie*, 146.

24. "Le duc de Richelieu à M-r Sicard," *SIRIO* 54 (1886): 630.

Chapter 4: THE GOVERNOR AND THE POET

1. This account is based on the eyewitness report in Morton, *Travels in Russia*, 333–35.

2. Tolstoy, *Hadji Murat*, 41–42.

3. Quoted in Rhinelander, *Prince Michael Vorontsov*, 45–46. I am grateful to Rhinelander's work for helping me to reconstruct the life and career of Mikhail Vorontsov.

4. Pushkin to Wiegel, between Oct. 22 and Nov. 4, 1823, in *Letters of Alexander Pushkin*, trans. Shaw, 1: 139.

5. Pushkin to Lev Pushkin, Aug. 25, 1823, in *Letters of Alexander Pushkin*, trans. Shaw, 1: 136.

6. Morton, *Travels in Russia*, 202; Jesse, *Notes of a Half-Pay*, 1: 185.

7. Morton, *Travels in Russia*, 238.

8. Lyall, *Travels in Russia*, 1: 171.

9. Binyon, *Pushkin*, 158–60, quote to Wiegel on p. 158.

10. Vsevolozhskii, *Puteshestvie cherez iuzhnuiu Rossiiu*, 1: 94.

11. Morton, *Travels in Russia*, 355–58, describing two soirees in 1829.

12. Binyon, *Pushkin*, 162.

13. *PPSS*, 2: 420. For a brief description of the dacha, see Vsevolozhskii, *Puteshestvie cherez iuzhnuiu Rossiiu*, 1: 99.

14. Binyon, *Pushkin*, 173.

15. Quoted in Binyon, *Pushkin*, 175.

16. Bremner, *Excursions in the Interior of Russia*, 2: 500.

17. Spencer, *Travels in Circassia*, 2: 126.

18. Binyon, *Pushkin*, 176–77.

19. Pushkin to Vasilii Lvovich Davydov (?), first half of Mar. 1821, in *Letters of Alexander Pushkin*, trans. Shaw, 1: 79.

20. Moore, *Journey from London to Odessa*, 196.

21. Quoted in Binyon, *Pushkin*, 185.

22. Vorontsov, "Mémoires du prince M. Woronzow, 1819–1833," 78.

23. Morton, *Travels in Russia*, 368–85.

24. "Michele de Ribas to Prince Cassaro," Sept. 22, 1837, in de Ribas, *"Saggio sulla città di Odessa" e altri documenti*, 102.

25. Herlihy, *Odessa*, 144.

26. Hommaire de Hell, *Travels in the Steppes of the Caspian Sea*, 2.

27. Herlihy, *Odessa*, 140.

28. Innokentii, *Slovo pri pogrebenii*, 22.

Chapter 5: "THERE IS NOTHING NATIONAL ABOUT ODESSA"

1. Zipperstein, *Jews of Odessa*, 35.

2. Herlihy, *Odessa*, 124; Reuilly, *Travels in the Crimea*, in *Collection of Modern and Contemporary Voyages*, 5: 82.

3. Frederick William Skinner, "Odessa and the Problem of Urban Modernization," in Hamm, ed., *City in Late Imperial Russia*, 214.

4. John Ralli to State, July 12, 1856, NARA, M459, Reel 1.

5. Hommaire de Hell, *Travels in the Steppes of the Caspian Sea*, 13.

6. Mendele Moykher-Sforim, *Selected Works*, 298.

7. Vsevolozhskii, *Puteshestvie cherez iuzhnuiu Rossiiu*, 1: 92.

8. La Fite de Pellepore, *La Russie historique*, 2: 299.

9. Polishchuk, *Evrei Odessy i Novorossii*, 22.

10. Tarnopol, *Notices historiques*, 65.

11. Zipperstein, *Jews of Odessa*, 56–64. My treatment of Jewish enlightenment and the role of the *maskilim* in the city's history relies on Zipperstein's pathbreaking work.

12. Jesse, *Notes of a Half-Pay*, 1: 225.

13. Hagemeister, *Report on the Commerce of the Ports of New Russia*, 74.

14. Tarnopol, *Notices historiques*, 74.

15. Guthrie, *Tour, Performed in the Years 1795–6*, 6.

16. Herlihy, *Odessa*, 124.

17. Guthrie, *Through Russia*, 1: 284.

18. Hommaire de Hell, *Travels in the Steppes of the Caspian Sea*, 7; Wikoff, *Reminiscences of an Idler*, 231; Koch, *Crimea and Odessa*, 256; Oliphant, *Russian Shores of the Black Sea*, 234; Olenin, *Vek*, 9; Stephens, *Incidents of Travel*, 56.

19. Jesse, *Notes of a Half-Pay*, 1: 211.

20. Spencer, *Turkey, Russia, the Black Sea, and Circassia*, 242.

21. "Le duc de Richelieu à M-r Sicard," *SIRIO* 54 (1886): 537.

22. Puryear, "Odessa: Its Rise and International Importance, 1815–50," 195–96.

23. Harvey, "Development of Russian Commerce," 101.

24. John Ralli to State, Apr. 1, 1845, Jan. 1, 1848, and Jan. 1. 1849, NARA, M459, Roll 1.

25. Puryear, "Odessa: Its Rise and International Importance, 1815–50," 206–7; John Ralli to State, Jan. 1, 1849, NARA, M459, Roll 1.

26. Harvey, "Development of Russian Commerce," 104.

27. Jesse, *Notes of a Half-Pay*, 1: 177.

28. Gadsby, *Trip to Sebastopol*, 37.

29. Brooks, *Russians of the South*, 21.

30. Jesse, *Notes of a Half-Pay*, 1: 204.

31. Vsevolozhskii, *Puteshestvie cherez iuzhnuiu Rossiiu*, 1: 100.

32. Smol'ianinov, *Istoriia Odessy*, 101.

33. Herlihy, "Odessa: Staple Trade," 189–91.

34. Vorontsov, "Mémoires du prince M. Woronzow, 1819–1833," 101.

35. Castelnau, *Essai sur l'histoire ancienne*, 3: 36.

36. Lyall, *Travels in Russia*, 1: 169.

37. Herlihy, *Odessa*, 237.

38. Anderson, *Naval Wars*, 577–80.

39. John Ralli to State, Mar. 1, 1854, and Apr. 1, 1854, NARA, M459, Roll 1.

40. John Ralli to State, Oct. 18, 1855, NARA, M459, Roll 1.

41. Gadsby, *Trip to Sebastopol*, 61; Cunynghame, *Travels in the Eastern Caucasus*, 87. One of the *Tiger* guns can still be seen near the Pushkin statue on Primorsky Boulevard, while the base of the Richelieu statue contains a cannonball allegedly fired during the Allied bombardment.

42. John Ralli to State, Apr. 4 and 7, 1856, NARA, M459, Roll 1.

43. Gadsby, *Trip to Sebastopol*, 61.

44. Harvey, "Development of Russian Commerce," 147.

45. Harvey, "Development of Russian Commerce," 185.

46. I am grateful to Patricia Herlihy, whose research published in her *Odessa* and elsewhere established Odessa's relative economic decline after the Crimean War.

47. Stephen Ralli to State, Dec. 28, 1859/Jan. 9, 1860, NARA, M459, Roll 2.

48. Fal'kner, *Samoubiistva v Odesse*, 8–10, 16, 22.

49. Shuvalov, *"Predany vechnomu zabven'iu,"* 7–10.

50. Kohl, *Russia*, 419.

Chapter 6: SCHEMES AND SHADOWS

1. Trotsky, *My Life*, 48.

2. Trotsky, *My Life*, 58, 95.

3. Trotsky, *My Life*, 72.

4. See Adler, *Life on the Stage*.

5. Castelnau, *Essai sur l'histoire ancienne*, 3: 28.

6. Langeron, "Soobrazheniia gr. Lanzherona o neobkhodimosti obshirnyia prostranstva generalgubernatorstv: Pis'mo grafa Lanzherona k imperatoru Nikolaiu I," *Russkaia starina* (Jan.–March 1904), 228, quoted in Tanny, "City of Rogues and Schnorrers," 122.

7. Skinner, "Odessa and the Problem of Urban Modernization," in Hamm, ed., *City in Late Imperial Russia*, 209.

8. Hommaire de Hell, *Travels in the Steppes of the Caspian Sea*, 6.

9. Mendele Moykher-Sforim, "Fishke the Lame," in *Selected Works of Mendele Moykher-Sforim*, 292.

10. Jesse, *Notes of a Half-Pay*, 1: 208.

11. Cunynghame, *Travels in the Eastern Caucasus*, 86.

12. Hommaire de Hell, *Travels in the Steppes of the Caspian Sea*, 6; Scott, *Baltic*, 336; Stephens, *Incidents of Travel*, 56.

13. Heenan to State, May 7, Sept. 2, and Nov. 16, 1896, NARA, M459, Roll 6. In his dispatch, the consul may have intended the term "costume" to mean simply "suit," but the implication is that Whirlwind/Hampa needed a particular set of clothes in order to continue his profession.

14. Skinner, "Odessa and the Problem of Urban Modernization," in Hamm, ed., *City in Late Imperial Russia*, 212.

15. Skinner, "Odessa and the Problem of Urban Modernization," in Hamm, ed., *City in Late Imperial Russia*, 211.

16. *Odesskii listok*, Aug. 18 (31), 1899.

17. *Odesskii listok*, Aug. 28 (Sept. 9), 1899.

18. Sylvester, *Tales of Old Odessa*, 55.

19. *Odesskii listok*, June 25 (July 7), 1895.

20. See Sylvester, *Tales of Old Odessa*, chaps. 4–5. I am grateful to Sylvester's work on the relationship between middle-class values and sensational crime.

21. *Odesskii listok*, Sept. 26 (Oct. 8), 1894.

22. *Odesskii listok*, Oct. 7 (19), 1894.

23. Jabotinsky, "Memoirs by My Typewriter," in Dawidowicz, ed., *Golden Tradition*, 398.

24. Kokhanskii, *Odessa za 100 let*, 41–46.

25. Babel, "The End of the Almshouse," in *Complete Works of Isaac Babel*, 179.

26. Pallas, *Travels through the Southern Provinces*, 1: 489.

27. My account of the Odessa quarantine experience is based on Stephens, *Incidents of Travel*, 53–55; Oliphant, *Russian Shores of the Black Sea*, 230; Hommaire de Hell, *Travels in the Steppes of the Caspian Sea*, 3–5; and Slade, *Records of Travels*, 1: 252.

28. Hommaire de Hell, *Travels in the Steppes of the Caspian Sea*, 5.

29. Gadsby, *Trip to Sebastopol*, 26.

30. Brooks, *Russians of the South*, 33; Oliphant, *Russian Shores of the Black Sea*, 230; Herlihy, *Odessa*, 141.

31. My account of Mechnikov's life and work is based on Metchnikoff, *Life of Élie Metchnikoff*, and Shum'ko and Anserova, eds., *Il'ia Il'ich Mechnikov*.

32. Quoted in Metchnikoff, *Life of Élie Metchnikoff*, 67–68.

33. See Mechnikov, *Etudes sur la nature humaine*, and *idem*, *Essais optimistes*.

34. Mechnikov to A. O. Kovalevsky, Jan. 13, 1883, in Mechnikov, *Pis'ma (1863–1916 gg)*, 114.

Chapter 7: BLOOD AND VENGEANCE

1. Adler, *Life on the Stage*, 6.

2. Weinberg, *Revolution of 1905 in Odessa*, 16–17.

3. Polishchuk, *Evrei Odessy i Novorossii*, 319-21.

4. Smith to State, Apr. 22, 1871, NARA, M459, Roll 3.

5. Zipperstein, *Jews of Odessa*, 122.

6. Smith to State, Apr. 22, 1871, NARA, M459, Roll 3; Herlihy, *Odessa*, 301-3.

7. John D. Klier, "The Pogrom Paradigm in Russian History," in Klier and Lambroza, eds., *Pogroms,* 13–38.

8. Herlihy, *Odessa*, 252.

9. References to Jabotinsky's *The Five* are to Michael R. Katz's sparkling translation published by Cornell University Press, 2005.

10. Jabotinsky, *Five*, 15.

11. Jabotinsky, *Five*, 138.

12. Weinberg, *Revolution of 1905 in Odessa*, 20–23. I am grateful to Patricia Herlihy, whose research first established a clear portrait of Odessa's economic plight in the run-up to 1905. See especially her *Odessa*, chaps. 8–9.

13. Heenan to State, Sept. 27, 1904, NARA, M459, Roll 7.

14. Heenan to State, Jan. 2, 1906, NARA, M459, Roll 7.

15. Heenan to U.S. embassy in St. Petersburg, July 4, 1905, NARA, M459, Roll 7. See also Smith to Marquess of Landsdowne, Nov. 28, 1905, NAUK, FO 65/1712.

16. Washburn, *The Cable Game*, 95.

17. L. A. Girs Diaries, Oct. 19, 1905, Aleksei and Liubov' Girs Papers, Bakhmeteff Archive, CUR.

18. Savchenko, *Anarkhisty-terroristy*, 218–19.

19. See the survey in the guidebook by Kokhanskii, *Odessa za 100 let*.

20. Jabotinsky, *Five*, 170–71.

21. Katz, *Lone Wolf*, 13–21.

22. Jabotinsky, "Memoirs by My Typewriter," in Dawidowicz, ed., *Golden Tradition*, 399.

23. Jabotinsky, "Memoirs by My Typewriter," in Dawidowicz, ed., *Golden Tradition*, 401.

24. Quoted in Katz, *Lone Wolf*, 26.

25. Dubnow, *Kniga zhizni*, 1: 407.

26. Jabotinsky, *Povest' moikh dnei*, 44.

27. Shlaim, *Iron Wall*, 11–16.

28. Jabotinsky to Mussolini, July 16, 1922, JIA.

29. Jabotinsky, *Political and Social Philosophy of Ze'ev Jabotinsky*, 2–3.

30. See Stanislawski, *Zionism and the Fin de Siècle*, chap. 9.

Chapter 8: NEW WORLD

1. Wightman, *Diary of an American Physician*, 156.

2. Kenez, *Civil War in South Russia, 1919–1920*, 185.

3. Derby to Curzon, June 14, 1919, NAUK, FO 608/207, 297–304.

4. Theodore Gordon Ellyson to Helen Ellyson, Feb. 9, 10, and 11, 1920, Box 3, Folder 3, TGE.

5. Rowan-Hamilton, *Under the Red Star*, 194. See also Sheridan, *Across Europe with Satanella*, 184.

6. "Statisticheskii otchet Odesskoi raionnoi komissii Evreiskogo obshchest-vennogo komiteta o rezul'tatakh bezhenskoi massy, postradavshei ot pog-romov," GAOO, f. R-5275, op. 1, d. 144, ll. 1–12 verso.

7. See Gatrell, *Whole Empire Walking*.

8. Polishchuk, *Evrei Odessy i Novorossii*, 345–46.

9. *Oktiabr'* 3 (1924): 196–97, quoted in Sicher, "Trials of Isaak," 15.

10. Babel, "The Father," in *Complete Works of Isaac Babel*, 163.

11. Babel, "Froim Grach," in *Complete Works of Isaac Babel*, 173.

12. Report of Mr. Simmonds (n.d.), NAUK, FO 371/22301, 198–208.

13. Eisenstein, *Beyond the Stars*, 179; Taylor, ed., *Eisenstein Reader*, 65.

14. Quoted in Barna, *Eisenstein*, 94.

15. Eisenstein, *Beyond the Stars*, 173.

16. Barna, *Eisenstein*, 98.

17. Seton, *Sergei M. Eisenstein*, 87.

18. Barna, *Eisenstein*, 111.

19. Eisenstein, *Beyond the Stars*, 162–66. The naval advisor on set was scandalized when Eisenstein first suggested adding the tarpaulin scene, since it deviated so radically from historical fact. Barna, *Eisenstein*, 98.

20. Taylor, ed., *Eisenstein Reader*, 62.

21. Quoted in Seton, *Sergei M. Eisenstein*, 78.

22. Taylor, ed., *Eisenstein Reader*, 65.

23. Pirozhkova, *At His Side*, 93.

24. Pirozhkova, *At His Side*, 113.

25. Borovoi, *Vospominaniia*, 71.

26. Koval'chuk and Razumov, eds., *Odesskii martirolog*, 1: 678.

Chapter 9: THE FIELDS OF TRANSNISTRIA

1. USHMM, RG-25.004M, Reel 150; Litani, "Destruction of the Jews of Odessa," 138.

2. See Macici to Iacobici, Oct. 27, 1941, and telegrams on the demining operation, USHMM, RG-25.003M, Reel 12.

3. Mazower, *Hitler's Empire*, 171.

4. USHMM, RG-25.003M, Reel 12; RG-25.004M, Reel 150. See also Litani, "Destruction of the Jews of Odessa," 139; Ioanid, *Holocaust in Romania*, 179.

5. Ioanid, *Holocaust in Romania*, 289; Deletant, *Hitler's Forgotten Ally*, 171.

6. Arad, "Holocaust of Soviet Jewry," 7; Levin, "Fateful Decision," 142.

7. Dennis Deletant, "Transnistria and the Romanian Solution to the 'Jewish Problem,'" in Brandon and Lower, eds., *Shoah in Ukraine*, 158, 182n.

8. See Litani, "Destruction of the Jews of Odessa," 135–54. Another estimate puts the total number of evacuees at 350,000 people, or roughly half the prewar population. Manley, *To the Tashkent Station*, 57.

9. Pântea to Antonescu, n.d. [1941], USHMM, RG-25.004M, Reel 30.

10. Borovoi, *Vospominaniia*, 240.

11. On wartime evacuees, see the excellent treatment by Manley, *To the Tashkent Station*.

12. Testimony of Boris Kalika, YVA, O-3/5177.

13. Arad, *Holocaust in the Soviet Union*, 128; Angrick, *Besatzungspolitik und Massenmord*, 294–307.

14. Rubenstein and Altman, eds., *Unknown Black Book*, 115–18, 132.

15. Davidescu to "Vrancea I" (Military Command Odessa), Oct. 23, 1941, in Carp, *Cartea neagră*, 3: 214–15.

16. See the correspondence in USHMM, RG-25.003M, Reel 12, and Ioanid, *Holocaust in Romania*, 179–80.

17. Stănculescu to Tătăranu, Oct. 23, 1941, USHMM, RG-25.003M, Reel 12.

18. Dallin, *Odessa*, 74.

19. Angrick, *Besatzungspolitik und Massenmord*, 302.

20. Quoted in *Report of the International Commission on the Holocaust in Romania*, 5: 54.

21. See USHMM, RG-25.004M, Reel 150; Litani, "Destruction of the Jews of Odessa," 139; Ioanid, *Holocaust in Romania*, 182.

22. See Desbois, *Holocaust by Bullets*.

23. See Alexianu's report to Antonescu on the state of Odessa, Nov. 7, 1941, USHMM, RG-31.004M, Reel 1.

24. "Raport," Nov. 19, 1941, GAOO, f. R-2262, op. 1, d. 1, l. 2.

25. "Înțelegeri asupra siguranței, administrației si exploatarei economice a teritoriilor între Nistru şi Bug (Transnistria) şi Bug-Nipru (regiunea Bug-Nipru)," Aug. 30, 1941, USHMM, RG-25.003M, Reel 12.

26. "Ordonanța No. 35," Jan. 2, 1942, USHMM, RG-31.004M, Reel 1. See also "Instrucțiuni pentru evacuarea populației evreeşti din municipiului Odesa şi împrejurimi," USHMM, RG-31.004M, Reel 1; ibid., RG 25.003M, Reel 394; Litani, "Destruction of the Jews of Odessa," 144–47; Ioanid, *Holocaust in Romania*, 208–10.

27. Arad, *Holocaust in the Soviet Union*, 244.

28. Velcescu to Transnistrian government, Feb. 13, 1942, USHMM, RG-31.004M, Reel 3.

29. See the declarations and signature lists in USHMM, RG-25.003M, Reel 394.
30. I have reconstructed the story of Tănase and Sepel from "Ordinul C.2.A, Serv. Pretoral Nr. 4057/14.I.1942," USHMM, RG-25.003M, Reel 394, and "Ordin de zi, nr. 217," Feb. 9, 1942, USHMM, RG-25.003M, Reel 394.
31. Velcescu to Transnistrian government, Apr. 11, 1942, USHMM, RG-31.004M, Reel 3.
32. "Deciz 2927," Dec. 7, 1943, USHMM, RG-31.004M, Reel 3.
33. Litani, "Destruction of the Jews of Odessa," 152.
34. Dallin, *Odessa*, 162, fn56.
35. Werth, *Russia at War, 1941–1945*, 825.
36. Alexianu to Antonescu, Nov. 7, 1941, USHMM, RG-31.004M, Reel 1.
37. See USHMM, RG-31.004M, Reel 14.
38. Velcescu to Alexianu, Feb. 13, 1942, USHMM, RG-31.004M, Reel 3.
39. See correspondence between Alexianu and Inspectorate of the Gendarmerie, May 1942, and case files of Daria Ovselevici, 1943, USHMM, RG-31.004M, Reel 3.
40. See Case, *Between States*, and Solonari, *Purifying the Nation*.
41. "Ordonanţa No. 89," Sept. 28, 1942, USHMM, RG-31.004M, Reel 1.
42. "Odesa de eri şi de astăzi," *Gazeta Odesei*, Jan. 17, 1943, reproduced in *DCFRJ*, 4: 429–30.
43. I am grateful to Vladimir Solonari for several conversations about these issues.
44. See USHMM, RG-31.004M, Reel 2; and "Memoriu cu privire la problemele practice, pe care le ridică în toamna 1942 românii de peste Bug," Sept. 21, 1942, GAOO, f. R-2249, op. 3, d. 111, ll. 11–15.
45. Brătianu, "Notes sur un voyage en Crimée," 176–82.
46. "Raport," Nov. 19, 1941, GAOO, f. R-2262, op. 1, d. 1, l. 1.

Chapter 10: "I WOULD LIKE TO BRING TO YOUR ATTENTION THE FOLLOWING"

1. See Cherkasov, *Okkupatsiia Odessy*.
2. GAOO, f. R-2262, op. 1, d. 1, ll. 3–8, 9–12.
3. "Raport," Nov. 28, 1941, GAOO, f. R-2262, op. 1, d. 1, l. 13.
4. "Raport," Nov. 28, 1941, GAOO, f. R-2262, op. 1, d. 1, l. 13.
5. "Raport," n.d. [1941], GAOO, f. R-2262, op. 1, d. 1, l. 32.
6. "Raport," Nov. 26, 1941, GAOO, f. R-2262, op. 1, d. 1, l. 36.

7. "Raport," Nov. 19, 1941, GAOO, f. R-2262, op. 1, d. 1, l. 64. See also ibid., ll. 69, 153; ibid., d. 8, l. 38; ibid., d. 2, ll. 4-6.

8. "Comunicare," Feb. 22, 1942, USHMM, RG-31.004M, Reel 3.

9. See Sheila Fitzpatrick, "Signals from Below: Soviet Letters of Denunciation of the 1930s," in Fitzpatrick and Gellately, eds., *Accusatory Practices*, 85–120; Fitzpatrick, "Supplicants and Citizens"; and Fitzpatrick, *Tear Off the Masks!*.

10. "Raport," Nov. 20, 1941, GAOO, f. R-2662, op. 1, d. 2, l. 19. On the earlier history of denunciation, see Grünewald, "Jewish Workers in Odessa."

11. David Senyaver Collection, USHMM. See also Semyon Tarantor Collection and Efim Yurkovetski Collection, USHMM.

12. Liudmila Kalika, "Odessa. 820 dnei v podzeml'e," in Rashkovetskii, Naidis, Dusman, and Belousova, eds., *Istoriia Kholokosta v Odesskom regione*, 96–110.

13. "Raport," n.d. [Dec. 1941], GAOO, f. R-2262, op. 1, d. 3, l. 17. On "revenge" see also ibid., d. 22, l. 9.

14. "Raport," Apr. 15, 1942, GAOO, f. R-2262, op. 1, d. 8, l. 30; Ioanid, *Holocaust in Romania*, 187–94.

15. Litani, "Destruction of the Jews of Odessa," 150, mentions his university background. Other biographical information on Pântea and his role in the deportations is taken from his signed declaration to the Romanian Communist authorities, June 22, 1950, in USHMM, RG-25.004M, Reel 30, and Colesnic, *Sfatul Țării*, 231.

16. Pântea to Antonescu, n.d. [1941], USHMM, RG-25.004M, Reel 30.

17. See Pântea's own 1950 statement, cited above, as well as those of Matei Velcescu, Apr. 1 and June 17, 1950; and of Constantin Vidrașcu, June 17, 1950, USHMM, RG-25.004M, Reel 30.

18. Chelovan' to Odessa municipality, n.d. [1941], GAOO, f. R-2262, op. 1, d. 2, l. 35.

19. Dallin, *Odessa*, 91.

20. See "Dare de seama asupra activității subdirecției artelor pe lunile aprilie-mai-iunie [1943]," GAOO, f. R-2249, op. 3, d. 89, ll. 10–12; "Dare de seama despre reconstruirea Teatrului de opera și balet din Odessa [January 1943]," ibid., ll. 41–46; "Tablou de spectacole date de Teatrul de opera și balet Odessa în cursul trimestrului II-1943," ibid., ll. 115–16.

21. Declaration of Taisia Arnautu, July 23, 1956, USHMM, RG-25.004M, Reel 30. See also Fred Saraga, "În Transnistria: Primii pași: Odessa," *Sliha*, Apr. 5, 1956, reproduced in *DCFRJ*, 8: 547.

22. Dallin, *Odessa*, 85.

23. See GAOO, f. R-2249, op. 1, d. 266.

24. Werth, *Russia at War, 1941–1945*, 817.

25. Pântea to Alexianu, Jan. 20, 1942, USHMM, RG-25.004M, Reel 30.

26. See USHMM, RG-25.003M, Reel 10.

27. Pântea to Alexianu, Dec. 3, 1941, USHMM, RG-25.004M, Reel 30.

28. See Alexianu's postwar trial dossier in USHMM, RG-25.004M, Reel 33.

29. See USHMM, RG-25.004M, Reel 33.

30. See the Romanian high court decision of Jan. 1, 1956, USHMM, RG-25.004M, Reel 30.

31. See Pântea's file from the Romanian Information Service archives, USHMM, RG-25.004M, Reel 30.

32. Instead, Pântea made a direct request to Alexianu for clarification. Alexianu then predictably decreed that anyone attempting to notarize such a document was obviously a Jew and would therefore be removed from the city. See the Pântea-Alexianu correspondence, Feb. 4 and 14, 1942, USHMM, RG-31.004M, Reel 3. One survivor claimed that Pântea had also prevented several thousand Jews from being executed in Dalnik by instead having them deported. Many nevertheless died. Ioanid, *Holocaust in Romania*, 182.

33. Pântea to Antonescu, n.d. [1941], USHMM, RG-25.004M, Reel 30.

34. Alexander Kruglov, "Jewish Losses in Ukraine, 1941–1944," in Brandon and Lower, eds., *Shoah in Ukraine*, 284.

35. Jean Ancel, "'The New Jewish Invasion'—The Return of the Survivors from Transnistria," in Bankier, ed., *Jews Are Coming Back*, 231.

36. Blinov to Polianskii, July 19, 1945, YVA, M-46/11.

Chapter 11: HERO CITY

1. E. T. Samoilov, "Informatsiia," Dec. 5, 1941, GAOO, f. R-2262, op. 1, d. 3, l. 46.

2. Dallin, *Odessa*, 245.

3. Testimony of Aleksandr Bakman, YVA, O-3/6054.

4. See YVA, M-33/19967.

5. Testimony of Sura Sturmak, YVA, O-3/5178. See also testimony of Boris Kalika, YVA, O-3/5177.

6. Yaacov Roi, "The Reconstruction of Jewish Communities in the USSR, 1944–1947," in Bankier, ed., *Jews are Coming Back*, 194. For overviews of

Communist and Soviet antisemitism, see Gross, *Fear*, and Kostyrchenko, ed., *Gosudarstvennyi antisemitizm*.

7. Borovoi, *Vospominaniia*, 290.

8. Draitser, *Shush!*, 18.

9. Tanny, "City of Rogues and Schnorrers," 303–4. Tanny's magnificent dissertation is an exhaustive study of the myth of "Old Odessa" from the nineteenth century forward.

10. Eisenstein, *Beyond the Stars*, 177.

11. Yekelchyk, *Stalin's Empire of Memory*, 115.

12. Yevgeny Yevtushenko, "On liubil tebia, zhizn' . . . ," in Bernes-Bodrova, ed., *Mark Bernes*, 156.

13. Mark Bernes, "Odin iz 'dvukh boitsov,'" in Bernes-Bodrova, ed., *Mark Bernes*, 59–61.

14. Rybak, *Mark Bernes*, 60.

15. Andzhei Bin'kovskii and Ezhi Ol'shtyn'skii, "Mark Bernes," in Bernes-Bodrova, ed., *Mark Bernes*, 199–201.

16. N. Smirnova, "Obrazy i pesni Marka Bernesa," in Bernes-Bodrova, ed., *Mark Bernes*, 11; Rybak, *Mark Bernes*, 10–16.

17. Utesov, *Spasibo serdtse!*, 22–23.

18. Tanny, "City of Rogues and Schnorrers," 305, 309.

19. *Odesskaia turisticheskaia baza*, 4.

20. See Friedberg, *How Things Were Done in Odessa*, 10–15.

Chapter 12: TWILIGHT

1. *Brooklyn Eagle*, May 5, 1918.

2. *New York Daily News*, Dec. 14, 1979.

3. Annelise Orleck, "The Soviet Jews: Life in Brighton Beach, Brooklyn," in Foner, ed., *New Immigrants in New York*, 273.

4. Quoted in Michael Specter, "In Musical Odessa, Playing On for the Love of It," *New York Times*, Apr. 11, 1994.

5. *Brooklyn Eagle*, Sept. 25, 1916, and Sept. 10, 1918.

6. *Itogi vsesoiuznoi perepisi naseleniia 1959 goda: Ukrainskaia SSR*, 184.

7. Oleg Gubar and Patricia Herlihy, "The Persuasive Power of the Odessa Myth," in Czaplicka, Gelazis, and Ruble, eds., *Cities after the Fall of Communism*, 153.

8. Patricia Herlihy, "How Ukrainian is Odesa?" in Ramer and Ruble, eds., *Place, Identity, and Urban Culture*, 24, fn3.

BIBLIOGRAPHY

ARCHIVES

British National Archives, Kew
    Foreign Office Records
Brooklyn Public Library, New York
    Brooklyn Collection
Columbia University Rare Book and Manuscript Library, New York
    Aleksei and Liubov' Girs Papers, Bakhmeteff Archive
Library of Congress, Washington, DC
    Theodore Gordon Ellyson Papers
    John Paul Jones Papers
National Archives and Records Administration, College Park, MD
    Consular Despatches, Odessa
State Archive of the Odessa Region, Odessa
    Files from the Period of German-Romanian Occupation
        Directorate of Culture, Governorship of Transnistria
        Directorate of Economic Affairs, Governorship of Transnistria
        Directorate of Culture, Municipality of Odessa
        Odessa Central Prison
        Odessa Mayoralty
        Odessa Prefecture of Police
        Office of Military Propaganda, Military Command, Odessa
    Odessa District Commission, Jewish Public Committee for Aiding the
        Victims of Pogroms (Evobshchestkom)
    Odessa Regional Executive Committee, Soviet of Workers, Peasants, and
        Red Army Deputies (Okrispolkom/Oblispolkom)

United States Holocaust Memorial Museum Archives, Washington, DC
    Romanian National Archives Collection
    Romanian Ministry of Defense Archives Collection
    David Senyaver Collection
    State Archive of Odessa Region Collection
    Steven Spielberg Film and Video Archive
    Semyon Tarantor Collection
    Efim Yurkovetski Collection
Yad Vashem Archives, Jerusalem
    Council for Religious Matters in the Soviet Union Collection
    Extraordinary State Commission to Investigate German-Fascist Crimes
        Collection
    Central Archive for Public Organizations in Ukraine Collection
    Central Government Archive of Ukraine Collection
    Yad Vashem Photograph Archive
    Yad Vashem Testimonials
YIVO Institute Archives, Center for Jewish History, New York
    Dr. Joseph A. Rosen Papers
    Moisei Borisovitch Bernstein Papers

BOOKS, ARTICLES, AND OTHER SOURCES

Abou-el-Haj, Rifaat A. "The Formal Closure of the Ottoman Frontier in Europe: 1699–1703." *Journal of the American Oriental Society* 89, no. 3 (July–September 1969): 467–75.

Adler, Jacob. *A Life on the Stage*. New York: Knopf, 1999.

Ainsworth, John. "Sidney Reilly's Reports from South Russia, December 1918–March 1919." *Europe-Asia Studies* 50, no. 8 (1998): 1447–70.

Alcock, Thomas. *Travels in Russia, Persia, Turkey, and Greece, in 1828–9*. London: E. Clarke and Sons, 1831.

Alexopoulos, Golfo. *Stalin's Outcasts: Aliens, Citizens, and the Soviet State, 1926–1936*. Ithaca: Cornell University Press, 2003.

Ancel, Jean. "Antonescu and the Jews." *Yad Vashem Studies* 23 (1993): 213–80.

——, ed. *Documents concerning the Fate of Romanian Jewry during the Holocaust*. 12 vols. New York: Beate Klarsfeld Foundation, 1986.

——. *The Economic Destruction of Romanian Jewry*. Jerusalem: Yad Vashem, 2007.

——. *Transnistria, 1941–1942*. 3 vols. Tel Aviv: Goldstein-Goren Diaspora Research Center, Tel Aviv University, 2003.

Anderson, R. C. *Naval Wars in the Levant, 1559–1853*. Liverpool: Liverpool University Press, 1952.

Angrick, Andrej. *Besatzungspolitik und Massenmord: Die Einsatzgruppe D in der südlichen Sowjetunion, 1941–1943*. Hamburg: Hamburger Edition, 2003.

Ansky, S. *The Enemy at His Pleasure: A Journey through the Jewish Pale of Settlement during World War I*. Joachim Neugroschel, trans. New York: Metropolitan Books, 2002.

Anthoine de Saint-Joseph, Antoine-Ignace. *Essai historique sur le commerce et la navigation de la Mer-Noire*. 2nd ed. Paris: L'Imprimerie de Mme. Veuve Agasse, 1820.

Arad, Yitzhak. *The Holocaust in the Soviet Union*. Lincoln and Jerusalem: University of Nebraska Press and Yad Vashem, 2009.

———. "The Holocaust of Soviet Jewry in the Occupied Territories of the Soviet Union." *Yad Vashem Studies* 21 (1991): 1–47.

Aragon, Le Marquis de. *Le prince Charles de Nassau-Siegen, d'après sa correspondance originale inédite*. Paris: E. Plon, Nourrit, et Cie., 1893.

Arrianus, Flavius. *Arrian's Voyage round the Euxine Sea, Translated; and Accompanied with a Geographical Dissertation, and Maps*. Oxford: J. Cooke, 1805.

Astarita, Tommaso. *Between Salt Water and Holy Water: A History of Southern Italy*. New York: W. W. Norton, 2005.

Atlas, D. G. *Staraia Odessa: Ee druz'ia i nedrugi*. Odessa: Tekhnik, 1991; reprint Odessa: Lasmi, 1992.

Babel, Isaac. *The Complete Works of Isaac Babel*. Peter Constantine, trans. New York: W. W. Norton, 2002.

———. *Isaac Babel: The Lonely Years, 1925–1939*. Andrew R. MacAndrew and Max Hayward, trans. New York: Farrar, Straus, 1964; reprint Boston: Verba Mundi, 1995.

Balard, Michel. *La Romanie génoise (XIIe-début du XVe siècle)*. 2 vols. Rome: Ecole Française de Rome, 1978.

Bankier, David, ed. *Jews Are Coming Back: The Return of the Jews to Their Countries of Origin after WWII*. Jerusalem: Yad Vashem, 2005.

Barna, Yon. *Eisenstein*. Bloomington: Indiana University Press, 1973.

Baron, Nick, and Peter Gatrell. "Population Displacement, State-Building, and Social Identity in the Lands of the Former Russian Empire, 1917–1923." *Kritika* 4, no. 1 (2003): 51–100.

Baschmakoff, Alexandre. *La synthèse des périples pontiques: Méthode de precision en paléo-ethnologie*. Paris: Librairie orientaliste Paul Geuthner, 1948.

Bascomb, Neal. *Red Mutiny: Eleven Fateful Days on the Battleship Potemkin*. New York: Houghton Mifflin, 2007.

Beauplan, Guillaume Le Vasseur, Sieur de. *A Description of Ukraine*. Andrew B. Pernal and Dennis F. Essar, trans. Cambridge, MA: Harvard Ukrainian Research Institute, 1993.

Begicheva, N. *Ot Odessy do Ierusalima: Putevyia pis'ma*. St. Petersburg: Tipografiia Glavnago upravleniia udelov, 1898.

Belousova, L. G., and T. E. Volkova, eds. *Evrei Odessy i iuga Ukrainy: Istoriia v dokumentakh*. Odessa: Studiia Negotsiant, 2002.

Bergan, Ronald. *Eisenstein: A Life in Conflict*. New York: Overlook Press, 1997.

Berkhoff, Karel C. *Harvest of Despair: Life and Death in Ukraine under Nazi Rule*. Cambridge, MA: Belknap Press of Harvard University Press, 2004.

Bernes-Bodrova, L. M., ed. *Mark Bernes*. Moscow: Iskusstvo, 1980.

Binyon, T. J. *Pushkin: A Biography*. New York: Knopf, 2003.

Bloom, Harold, ed. *Isaac Babel: Modern Critical Views*. New York: Chelsea House Publishers, 1987.

Boardman, John. *The Greeks Overseas: Their Early Colonies and Trade*. London: Thames and Hudson, 1980.

Borovoi, Saul [S. Ia.]. *Gibel' evreiskogo naseleniia Odessy vo vremia fashistskoi okkupatsii*. Kiev: Institut istorii Ukrainy, 1991.

———. *Vospominaniia*. Moscow and Jerusalem: Jewish University in Moscow, 1993.

Braham, Randolph L., ed. *The Tragedy of Romanian Jewry*. New York: Columbia University Press, 1994.

Brandon, Ray, and Wendy Lower, eds. *The Shoah in Ukraine: History, Testimony, Memorialization*. Bloomington: Indiana University Press, 2008.

Brătianu, Gheorghe Ioan. *La mer Noire: Des origines à la conquête ottomane*. Munich: Romanian Academy Society, 1969.

———. "Notes sur un voyage en Crimée." *Revue historique du sud-est européen* 19, no. 1 (1942): 176–82.

Bremner, Robert. *Excursions in the Interior of Russia*. 2 vols. London: Henry Colburn, 1839.

Brooks, Shirley. *The Russians of the South*. London: Longman, Brown, Green, and Longmans, 1854.

Brower, Daniel R. *The Russian City between Tradition and Modernity, 1850–1900*. Berkeley: University of California Press, 1990.

Brown, James Baldwin. *Memoirs of Howard, Compiled from His Diary, His Confidential Letters, and Other Authentic Documents*. Abridged ed. Boston: Lincoln and Edmands, 1831.

Brown, Kate. *A Biography of No Place: From Ethnic Borderland to Soviet Heartland*. Cambridge, MA: Harvard University Press, 2004.

Brumfield, William Craft, Boris V. Anan'ich, and Yuri A. Petrov, eds. *Commerce in Russian Urban Culture, 1861–1914.* Washington, DC, and Baltimore: Woodrow Wilson Center Press and Johns Hopkins University Press, 2001.

Bryer, Anthony, ed. *The Byzantine Black Sea.* Special issue of *Archeion Pontou* 35 (1979).

Cameron, Evan P. *Goodbye Russia.* London: Hodder and Stoughton, 1934.

Carp, Matatias. *Cartea neagră: Suferințele evreilor din România, 1940–1944.* 2nd ed. 3 vols. Bucharest: Editura Diogene, 1996.

Case, Holly. *Between States: The Transylvanian Question and the European Idea during World War II.* Stanford: Stanford University Press, 2009.

Castelnau, Gabriel de. *Essai sur l'histoire ancienne et moderne de la Nouvelle Russie.* 3 vols. Paris: Rey et Gravier, 1820.

Cesarani, David. *Port Jews: Jewish Communities in Cosmopolitan Maritime Trading Centres, 1550–1950.* London: Frank Cass, 2002.

Charyn, Jerome. *Savage Shorthand: The Life and Death of Isaac Babel.* New York: Random House, 2005.

Cherkasov, A. A. *Okkupatsiia Odessy: god 1941.* Odessa: Optimum, 2007.

Chistovich, N. Ia. *I. I. Mechnikov.* Berlin: Z. I. Grzhebina, 1923.

Clarke, Edward Daniel. *Travels to Russia, Tartary, and Turkey.* New York: Arno Press, 1970; reprint of vol. 1 of his *Travels in Various Countries of Europe, Asia, and Africa,* London: 1811.

Clogg, Richard, ed. *Balkan Society in the Age of Greek Independence.* Totowa, NJ: Barnes and Noble Books, 1981.

Colesnic, Iurie. *Sfatul Țării: Enciclopedie.* Chisinau: Museum, 1998.

Cox, Cynthia. *Talleyrand's Successor.* London: Arthur Baker, 1959.

Coxe, William. *Travels in Russia,* from his *Travels in the Northern Countries of Europe.* London, 1802. In John Pinkerton, ed., *A General Collection of the Best and Most Interesting Voyages and Travels in All Parts of the World.* 17 vols. London: Longman, Hurst, Rees, and Orme, 1808–1814.

Craven, Elizabeth Lady. *A Journey through the Crimea to Constantinople.* Dublin: H. Chamberlaine, et al., 1789; reprint New York: Arno Press, 1970.

Cunynghame, Sir Arthur Thurlow. *Travels in the Eastern Caucasus.* London: John Murray, 1872.

Czaplicka, John, Nida Gelazis, and Blair Ruble, eds. *Cities after the Fall of Communism: Reshaping Cultural Landscapes and European Identity.* Washington, DC, and Baltimore: Woodrow Wilson Center Press and Johns Hopkins University Press, 2009.

Dallin, Alexander. *Odessa, 1941–1944: A Case Study of Soviet Territory under Foreign Rule.* Iași: Center for Romanian Studies, 1998.

Davies, Brian L. *Warfare, State, and Society on the Black Sea Steppe, 1500–1700*. London: Routledge, 2007.

Dawidoff, Nicholas. *The Fly Swatter: How My Grandfather Made His Way in the World*. New York: Pantheon, 2002.

de Madariaga, Isabel. *Russia in the Age of Catherine the Great*. New Haven: Yale University Press, 1981.

De-Ribas, L. M., ed. *Iz proshlago Odessy: sbornik statei*. Odessa: L. Kirkhner, 1894.

de Ribas, Michele. *"Saggio sulla città di Odessa" e altri documenti dell'Archivio di Stato di Napoli*. Giovanna Moracci, ed. Genoa: Cassa di Risparmio di Genova, 1988.

de Voland, Franz. *Moia zhizn' v Rossii*. Odessa: Optimum, 2002.

Dearborn, Henry A. S. *A Memoir of the Commerce and Navigation of the Black Sea, and the Trade and Maritime Geography of Turkey and Egypt*. 2 vols. Boston: Wells and Lilly, 1819.

Deletant, Dennis. *Hitler's Forgotten Ally: Ion Antonescu and His Regime, Romania 1940–1944*. Basingstoke, UK: Palgrave Macmillan, 2006.

Deribas, Aleksandr. *Staraia Odessa: zabytie stranitsy*. Kiev: Mistetstvo, 2004.

Desbois, Patrick. *The Holocaust by Bullets*. New York: Palgrave Macmillan, 2008.

Deutscher, Isaac. *The Prophet Armed: Trotsky, 1879–1921*. New York: Oxford University Press, 1954.

———. *The Prophet Outcast: Trotsky, 1929–1940*. New York: Oxford University Press, 1963.

Diller, Aubrey. *The Tradition of the Minor Greek Geographers*. New York: American Philological Association, 1952.

Dobroliubskii, Andrei, Oleg Gubar', and Andrei Krasnozhon. *Borisfen-Khadzhibei-Odessa: Istoriko-arkheologicheskie ocherki*. Odessa and Chisinau: Vysshaia antropologicheskaia shkola, 2002.

Dontsova, Tat'iana. *Moldavanka: Zapiski kraeveda*. Odessa: Druk, 2001.

Draitser, Emil. *Shush! Growing Up Jewish under Stalin*. Berkeley: University of California Press, 2008.

Dubnow, S. M. *Kniga zhizni*. 3 vols. Riga and New York: Jaunātnes Grāmata and Soiuz russkikh evreev, 1934–57.

Duţu, Alesandru, and Petre Otu, eds. *Pe Ţărmul nord pontic (17 iulie 1941–4 iulie 1942)*. Bucharest: Editura Fundaţiei Culturale Române, 1999.

Eisenstein, Sergei. *Beyond the Stars: The Memoirs of Sergei Eisenstein*. Richard Taylor, ed. Calcutta: Seagull Books, 1995.

———. *Notes of a Film Director*. New York: Dover, 1970.

Faitel'berg-Blank, Viktor, and Tat'iana Kolesnichenko. *Zolotoi vek iuzhnoi Pal'miry*. Odessa: Optimum, 2006.

Fal'kner, I. S. *Samoubiistva v Odesse*. Odessa: Tipografiia "Odesskago Listka," 1890.

Feinstein, Elaine. *Pushkin: A Biography*. Hopewell, NJ: Ecco, 1998.

Finlay, George. *History of the Greek Revolution*. Reprint ed. 2 vols. London: Zeno, 1971.

Fisher, Julius S. *Transnistria: The Forgotten Cemetery*. London: Thomas Yoseloff, 1969.

Fitzpatrick, Sheila. *The Cultural Front: Power and Culture in Revolutionary Russia*. Ithaca: Cornell University Press, 1992.

———. *Everyday Stalinism*. New York: Oxford University Press, 1999.

———, ed. *Stalinism: New Directions*. London: Routledge, 2000.

———. "Supplicants and Citizens: Public Letter-Writing in Soviet Russia in the 1930s." *Slavic Review* 55, no. 1 (Spring 1996): 78–105.

———. *Tear Off the Masks! Identity and Imposture in Twentieth-Century Russia*. Princeton: Princeton University Press, 2005.

———. "The World of Ostap Bender: Soviet Confidence Men in the Stalin Period." *Slavic Review* 61, no. 3 (2002): 535–57.

Fitzpatrick, Sheila, and Robert Gellately, eds. *Accusatory Practices: Denunciation in Modern European History, 1789–1989*. Chicago: University of Chicago Press, 1997.

Fitzpatrick, Sheila, Alexander Rabinowitch, and Richard Stites, eds. *Russia in the Era of NEP*. Bloomington: Indiana University Press, 1991.

Foner, Nancy, ed. *New Immigrants in New York*. New York: Columbia University Press, 2001.

Formaleoni, Vincenzio Antonio. *Histoire philosophique et politique du commerce, de la navigation, et des colonies des anciens dans la Mer-Noire, avec l'hydrographie du Pont-Euxin, publiée d'après une carte ancienne conservée dans la Bibliothèque de S. Marc*. Le Chev. d'Henin, trans. 2 vols. Venice: Charles Palese, 1789.

Friedberg, Maurice. *How Things Were Done in Odessa: Cultural and Intellectual Pursuits in a Soviet City*. Boulder, CO: Westview, 1991.

Gadsby, John. *A Trip to Sebastopol, Out and Home*. London: Gadsby, 1858.

Gaivoron, Arkadii. *Odessa, moi gorod rodnoi*. Odessa: Odesskoe knizhnoe izdatel'stvo, 1963.

Gallenga, Antonio. *A Summer Tour in Russia*. London: Chapman and Hall, 1882.

Gamaleia, N. F. *Kholera v Odesse*. Odessa: Tipografiia Aktsionernago iuzhno-russkago obshchestva pechatnago dela, 1909.

Gatrell, Peter. *A Whole Empire Walking: Refugees in Russia during World War I*. Bloomington: Indiana University Press, 1999.

Gerasimov, Ilya. "My ubivaem tol'ko svoikh: prestupnost' kak marker mezhetnicheskikh granits v Odesse nachala XX veka." *Ab Imperio* 1 (2003): 208–60.

Geyer, Michael, and Sheila Fitzpatrick, eds. *Beyond Totalitarianism: Stalinism and Nazism Compared*. Cambridge: Cambridge University Press, 2009.

Gitelman, Zvi, ed. *Bitter Legacy: Confronting the Holocaust in the USSR*. Bloomington: Indiana University Press, 1997.

Goldman, Wendy Z. *Terror and Democracy in the Age of Stalin*. Cambridge, UK: Cambridge University Press, 2007.

Gorod vechnoi iunosti. Odessa: Knizhnoe izdatel'stvo, 1960.

Grill, Tobias. "Odessa's German Rabbi: The Paradigmatic Meaning of Simon Leon Schwabacher (1861–1888)." *Jahrbuch des Simon-Dubnow-Instituts* 2 (2003): 199–222.

Gross, Jan T. *Fear: Anti-Semitism in Poland after Auschwitz*. New York: Random House, 2006.

———. *Neighbors: The Destruction of the Jewish Community in Jedwabne, Poland*. Princeton: Princeton University Press, 2001.

Grünewald, Jörn. "Jewish Workers in Odessa: Cultural Practices and Beliefs in the 1920s." *Jahrbuch des Simon-Dubnow-Instituts* 2 (2003): 315–32.

Gubar', Oleg. *Novye voprosy o staroi Odesse*. Odessa: Optimum, 2007.

Guthrie, Katherine Blanche. *Through Russia*. 2 vols. London: Hurst and Blackett, 1874; reprint New York: Arno Press, 1970.

Guthrie, Marie. *A Tour, Performed in the Years 1795–6, through the Taurida, or Crimea*. London: T. Cadell, Jr., and W. Davies, 1802.

Hagemeister, Julius de [Iulii Andreevich Gagemeister]. *Report on the Commerce of the Ports of New Russia, Moldavia, and Wallachia*. T. F. Triebner, trans. London: Effingham Wilson, 1836.

Hamm, Michael F., ed. *The City in Late Imperial Russia*. Bloomington: Indiana University Press, 1986.

———, ed. *The City in Russian History*. Lexington: University Press of Kentucky, 1976.

Harvey, Mose Lofley. "The Development of Russian Commerce on the Black Sea and Its Significance." PhD dissertation. University of California, Berkeley, 1938.

Herlihy, Patricia. *Odessa: A History, 1794–1914*. Cambridge, MA: Harvard University Press and Harvard Ukrainian Research Institute, 1986.

———. "Odessa: Staple Trade and Urbanization in New Russia." *Jahrbücher für Geschichte Osteuropas* 21, no. 2 (1973): 121–32.

———. "Port Jews of Odessa and Trieste: A Tale of Two Cities." *Jahrbuch des Simon-Dubnow-Instituts* 2 (2003): 183–98.

Herodotus. *The Histories*. Aubrey de Sélincourt, trans. New ed. London: Penguin, 1996.

Higham, Robin, and Frederick W. Kagan, eds. *The Military History of the Soviet Union*. New York: Palgrave, 2002.

Hilbrenner, Anke. "Nationalization in Odessa: Simon Dubnow and the Society for the Dissemination of Enlightenment among the Jews in Russia." *Jahrbuch des Simon-Dubnow-Instituts* 2 (2003): 223–39.

Hofmeister, Alexis. "Palestinophilism and Zionism among Russian Jews: The Case of the Odessa Committee." *Jahrbuch des Simon-Dubnow-Instituts* 2 (2003): 241–65.

Holderness, Mary. *New Russia: Journey from Riga to the Crimea, by Way of Kiev*. London: Sherwood, Jones, 1823.

Holquist, Peter. "Violent Russia, Deadly Marxism? Russia in the Epoch of Violence, 1905–21," *Kritika* 4, no. 3 (2003): 627–52.

Hommaire de Hell, Xavier. *Travels in the Steppes of the Caspian Sea, the Crimea, the Caucasus, &c*. London: Chapman and Hall, 1847.

Honcharuk, T. H., ed. *Istoriia Khadzhibeiia (Odesi), 1415–1796 rr. v dokumentakh*. Odessa: AstroPrynt, 2000.

Horowitz, Brian. *Jewish Philanthropy and Enlightenment in Late-Tsarist Russia*. Seattle: University of Washington Press, 2009.

Horwitz, Gordon. *Ghettostadt: Łódź and the Making of a Nazi City*. Cambridge, MA: Harvard University Press, 2008.

Hough, Richard. *The Potemkin Mutiny*. Annapolis: Naval Institute Press, 1960.

Il'f, Iliia, and Evgenii Petrov. *The Golden Calf*. New York: Random House, 1962.

———. *The Twelve Chairs*. New York: Vintage Books, 1961.

Iljine, Nicolas V., ed. *Odessa Memories*. Seattle: University of Washington Press, 2003.

Inalcik, Halil, ed., with Donald Quataert. *An Economic and Social History of the Ottoman Empire*. 2 vols. Cambridge, UK: Cambridge University Press, 1997.

Innokentii, Archbishop of Kherson and Tavrida. *Slovo pri pogrebenii generalfel'dmarshala, svetleishago kniazia, Mikhaila Semenovicha Vorontsova*. Odessa: P. Frantsov, 1856.

Ioanid, Radu. *The Holocaust in Romania*. Chicago: Ivan Dee, 2000.

Itogi vsesoiuznoi perepisi naseleniia 1959 goda: Ukrainskaia SSR. Moscow: Gosstatizdat, 1963.

Itogi vsesoiuznoi perepisi naseleniia 1970 goda. Moscow: Statistika, 1973.

Itogi vsesoiuznoi perepisi naseleniia 1979 goda. Moscow: Goskomitet statistiki, 1989.

Iurenev, R. N. *Eizenshtein v vospominaniiakh sovremennikov*. Moscow: Isskustvo, 1974.

Jabotinsky, Vladimir. *The Five*. Michael R. Katz, trans. Ithaca: Cornell University Press, 2005.

———. *Kritiki Sionizma*. Odessa: Kadima, 1906.

———. "Memoirs by My Typewriter." In Lucy S. Dawidowicz, ed. *The Golden Tradition: Jewish Life and Thought in Eastern Europe*. New York: Schocken Books, 1984.

———. *Nedrugam Siona*. 3rd ed. Odessa: S. D. Zal'tsman, 1906.

———. *A Pocket Edition of Several Stories Mostly Reactionary*. Paris: n.p., 1925.

———. *The Political and Social Philosophy of Ze'ev Jabotinsky: Selected Writings*. Mordechai Saris, ed. London: Vallentine Mitchell, 1999.

———. *Polnoe sobranie sochinenii*. Vol. 1. Minsk: Met, 2008.

———. *Povest' moikh dnei*. Tel Aviv: Biblioteka-Aliia, 1985.

Jesse, William. *Notes of a Half-Pay in Search of Health: or Russia, Circassia, and the Crimea, in 1839–40*. 2 vols. London: James Madden, 1841.

Jones, George Matthew. *Travels in Norway, Sweden, Finland, Russia, and Turkey; Also on the Coasts of the Sea of Azov and of the Black Sea*. 2 vols. London: John Murray, 1827.

Jones, John Paul. *Life of Rear-Admiral John Paul Jones*. Philadelphia: Grigg and Elliot, 1846.

Kappeler, Andreas, Zenon E. Kohut, Frank E. Sysyn, and Mark von Hagen, eds. *Culture, Nation, Identity: The Ukrainian-Russian Encounter (1600–1945)*. Edmonton: Canadian Institute of Ukrainian Studies Press, 2003.

Kataev, Valentin. *A Mosaic of Life, or the Magic Horn of Oberon*. Moira Budberg and Gordon Latta, trans. Chicago: J. Philip O'Hara, 1976.

Katz, Shmuel. *Lone Wolf: A Biography of Vladimir (Ze'ev) Jabotinsky*. 2 vols. New York: Barricade Books, 1996.

Kenez, Peter. *Civil War in South Russia, 1918*. Berkeley: University of California Press, 1971.

———. *Civil War in South Russia, 1919–1920*. Berkeley: University of California Press, 1977.

Khodarkovsky, Michael. *Russia's Steppe Frontier: The Making of a Colonial Empire, 1500–1800*. Bloomington: Indiana University Press, 2002.

Khrushchov, G. K. *Velikii russkii biolog I. I. Mechnikov*. Moscow: Pravda, 1951.

Kiaer, Christina, and Eric Naiman, eds. *Everyday Life in Early Soviet Russia*. Bloomington: Indiana University Press, 2006.

King, Charles. *The Black Sea: A History*. Oxford: Oxford University Press, 2004.

Klier, John D. *Russia Gathers Her Jews*. DeKalb: Northern Illinois University Press, 1986.

Klier, John D., and Shlomo Lambroza, eds. *Pogroms: Anti-Jewish Violence in Modern Russian History*. Cambridge, UK: Cambridge University Press, 1992.

Koch, Karl. *The Crimea and Odessa*. London: John Murray, 1855.

Kohl, J. G. *Russia*. London: Chapman and Hall, 1844.

Kokhanskii, V. *Odessa za 100 let*. Odessa: Tipografiia P. Frantsova, 1894.

Komroff, Manuel, ed. *Contemporaries of Marco Polo*. New York: Dorset Press, 1989.

Kostyrchenko, G. V., ed. *Gosudarstvennyi antisemitizm v SSSR ot nachala do kul'minatsii, 1938–1953*. Moscow: Mezhdunarodnyi fond "Demokratiia," 2005.

Koval'chuk, L. V., and G. A. Razumov, eds. *Odesskii martirolog*. 3 vols. Odessa: OKFA, 1997–2005.

Kriwaczek, Paul. *Yiddish Civilization: The Rise and Fall of a Forgotten Nation*. New York: Vintage, 2005.

La Fite de Pellepore, Vladimir de [Piotre Artamof]. *La Russie historique, monumentale et pittoresque*. 2 vols. Paris: Imprimerie de Ch. Lahure, 1862–65.

Lagarde, Auguste, comte de. *Voyage de Moscou à Vienne*. Paris: Treuttel et Würtz, 1824.

Lancaster, Jordan. *In the Shadow of Vesuvius: A Cultural History of Naples*. London: I. B. Tauris, 2005.

Lechevalier, Jean-Baptiste. *Voyage de la Propontitude et du Pont-Euxin*. 2 vols. Paris: Dentu, 1800.

Levin, Dov. "The Fateful Decision: The Flight of the Jews into the Soviet Interior in the Summer of 1941." *Yad Vashem Studies* 20 (1990): 115–42.

Libin, Aleksandr, and Natal'ia Makovets, eds. *Sto velikikh odessitov*. Odessa: Optimum, 2009.

Ligne, Charles-Joseph de. *Letters and Reflections of the Austrian Field-Marshal Prince de Ligne*. 2 vols. D. Boileau, trans. Philadelphia: Bradford and Inskeep, 1809.

———. *Mémoires*. Paris: Edouard Champion, 1914.

Litani, Dora. "The Destruction of the Jews of Odessa in Light of Rumanian Documents." *Yad Vashem Studies* 6 (1967): 135–54.

Livezeanu, Irina. *Cultural Politics in Greater Romania: Regionalism, Nation Building, and Ethnic Struggle, 1918–1920*. Ithaca: Cornell University Press, 1995.

Lyall, Robert. *Travels in Russia, the Krimea, the Caucasus, and Georgia*. 2 vols. London: T. Cadell, 1825.

Makolkin, Anna. *A History of Odessa, the Last Italian Black Sea Colony*. Lewiston, NY: Edwin Mellen Press, 2004.

———. *The Nineteenth Century in Odessa*. Lewiston, NY: Edwin Mellen Press, 2007.

Malakhov, V. P., and B. A. Stepanenko. *Odessa, 1900–1920: Liudi, sobytiia, fakty*. Odessa: Optimum, 2004.

———. *Odessa, 1920–65: Liudi, sobytiia, fakty*. Odessa: Nauka i tekhnika, 2008.

Manley, Rebecca. *To the Tashkent Station: Evacuation and Survival in the Soviet Union at War*. Ithaca: Cornell University Press, 2009.

Marigny, E. Taitbout de. *Atlas de la Mer Noire et de la Mer d'Azov*. Odessa: Nitzsche, 1850.

———. *Plans de golfes, baies, ports et rades de la mer Noire et de la mer d'Azov*. Odessa: Lithographie de Alexandre Braun, 1850.

———. *Three Voyages in the Black Sea to the Coast of Circassia: Including Descriptions of the Ports, and the Importance of Their Trade*. London: John Murray, 1837.

Materialy k serii "Narody Sovetskogo Soiuza": Perepis' 1939 goda. 15 vols. Moscow: Akademiia Nauk SSSR, 1990.

Mayer, David. *Sergei M. Eisenstein's Potemkin: A Shot-by-Shot Presentation*. New York: Grossman, 1972.

Mazower, Mark. *Hitler's Empire: How the Nazis Ruled Europe*. New York: Penguin, 2008.

McNeill, William. *Europe's Steppe Frontier, 1500–1800*. Chicago: University of Chicago Press, 1964.

Mechnikov, Ilya [Elie Metchnikoff]. *Essais optimistes*. Paris: A. Maloine, 1907.

———. *Etudes sur la nature humaine*. Paris: Masson, 1903.

———. *Pis'ma (1863–1916 gg)*. Moscow: Nauka, 1974.

———. *Pis'ma k O. N. Mechnikovoi (1900–1914)*. Moscow: Nauka, 1980.

Mendele Moykher-Sforim. *Selected Works of Mendele Moykher-Sforim*. Marvin Zuckerman, Gerald Stillman, and Marion Herbst, eds. N.p.: Pangloss Press, 1991.

Merry del Val, Diego. *El súbdito de la Zarina*. Barcelona: Roca Editorial, 2008.

Metchnikoff, Olga. *The Life of Élie Metchnikoff, 1845–1916*. London: Constable, 1921.

Minns, Ellis H. *Scythians and Greeks: A Survey of Ancient History and Archaeology on the North Coast of the Euxine from the Danube to the Caucasus*. Cambridge, UK: Cambridge University Press, 1913.

Montefiore, Simon Sebag. *Prince of Princes: The Life of Potemkin*. London: Weidenfeld and Nicolson, 2000.

Moore, John A. *A Journey from London to Odessa*. Paris: A. and W. Galignani, 1833.

Morton, Edward. *Travels in Russia, and a Residence at St. Petersburg and Odessa, in the Years 1827–1829*. London: Longman, Rees, Orme, Brown, and Green, 1830.

Morton, Jamie. *The Role of the Physical Environment in Ancient Greek Seafaring*. Leiden: Brill, 2001.

Moskvich, Grigorii. *Illiustrirovannyi prakticheskii putevoditel' po Odesse*. Odessa: Tipografiia L. Nitche, 1904.

Moss, Kenneth B. *Jewish Renaissance in the Russian Revolution.* Cambridge, MA: Harvard University Press, 2009.

Nadler, V. K. *Odessa v pervyia epokhi eia sushchestvovaniia.* Odessa: V. V. Kirkhner, 1893; reprint Odessa: Optimum, 2007.

Nakhimovsky, Alice. "Vladimir Jabotinsky, Russian Writer." *Modern Judaism* 7, no. 2 (1987): 151–73.

Nathans, Benjamin. *Beyond the Pale: The Jewish Encounter with Late Imperial Russia.* Berkeley: University of California Press, 2002.

Nawotka, Krzysztof. *The Western Pontic Cities: History and Political Organization.* Amsterdam: Adolf M. Hakkert, 1997.

Nekliudov, N. *Chernoe more: Spravochnik-putevoditel'.* Moscow: Narkomvod, 1936.

Nistor, Ion. *Istoria Bucovinei.* Bucharest: Humanitas, 1991.

Odessa 1794–1894. Odessa: A. Shul'tse, 1895.

Odessa: Kto est' kto, 1794–1994. Odessa: Okfa, 1999.

Odesskaia turisticheskaia baza. Odessa: Maiak, 1972.

Ofer, Dalia. "Life in the Ghettos of Transnistria." *Yad Vashem Studies* 25 (1996): 229–74.

Olenin, K. L. *Vek: Odesskii istoricheskii al'bom, 1794–1894.* Odessa: Tipografiia G. N. Karakta, 1894.

Oliphant, Laurence. *The Russian Shores of the Black Sea in the Autumn of 1852.* 3rd ed. London: Redfield, 1854; reprint New York: Arno Press, 1970.

Orbach, Alexander. *New Voices of Russian Jewry.* Leiden: E. J. Brill, 1980.

Orlov, A. *Istoricheskii ocherk Odessy s 1794 po 1803 god.* Odessa: A. Shul'tse, 1885.

Ostapchuk, Victor. "The Human Landscape of the Ottoman Black Sea in the Face of the Cossack Naval Raids." *Oriente Moderno* 20, no. 1 (2001): 23–95.

Ovid. *Poems of Exile.* Peter Green, trans. New York: Penguin, 1994.

Pachymeres, George. *Relations historiques.* Vitalien Laurent, trans. 2 vols. Paris: Belles Lettres, 1984.

Pallas, Peter Simon. *Travels through the Southern Provinces of the Russian Empire, in the Years 1793 and 1794.* 2 vols. London: T. N. Longman and O. Rees, et al., 1802–3.

Paustovsky, Konstantin. *The Story of a Life.* New York: Pantheon, 1964.

Paxson, Margaret. *Solovyovo: The Story of Memory in a Russian Village.* Bloomington and Washington, DC: Indiana University Press and Woodrow Wilson Center Press, 2005.

Pegolotti, Francesco Balducci. *La pratica della mercatura.* Allen Evans, ed. Cambridge, MA: Medieval Academy of America, 1936.

Phillips, Edward J. *The Founding of Russia's Navy: Peter the Great and the Azov Fleet, 1688–1714.* Westport, CT: Greenwood Press, 1995.

Pinkerton, Robert. *Russia*. London: Seeley and Sons, 1833.

Pirozhkova, A. N. *At His Side: The Last Years of Isaac Babel*. Anne Frydman and Robert L. Busch, trans. South Royalton, VT: Steerforth Press, 1996.

———. "Years at His Side (1932–1939) and Beyond." *Canadian Slavonic Papers* 36, nos. 1–2 (1994): 169–240.

Pliny the Elder. *Natural History*. H. Rackham, trans. Cambridge, MA: Harvard University Press, 1949.

Polishchuk, Mikhail. *Evrei Odessy i Novorossii*. Moscow: Mosty kul'tury, 2002.

Polo, Marco. *The Travels of Marco Polo*. Ronald Latham, trans. Harmondsworth, UK: Penguin, 1958.

Ponting, Clive. *The Crimean War: The Truth behind the Myth*. London: Chatto and Windus, 2004.

Proctor, Edna Dean. *A Russian Journey*. Boston: James R. Osgood, 1872.

Prousis, Theophilus C. "Demetrios S. Inglezes: Greek Merchant and City Leader of Odessa." *Slavic Review* 50, no. 3 (1991): 672–79.

Puryear, Vernon T. "Odessa: Its Rise and International Importance, 1815–50." *Pacific Historical Review* 3, no. 2 (1934): 192–215.

Pushkin, Alexander. *The Letters of Alexander Pushkin*. J. Thomas Shaw, trans. and ed. 2 vols. Madison: University of Wisconsin Press, 1967.

———. *Polnoe sobranie sochinenii*. 2nd ed. 19 vols. Moscow: Voskresen'e, 1994–97.

Putevoditel' po Odesse. Odessa: Tipografiia L. Nitche, 1867.

Putevoditel' po Pushkinu. St. Petersburg: Akademicheskii proekt, 1997.

Ramer, Samuel C., and Blair A. Ruble, eds. *Place, Identity, and Urban Culture: Odesa and New Orleans*. Kennan Institute Occasional Paper 301. Washington, DC: Woodrow Wilson International Center for Scholars, 2008.

Rashkovetskii, Mikhail, Inna Naidis, Leonid Dusman, and Liliia Belousova, eds. *Istoriia Kholokosta v Odesskom regione*. Odessa: Migdal' and Studiia Negotsiant, 2006.

Reikhel't, Nikolai N. [N. Lender]. *Po Chernomu moriu*. St. Petersburg: A. S. Suvorin, 1891.

Report of the International Commission on the Holocaust in Romania, 2004. Available at http://yad-vashem.org.il/about_yad/what_new/data_whats_new/report1.html.

Reuilly, Jean, Baron de. *Travels in the Crimea, and along the Shores of the Black Sea, Performed during the Year 1803*. In *A Collection of Modern and Contemporary Voyages and Travels*. Vol. 5. London: Richard Phillips, 1807.

Rhinelander, Anthony L. H. *Prince Michael Vorontsov: Viceroy to the Tsar*. Montreal: McGill-Queen's University Press, 1990.

Richardson, Tanya. *Kaleidoscopic Odessa: History and Place in Contemporary Ukraine*. Toronto: University of Toronto Press, 2008.

Romm, James S. *The Edges of the Earth in Ancient Thought: Geography, Exploration, and Fiction*. Princeton: Princeton University Press, 1992.

Rothstein, Robert A. "How It Was Sung in Odessa: At the Intersection of Russian and Yiddish Folk Culture." *Slavic Review* 60, no. 4 (2001): 781–801.

Rowan-Hamilton, Norah. *Under the Red Star*. London: Herbert Jenkins, 1930.

Rubenstein, Joshua, and Ilya Altman, eds. *The Unknown Black Book: The Holocaust in the German-Occupied Soviet Territories*. Bloomington: Indiana University Press, 2008.

Ruble, Blair A. *Second Metropolis: Pragmatic Pluralism in Gilded Age Chicago, Silver Age Moscow, and Meiji Osaka*. Cambridge, UK: Cambridge University Press, 2001.

Rybak, Lev. *Mark Bernes*. Moscow: Isskustvo, 1976.

Sade, Marquis de. *Voyage d'Italie*. 2 vols. Paris: Fayard, 1995.

Sapozhnikov, I. V., and G. V. Sapozhnikova. *Zaporozhskie i chernomorskie kazaki v Khadzhibee i Odesse*. Odessa: OKFA, 1998.

Sargent, A. J. *Seaways of the Empire: Notes on the Geography of Transport*. London: A. and C. Black, 1918.

Savchenko, Viktor. *Anarkhisty-terroristy v Odesse (1903–1913)*. Odessa: Optimum, 2006.

Schechtman, Joseph B. *Fighter and Prophet: The Vladimir Jabotinsky Story*. New York: Thomas Yoseloff, 1961.

——. "The Jabotinsky-Slavinsky Agreement: A Chapter in Ukrainian-Jewish Relations." *Jewish Social Studies* 17, no. 4 (1955): 289–306.

——. *Rebel and Statesman: The Vladimir Jabotinsky Story*. New York: Thomas Yoseloff, 1956.

Scott, Charles Henry. *The Baltic, the Black Sea, and the Crimea*. London: Richard Bentley, 1854.

Sebastian, Mihail. *Journal, 1935–1944*. Patrick Camiller, trans. Chicago: Ivan R. Dee, 2000.

Ségur, Louis-Philippe, comte de. *Memoirs and Recollections of Count Ségur, Ambassador from France to the Courts of Russia and Prussia*. 3 vols. London: H. Colburn, 1825–1827.

Seton, Marie. *Sergei M. Eisenstein*. New York: A. W. Wyn, 1952.

Sheridan, Clare. *Across Europe with Satanella*. New York: Dodd, Mead, 1925.

Shilov, Konstantin V. *Mark Bernes v vospominaniiakh sovremennikov*. Moscow: Molodaia gvardiia, 2005.

Shkliaev, Igor'. *Odessa v smutnoe vremia*. Odessa: Studiia Negotsiant, 2004.

Shlaim, Avi. *The Iron Wall: Israel and the Arab World*. New York: W. W. Norton, 2001.

Sholem Aleichem. *The Letters of Menakhem-Mendl and Sheyne-Mendl and Motl, the Cantor's Son*. New Haven: Yale University Press, 2002.

Shternshis, Anna. *Soviet and Kosher: Jewish Popular Culture in the Soviet Union, 1923–1939*. Bloomington: Indiana University Press, 2006.

Shum'ko, L. V., and N. M. Anserova, eds. *Il'ia Il'ich Mechnikov, 1845–1916*. Moscow: Nauka, 2005.

Shuvalov, R. A. *"Predany vechnomu zabven'iu."* Odessa: OKFA, 1998.

Sicard, Charles [Karl Sikar']. *Pis'ma ob Odesse*. St. Petersburg: Tipografiia Karla Kraia, 1818.

Sicher, Efraim. "The Trials of Isaak: A Brief Life." *Canadian Slavonic Papers* 36, nos. 1–2 (1994): 7–42.

Sidorov, Vasilii. *Okol'noi dorogoi: Putevyia zametki i vpechatleniia*. St. Petersburg: Tipografiia A. Katanskago, 1891.

Siegelbaum, Lewis. "The Odessa Grain Trade: A Case Study in Urban Growth and Development in Tsarist Russia." *Journal of European Economic History* 9, no. 1 (1980): 113–51.

Siniaver, Moisei. *Arkhitektura staroi Odessy*. Leningrad: Izdatel'stvo Leningradskogo oblastnogo soiuza sovetskikh khudozhnikov, 1935.

Skal'kovskii, A. *Pervoe tridtsatiletie istorii goroda Odessy, 1793–1823*. Odessa: Gorodskaia tipografiia, 1837; reprint Odessa: OKFA, 1995.

Skinner, Frederick William. "City Planning in Russia: The Development of Odessa, 1789–1892." PhD dissertation. Princeton University, 1973.

Slade, Adolphus. *Records of Travels in Turkey, Greece, etc., and of a Cruise in the Black Sea, with the Capitan Pasha, in the Years 1829, 1830, and 1831*. 2 vols. Philadelphia: E. L. Carey and A. Hart, 1833.

Smith, Douglas, ed. and trans. *Love and Conquest: Personal Correspondence of Catherine the Great and Prince Grigory Potemkin*. DeKalb: Northern Illinois University Press, 2004.

Smol'ianinov, Konstantin. *Istoriia Odessy*. Odessa: Gorodskaia Tipografiia, 1853; reprint Odessa: Optimum, 2007.

Sokolyansky, Mark. "Reflecting Odessa's Jews: The Works of Saul Borovoi, 1903–1989." *Jahrbuch des Simon-Dubnow-Instituts* 2 (2003): 359–72.

Solonari, Vladimir. " 'Model Province': Explaining the Holocaust of Bessarabian and Bukovinian Jewry." *Nationalities Papers* 34, no. 4 (2006): 471–500.

———. *Purifying the Nation: Population Exchange and Ethnic Cleansing in Nazi-*

Allied Romania. Baltimore and Washington, DC: Johns Hopkins University Press and Woodrow Wilson Center Press, 2010.

Spencer, Edmund. *Travels in Circassia, Krim-Tartary, &c., Including a Steam Voyage down the Danube, from Vienna to Constantinople, and round the Black Sea*. 3rd ed. 2 vols. London: Henry Colburn, 1839.

———. *Turkey, Russia, the Black Sea, and Circassia*. London: George Routledge, 1854.

Stadelmann, Matthias. "Von jüdischen Ganoven zu sowjetischen Helden: Odessas Wandlungen in den Liedern Leonid Utesovs." *Jahrbuch des Simon-Dubnow-Instituts* 2 (2003): 333–58.

Stanislawski, Michael. *Zionism and the Fin de Siècle: Cosmopolitanism and Nationalism from Nordau to Jabotinsky*. Berkeley: University of California Press, 2001.

Stanton, Rebecca Jane. "Odessan Selves: Identity and Mythopoesis in Works of the 'Odessa School.'" PhD dissertation. Columbia University, 2004.

Starodinskii, David Z. *Odesskoe getto: Vospominaniia*. Odessa: Khaitekh, 1991.

Starr, S. Frederick. *Red and Hot: The Fate of Jazz in the Soviet Union, 1917–1980*. New York: Limelight Editions, 1985.

Stephens, J. L. *Incidents of Travel in Greece, Turkey, Russia, and Poland*. Edinburgh: William and Robert Chambers, 1851.

Stevens, Robert. *An Account of Odessa*. Newport, RI: William Simons, 1819.

Stites, Richard. *Soviet Popular Culture*. Cambridge, UK: Cambridge University Press, 1992.

———, ed. *Culture and Entertainment in Wartime Russia*. Bloomington: Indiana University Press, 1995.

Strabo. *The Geography of Strabo*. Horace Leonard Jones, trans. 8 vols. New York: G. P. Putnam's Sons, 1917–1932.

Stremenovskii, S. N. *Mestnoe samoupravlenie g. Odessy v seredine XIX stoletiia*. Odessa: Iurydychna literatura, 2002.

Sunderland, Willard. *Taming the Wild Field. Colonization and Empire on the Russian Steppe*. Ithaca: Cornell University Press, 2004.

Sylvester, Roshanna P. *Tales of Old Odessa: Crime and Civility in a City of Thieves*. DeKalb: Northern Illinois University Press, 2005.

Tanny, Jarrod Mitchell. "City of Rogues and Schnorrers: The Myth of Old Odessa in Russian and Jewish Culture." PhD dissertation. University of California, Berkeley, 2008.

———. "The Many Ends of Old Odessa: Memories of the Gilded Age in Russia's City of Sin." Berkeley Program in Soviet and Post-Soviet Studies Working Paper, University of California, Berkeley, 2007.

Tarnopol, Joachim. *Notices historiques et caractéristiques sur les Israelites d'Odessa.* Odessa: A. Braun, 1855.

Taylor, Richard, ed. *The Eisenstein Reader.* London: British Film Institute, 1998.

Thomas, Evan. *John Paul Jones.* New York: Simon and Schuster, 2003.

Tilley, Henry Arthur. *Eastern Europe and Western Asia.* London: Longman, Green, Longman, Roberts, and Green, 1864.

Tolmacheva, Marina A. "The Cossacks at Sea: Pirate Tactics in the Frontier Environment." *East European Quarterly* 24, no. 4 (1990): 483–512.

Tolstoy, Leo. *Hadji Murat.* Hugh Alpin, trans. London: Hesperus Classics, 2003.

Treaties and Other Documents Relating to the Black Sea, the Dardanelles, and the Bosphorus: 1535–1877. London: Harrison and Sons, 1878.

Troinitskii, N. A., ed. *Obshchii svod po imperii rezul'tatov razrabotki dannykh 1-i vseobshchei perepisi naseleniia.* 2 vols. St. Petersburg: N. L. Nyrkin, 1905.

Trotsky, Leon. *My Life.* Mineola, NY: Dover Publications, 2007.

Tsetskhladze, Gocha R., ed. *The Greek Colonisation of the Black Sea Area: Historical Interpretation of Archaeology.* Stuttgart: Franz Steiner, 1998.

———, ed. *North Pontic Archaeology: Recent Discoveries and Studies.* Leiden: Brill, 2001.

Twain, Mark. *The Complete Travel Books of Mark Twain.* 2 vols. Garden City, NY: Doubleday, 1966–67.

Tyrkova-Williams, Ariadna. *Zhizn' Pushkina.* 2 vols. Paris: n.p., 1929.

United States War Department, Military Intelligence Division. *Russia: Black Sea Entrances to Russia.* Washington, DC: Government Printing Office, 1919.

Utesov, Leonid. *Spasibo serdtse!* Moscow: Vagrius, 1999.

Veidlinger, Jeffrey. *Jewish Public Culture in the Late Russian Empire.* Bloomington: Indiana University Press, 2009.

Von Geldern, James, and Richard Stites, eds. *Mass Culture in Soviet Russia.* Bloomington: Indiana University Press, 1995.

Vorontsov, Mikhail. "Mémoires du prince M. Woronzow, 1819–1833." *Arkhiv kniazia Vorontsova* 37 (1891): 65–102.

Vsesoiuznaia perepis' naseleniia 1926 g.: Kratkie svodki. 10 vols. Moscow: TsSU SSSR, 1927.

Vsesoiuznaia perepis' naseleniia 1939 g.: Osnovnye itogi. 5 vols. Moscow: Gosplan SSSR, 1940.

Vsevolozhskii, N. S. *Dictionnaire géographique-historique de l'empire de Russie.* 2nd ed. 2 vols. Moscow: Imprimerie d'Auguste Semen, 1823.

———. *Puteshestvie cherez iuzhnuiu Rossiiu, Krym i Odessu.* 2 vols. Moscow: Tipografiia Avgusta Semena, 1839.

Washburn, Stanley. *The Cable Game: The Adventures of an American Press-Boat in Turkish Waters during the Russian Revolution*. Boston: Sherman, French, 1912.

Weinberg, Robert. *The Revolution of 1905 in Odessa: Blood on the Steps*. Bloomington: Indiana University Press, 1993.

Weiner, Amir. *Making Sense of War: The Second World War and the Fate of the Bolshevik Revolution*. Princeton: Princeton University Press, 2001.

Werth, Alexander. *Russia at War, 1941–1945*. New York: E. P. Dutton, 1964.

Wightman, Orrin Sage. *The Diary of an American Physician in the Russian Revolution 1917*. New York: Brooklyn Daily Eagle, 1928.

Wikoff, Henry. *The Reminiscences of an Idler*. New York: Fords, Howard, and Hulbert, 1880.

Yekelchyk, Serhy. *Stalin's Empire of Memory*. Toronto: University of Toronto Press, 2004.

Zapadnyi tsentral'nyi komitet samooborona Paole-Zion. *Odesskii pogrom i samooborona*. Paris: Ch. Noblet, 1906.

Zipperstein, Steven J. *Imagining Russian Jewry: Memory, History, Identity*. Seattle: University of Washington Press, 1999.

———. *The Jews of Odessa: A Cultural History, 1794–1881*. Stanford: Stanford University Press, 1986.

———. "Reflecting on the Writing of Odessa Jewry's History." *Jahrbuch des Simon-Dubnow-Instituts* 2 (2003): 373–84.

INDEX